The Visitor's Guide
to
THE ITALIAN LAKES

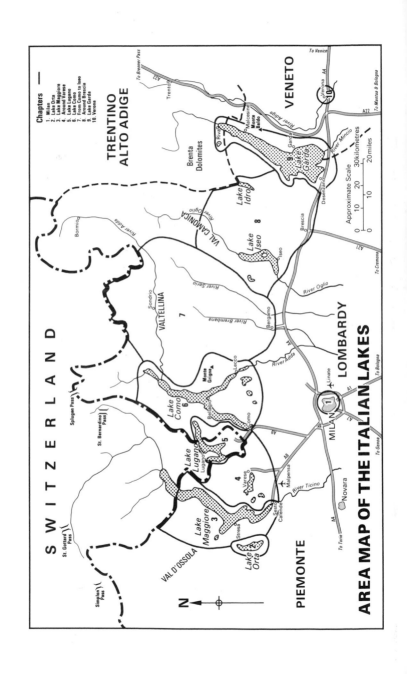

AREA MAP OF THE ITALIAN LAKES

Chapters
1. Milan
2. Lake Orta
3. Lake Maggiore
4. Around Varese
5. Lake Lugano
6. Lake Como
7. From Como to Iseo
8. Around Brescia
9. Lake Garda
10. Verona

SWITZERLAND

TRENTINO ALTO ADIGE

VENETO

LOMBARDY

PIEMONTE

Simplon Pass

St. Gotthard Pass

St. Bernardino Pass

Splugen Pass

To Brenner Pass

To Venice

Trento

River Adige

Verona

A4

A22

To Mantua & Bologna

Bormio

River Adda

VALTELLINA

Sondrio

Monte Girigna

Lecco

River Serio

River Brembana

Bergamo

River Oglio

Brescia

A21

To Cremona

Desenzano

River Mincio

VAL CAMONICA

River Oglio

Lake Idro

Lake Seo

Iseo

Lake Garda

Malcesine
Monte Baldo

Riva

Garda

Brenta Dolomites

Lake Como

Monte Girigna

Bellagio

Como

Lecco

River Adda

A9

A8

MILAN

Linate

A1

A4

To Genoa

To Bologna

To Turin

Novara

River Ticino

Malpensa

Sesto Calende

Varese

Lake Lugano

Lugano

Lake Maggiore

Stresa

Lake Orta

VAL D'OSSOLA

Approximate Scale

0   10   20   30 kilometres
0   20 miles

N

THE
VISITOR'S GUIDE TO
THE
ITALIAN LAKES

Richard Sale

MPC

HUNTER
PUBLISHING INC

British Library Cataloguing in
Publication Data:
Sale, Richard, *1946-*
 The Visitor's guide to the Italian
 Lakes.
 — (MPC Visitor's guides).
 1. Italy. Northern Italy. Italian
 Lakes.
 Visitor's guides
 I. Title
 914.5

Published by:
Moorland Publishing Co Ltd,
Moor Farm Road,
Airfield Estate,
Ashbourne,
Derbyshire DE6 1HD
England

ISBN 0 86190 220 3 (paperback)
ISBN 0 86190 219 X (hardback)

Published in the USA by:
Hunter Publishing Inc.,
300 Raritan Centre Parkway,
CN94, Edison, NJ 08818

ISBN 1 55650 074 2

Colour and black & white
origination by:
Quad Repro Ltd, Pinxton, Notts

Printed in the UK by:
Butler & Tanner Ltd, Frome,
Somerset

Cover photograph:
Sirmione, Lake Garda (Peter Baker)
(International Photobank).
Photographs have been supplied as
follows:
F. W. Ellis: pp90, 91; E. Fasola: pp102,
103, 110, 111, 114, 115, 119, 121, 122,
123, 126, 127, 130, 131, 134, 135; The
Italian State Tourist Office: pp31, 33,
35, 52, 53, 54, 59, 63, 66, 71, 75, 78,
79, 82, 117, 118, 124, 125, 129, 137,
139, 142 (top and bottom), 143, 146,
151, 154, 158, 159, 166-7, 170, 174,
178, 179, 187, 195, 196, 197, 199, 206,
214, 216, 221, 225, 226; R. Sale: pp25,
26, 27, 30, 32, 38, 39, 43, 47, 50, 51,
55, 58, 60, 67, 70, 83, 86-7, 94, 95, 98,
99, 106, 107, 138, 147, 150, 171, 175,
182-3, 186, 190, 191, 203, 208, 213,
219, 220, 224.

All maps drawn by Malcolm Barnes.

The author is indebted to the staff of
the Italian State Tourist Authority,
both in London and in the offices in
northern Italy.

 In particular he would like to offer
his sincere thanks to Erminio
Fasola, lately of the Tourist Office in
Como, for his considerable assistance, and for allowing the use of his
excellent personal photo library, and
also to Monica and Guiseppe of
Ermino's staff.

 He would also like to offer per-
sonal thanks to Chiara Canti of the
Tourist Office in Varese, and to Sgr
Carioli and his staff at Stresa.

CONTENTS

Key to Maps

AREA MAPS

⬭ Major towns/Cities	▬ Dual carriageway
○ Towns/Villages	▬ Main Roads
▪ ▪ ▪ International Borders	▬ Other Roads
▬ ▬ Regional Borders	⌣ Rivers
🗺 Nature Park	⬬ Lakes
✈ Airports	▲ Named Mountain

STREET PLANS

▬ Main Roads	⬬ Lakes
▬ Other Roads	**Museum** Places of Interest

The maps drawn for each chapter, while comprehensive, are not designed to be used as route maps, but rather to locate the main towns, villages and places of interest. An excellent 1:100,000 (1cm=1km) 'Tourist Map of the Lakes', which covers all the area except for Bergamo, is obtainable free from any local tourist office. Alternatively sheet D33 'Lombardia' at 1:200,000 (1cm=2km) is recommended, published by the Touring Club Italiano who also produce more detailed 1:50,000 maps suitable for walkers.

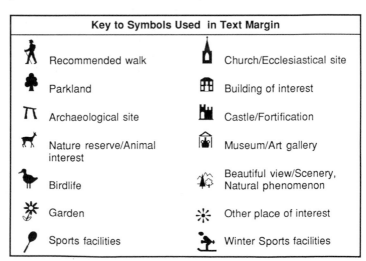

Key to Symbols Used in Text Margin	
🚶 Recommended walk	⛪ Church/Ecclesiastical site
♣ Parkland	🏛 Building of interest
� Archaeological site	🏰 Castle/Fortification
🦌 Nature reserve/Animal interest	🖼 Museum/Art gallery
🦆 Birdlife	🏕 Beautiful view/Scenery, Natural phenomenon
❀ Garden	☀ Other place of interest
🎾 Sports facilities	⛷ Winter Sports facilities

INTRODUCTION

Stendhal wrote — 'What can one say about Lake Maggiore, about the Borromean Islands, about Lake Como, unless it be that one pities those who are not madly in love with them'.

Dumas, arriving at Lake Maggiore after crossing the Simplon Pass, noted that 'the sky is pure, the air mild, and one recognises the land beloved of the gods, the happy land that neither barbarous invasions, nor civil discords could deprive of its heaven-sent blessings'.

These are just two examples of many that could be quoted, praising the delights of that area of Italy that lies between the plain of the river Po and the alpine chain. Its charm arises from its geography and history, a basic understanding of which is necessary for an appreciation of its delights.

This guide explores the area of the northern Italian lakes from west to east — from Orta to Garda.

The upland country between the lakes, including the large area between Lake Como and Lake Iseo, is covered, together with the cities that border the area, Varese, Bergamo, Brescia and Sondrio. For completeness, and because few visitors to the area will deny the call of Milan, Italy's richest city, or Verona, the city of Romeo and Juliet, these too are included, though they are dealt with only briefly.

Geography

On very rare days it is just possible to view, from the southern edge of the Alps, the Apennines, the ridge of mountains that form the bones of Italy's leg-shaped country. Similarly, it is a lucky visitor who sees the white alpine wall from the Apennines. Yet each of these mountain chains has helped to create the land that separates them, the Po plain, a wide valley covered with the deposits brought down by the rivers that drain the high peaks. But back in the Pleistocene era, during the time of the Quaternary Ice Age, it was not rivers, but glaciers that flowed south from the Alps towards what is now the Po plain. These glaciers were confined by the ridges of hard rock that still define the northern valleys, gouging out the bottoms of those valleys and depositing, as terminal and lateral moraine, the material they removed. The over-deepening of the valleys, and the thickness of the morainic deposits, produced deep basins that filled as the glaciers retreated, leaving huge lakes of fresh water bounded by rich bands of soil that separated them both from their confining ridges and the Po plain. The depth of both the lakes and the moraine deposits are impressive. Lake Garda, for example, is 346m (1,135ft) deep, the moraine deposits contributing 149m (484ft) to that depth. The lake's deepest point lies 281m (922ft) below sea level.

Lake Garda, though not unique in this thickness of morainic deposit, is slightly unusual, because the deposit's thickness allows it to extend far out of its valley into the plain. Alone of all the lakes, Garda has almost a third of its length beyond the end of its confining ridges. In common with the others, however, its more northerly end is confined by high ridges, the lakes pushing northward into the Alps so far that they have an almost fjord-like appearance at their extreme northern tips. The best example of this is Como, whose northern end is not only fjord-like, but shows quite spectacularly the V-formed cross-section of ridges that is such a characteristic of glacial valleys.

Travelling from Lake Garda in the east, westward towards Lake Maggiore, it is noticeable that the confining mountains of the lakes change. Initially the rock is calcareous, the dolomitic limestone that gives the peaks their name, the Dolomites. Ironically for a mountain area that is so famously characteristic of Italy, the name derives from that of a French geologist, Dolomieu, who first identified this magnesium-rich rock. Continuing westward there are occasional intrusions of crystalline rocks which become more frequent towards Lake Maggiore, by which time the mountains (strictly the pre-Alps, rather than the Alps themselves) are wholly crystalline, a mixture of schists and gneisses. This change of rock type changes the vegetation and its profusion. The most obvious change is in the woods, where the abundant and apparently ubiquitous chestnut trees grow only where the crystalline rocks intrude.

In general the western area has a more varied and luxuriant growth, but this really only applies to the upland areas. Near the lakes the growth is governed by the deposition of the lateral and terminal moraine, with Garda's considerable deposits giving its shorelines a richness that the other lakes can barely match.

To the south of the lakes, before and after the Ice Age, the moraines and the river-borne silts formed the immensely fertile Lombardy plain that constitutes the northern part of the Po plain. This was, and is still, the most productive area in Italy, and, as a consequence, has always been one of the most important areas in the country.

History

The area's fertility was noted in the wake of the glaciers that had carved the lake basins, retreating as the Ice Age ended, and was immediately exploited. The very early Bronze Age Remedello culture is named after the earliest known site, near Brescia, and there are also other very early sites, chiefly pile dwellings, at the edges of several of the smaller lakes. Later, Iron Age peoples also moved into the area, though the most famous of these, the Etruscans, are commemorated by the regional name Tuscany to the south. While the Etruscan civilisation was flowering, Romulus founded Rome — in 753BC according to legend — so that its first governors were Etruscans rather than Romans. These early Romans were defeated in northern Italy around 400BC by Gauls who swept across the Alps to found Cisalpine Gaul, Cisalpine meaning 'this side of the Alps'. It was to be more than a century before true Romans reconquered northern Italy as the Roman Empire expanded.

Surprisingly, the area covered by this book has very sparse Roman remains. Those at Brescia, dating from the first century AD, are about the best, though there are some isolated pieces at other places. The reason for this is partly the conversion of the Roman Empire to Christianity and the replacement of pagan temples with Christian churches on the same sites. The Emperor Nero presided over the first persecution of Christians in AD64. The persecution lasted for 250 years, and was at its most severe under Diocletian in AD303. He failed to reverse the tide of religious history, however, which flowed ever faster following the Edict of Milan in AD313 when Constantine the Great granted religious freedom to the empire's Christians. In AD391 Theodosius made Christianity the religion of the state. This reason for the apparent lack of Roman remains also partly explains the lack of very early Christian remains, later churches having been built on the sites of earlier ones. Some of the best preserved treasures from the early Christian era can also be seen at Brescia, in the Christian Museum.

Ironically, the two emperors Constantine and Theodosius assisted the fragmentation of the empire, but at the same time laid the foundation for later Italian greatness. In AD330 Constantine moved the capital of the empire to Byzantium, renaming it Constantinople, and in AD395 Theodosius divided it into eastern and western halves. The link with the east that followed this transfer of power had profound implications for the Italian city states in the early Middle Ages, while the division of the empire made the plundering of the western half by the northern barbarians easier, though it would almost certainly have happened at some stage even if there had been no division. The names of the 'barbarians at the gates' are now household words for the atrocious — Huns and Vandals — but they also included the Longobards or Lombards, who named the province which is mainly covered by this book. The origin of these people is not absolutely clear, though their route to Italy, across the Alps from the Danube basin, suggests somewhere around Hungary. They were pagan, but not really the barbarians of legend, having some impressively modern ideas. It is no coincidence that Lombard Street is the home of London's bankers.

The Lombards were converted to Christianity by Theodolinda, the daughter of a Bavarian duke, who married the Lombard king, and for this act of conversion Pope Gregory III sent her a 'True Nail'. This was incorporated into an iron crown, which was thereafter used to crown the kings of Lombardy and, later, Italy. Both Charlemagne in the eighth century and Napoléon in the nineteenth century were crowned with the Iron Crown, as were more than forty kings in the thousand years between those two. Today it can be seen at Monza Cathedral a little way north-east of Milan.

Charlemagne had defeated the Lombards in 794 taking the area into his Frankish kingdom, but the Lombards had retaken the crown by the ninth century following the invasion of the Magyars of Hungary who plundered the whole of northern Italy. The widow of King Lothar, who had been defeated and killed by King Berengar of Ivrea, appealed for help to the German emperor Otto. This plea was answered by invasion. Berengar was defeated, Otto married Adelheid and was crowned emperor in Rome. Thus began three centuries of German rule of the majority of Italy. This time was important for the rise of the Italian city states, and also for the conflict between the papacy and the emperors for overall control of the country.

This conflict was given voice by struggles between noblemen supporting either the pro-pope 'Guelfs' or the pro-emperor 'Ghibellines'. These two 'party' names are often encountered on museum visits, though neither had any direct bearing on Italian cultural or political history. The same is not true, however, of the rise of the city states. The towns of northern Italy were at the crossroads of the civilisations of west and east, on the pilgrimage routes to Rome and, most importantly, on the routes of the Crusades that kept the kings and noblemen of Europe active for many years around the twelfth century. Venice, Pisa and Genoa arose as ports, growing rich on trade from the east and on the transportation of soldiers. Milan, and later Florence, grew rich on their geographical position. Milan, in the fertile Po valley, was on trade routes inland from Genoa and Venice, Florence was on the trade route to Rome.

From earliest times the cities were controlled not by feudal lords, but by elected councils of rich merchants: Venice's Doge was an elected official, more mayor than duke. These councils encouraged innovations in agriculture and expanded markets in every possible direction. Feudalism required few innovations, power being maintained by keeping the peasants down. By contrast the merchants of the city states wanted increased efficiency and trade because that brought wealth. Marco Polo was a Venetian, and Leonardo Fibonacci, who brought Arabic numerals to Europe to replace the cumbersome Roman system, was Pisan. Later, when the city states were at the height of their power, their wealth encouraged art: Dante was born in Florence in 1265 and a century later the same city saw the work of Donatello. By the fifteenth century the Renaissance had created perhaps the finest artistic climate that has ever existed at any time, anywhere, with Michelangelo, Leonardo, Raphael and Titian all alive and working at the same time, and Palladio designing buildings that still inspire awe. The work of these masters make any visit to northern Italy worthwhile because, although only a limited amount of their work is visible, the effect of their presence on contemporaries and pupils is frequently seen.

However, the rise and domination of the city states was far from painless. There were frequent inter-city rivalries: Florence fought Pisa, Genoa fought Venice, Milan fought Como in the Ten Years' War (1118–27), destroying that city. Aided by Emperor Frederick I, known as Barbarossa — red beard — Como rose again, destroying the Island of Comacina in revenge and assisting the emperor against Milan. At first the emperor was successful, but the city states combined to form the Lombard League, defeating Barbarossa at Legnano in 1176 and winning significant concessions in the Treaty of Constance in 1183.

Later, some of the cities succumbed to lordships, though these remained chiefly benign. The Viscontis ruled Milan at first, later being replaced by the Sforzas, while the castles of Verona's Scaligeri family will be seen in almost every town on Lake Garda's shore.

Elsewhere in Italy the influence of the eastern states was declining. The Normans invaded Sicily and southern Italy around the same time as they were invading England. French influence was destroyed following the 'Sicilian Vespers' in 1282 when all Frenchmen were murdered or expelled. The House of Aragon which succeeded them supplied emperors for the Holy Roman Empire and ensured Spanish domination of much of Italy: Charles V's son, Phillip II, was given Milan in 1540 and it remained a Spanish colony for 150 years.

Eventually, a divided Italy with its small city states left the country open to attack by foreign powers. Not all of the business acumen of the cities failed however. In 1768 Genoa sold Corsica to France! By then, indeed 50 years before then as far as Lombardy was concerned, much of northern Italy had fallen under the rule of the Austrian Hapsburgs. Napoléon briefly freed the area, but declared himself king of Italy and replaced Hapsburg rule with small republics — the Cisalpine covering much of Lombardy, the Ligurian around Genoa — under the umbrella of France. When Austrian rule was re-established, Italians began to awaken to the fact that they had a national identity and that they could throw off foreign rule. A real voice was given to this awakening by the appearance of a newspaper *Il Risorgimento* in Turin in 1842. Its title was taken up by the disparate groups fighting for unity and freedom: Carlo Alberto, the Piemontian king of Sardinia, Count Camillo Cavour, from Piemonte, an ardent monarchist, Guiseppe Mazzine, an anti-monarchist from Genoa, and Guiseppe Garibaldi, an enigmatic but effective guerrilla leader. With help from France, particularly at the battles of Magenta and Solferino, much of northern Italy was freed from Austrian rule and voted, with the remainder of mainland Italy, for unity with Sardinia and for monarchy. In 1861 Vittorio Emanuele II, son of Carlo Alberto, was crowned king of Italy. Under his kingship war with Austria incorporated Venice into Italy, and World War I added South Tirol and Istria, apart from the city of Fiume.

Sadly, following World War I, the expansionist policy that had unified the country and brought the return of *Italia Irredenta* — 'Unrecovered Italy' — continued. Mussolini's fascists took over the government, Annunzio took Fiume, Abyssinia and Albania were invaded and the 'Pact of Steel' with Hitler came into being. Despite Mussolini's attempts at mediation, the latter brought Italy into the war with France and Britain in June 1940. In 1943 Italy changed sides, the fascists were routed and later Mussolini was shot, but in the Treaty of Paris Italy lost Istria to Yugoslavia. In 1946 King Vittorio Emanuele III abdicated and a national referendum abolished the monarchy. Today Italy is a respected member of the European Economic Community and of NATO.

Economy

Economically Italy is a country of staggering contrasts. In the north the standard of living is as high as in any country in Western Europe while in the south it is almost the equal of any economic low spot. This is in part due to the groundwork of the medieval free city states, in part to the climate, which is more amenable to agriculture in the north than in the very hot south, and in part due to the existence in the north of hydro-electricity and natural gas in a country that is chronically short of indigenous power sources. Milan, with a population of almost two million, is Italy's second biggest city behind Rome, but is the country's undoubted economic capital. Its shops, fashion houses, and restaurants are the equal of any other European city, and its artistic and architectural interest are considerable. Lombardy as a whole — Italy's fourth biggest region, of which Milan is regional capital — is equally rich.

The region does not, however, rely on its wealth alone to attract the visitor. It is of considerable artistic interest, of virtually unsurpassable scenic beauty — particularly the area of the lakes — and has a climate that is enviable. All in all there can be few more attractive areas to spend a holiday.

Travel

BY AIR
The Italian Lakes are served by Milan's two international airports. Linate is situated adjacent to the city's orbital *autostrada* (motorway) almost due east of the city centre. Flights from all the main European cities, including London Heathrow, land here, together with Italian internal flights.

Malpensa lies to the east of Gallarate, about 14km (9 miles) from the 'Busto Arsizio' exit of the A8 *autostrada*. This is the intercontinental airport with flights from all over the world, including New York, Montreal and Toronto. Both Linate and Malpensa are connected to Milan's Central Station by bus.

Orio sul Serio, Bergamo's airport, and Villafranca, Verona's airport, are situated beside the A4 *autostrada*. Although these are mainly used for Italian national flights, some charter flight companies in Britain are now using them with more regularity.

Full time students up to the age of 26 receive a 25 per cent discount on flight fares. A certificate from school, college or university must be presented to the flight operator.

All major Italian airports have duty free facilities.

By Rail

The cities of the Lombardy plain, Milan, Varese, Como, Bergamo and Brescia, together with Verona, are linked by a very efficient railway system. From the cities, branch lines penetrate some of the valleys that hold the lakes. The eastern shore of Lake Orta, and the western shore of Lake Maggiore as far as the river Toce, are served by lines that meet at Cuzzago in the Val d'Ossola before crossing into Switzerland via the Simplon tunnel.

The remainder of Lake Maggiore's western shore has no railway, though a line runs continuously along the eastern shore from Sesto Calende into Switzerland.

Lake Lugano is not well served by rail, though a line from Varese terminates at Porto Ceresio, and one from Como goes from Capolago along the lake to Lugano, after crossing the lake bridge.

On Lake Como the only railway line runs from Lecco up the eastern shore before serving the length of the Valtellina. A line runs up Lake Iseo's eastern shore and on up Val Camonica, but none of the Lake Garda towns, apart from Desenzano and Peschiera, are served by rail.

A French motorail service takes cars to Milan's Porta Garibaldi station. The journey's French terminus is either Paris or Boulogne, the latter being ideal for English travellers. The service is not cheap, but to leave Boulogne at around lunchtime one day and to wake (all passenger accommodation is in sleeper coaches) fresh, in time for a free breakfast at Milan, saving at least a day's holiday, is to many people worth the expense.

A second motorail service runs through the Simplon tunnel, cars loading and off-loading at each end, Brig and Varzo. This service is of more debatable merit, as the traveller saves little time and very few miles, those saved being through some of the finest rock-gorge scenery.

A 'travel-at-will' ticket — *Biglietto touristico libera circolazione* — iis available to tourists whose place of residence is outside of Italy. The ticket allows unlimited travel on the Italian railway system, and does not require a supplement for travel on the *Rapido* (see below). State tourist offices in your home country will have details of where the tickets can be purchased. In Italy they can only be obtained from a limited number of stations. In the area covered by this book, there are only two — Milan Central (Centrale) and Milan Porta Garibaldi. The tickets can be first or second class, and there is a 50 per cent reduction for children under 12. Other reductions, for circular journeys, 3-day returns, party and family tickets, are also available.

On all rail journeys children under 4 not occupying a seat travel free, children under 12 recieve a 50 per cent reduction.

Italian trains have the following specifications:

Super-Rapido *T E E*   Luxury first class only running between major cities. Special supplements charged, seat bookings obligatory.

Rapido   Fast trains between major cities. Some trains are first class only. Supplement charged (about 30 per cent of standard fare and children pay full supplement). On some trains seat booking is obligatory.

Espresso   Long-distance express trains, stopping at major stations only.

Diretto   Trains stopping at most stations.

Locale   Local trains, stopping at all stations.

Full-time students can obtain reduced rates on most tickets.

By Road

Coaches and Buses
Italy has an extensive long-distance coach system, and good local bus services. Most major cities offer specific bus tours.

Milan has an underground (*Metropolitano*) train service with a single-priced ticket, and a good tram service.

Car

Travelling from within Italy the area of the northern lakes is easily reached by the excellent *autostrada* system that uses Milan as a hub. From outside Italy the alpine chain must be breached, the most popular routes being through the Mont Blanc tunnel or Great St Bernard Pass to the Aosta valley which, though involving a drive of some distance to Milan (around 200km, 125 miles), does pass through some interesting countryside; the Simplon Pass from Brig in Switzerland to Domodossola and Lake Maggiore; the St Gotthard and San Bernardino Passes to Bellinzona and Lakes Maggiore, Lugano and Como; the Spluga Pass from Chur, the Maloja and Bernina Passes from St Moritz; the Ponte del Gallo and Stelvio Passes into the Valtellina; and the Brenner Pass from Austria into Trentino and the north tip of Lake Garda.

At any frontier crossing point that has an Italian Automobile Club (ACI) office (all the above crossings do) the visitor may buy a booklet of fuel coupons, either for northern or for southern Italy. The booklet for northern Italy contains vouchers for the lire equivalent of about 150 litres of fuel and offers a discount of about 10 per cent on pump prices. The coupons can be exchanged at most garages. The figures are approximate because the vouchers are for 'lire's worth' of fuel, not for 'litre's-worth', and so depend upon the current price.

In addition to the above benefits each booklet contains five 2,000 lire motorway toll vouchers. All Italian *autostradas* are tollways, the traveller taking a ticket from an automatic machine on entry to the system and paying on exit. Purchase of the booklet also entitles the buyer to call on the free breakdown assistance of the ACI (see 'Addresses' in Further Information section). For assistance dial 116 on any phone, or ask for ACI at the *autostrada* SOS columns, situated every 2km ($1^1/_4$ miles) along the roadside. Possession of a booklet entitles the driver whose car is off the road for at least 12 hours for repair after a breakdown or accident, to a free hire car for up to 10 days. This concession does not apply to coaches or motorcycles. To buy a coupon booklet the driver must be able to produce his vehicle registration document.

Speed limits on Italian roads are governed by engine size :

Engine Capacity	Autostradas	All other roads
Up to 600cc	90km/h (56mph)	80km/h (50mph)
Up to 900cc	110km/h (68mph)	90km/h (56mph)
Up to 1300cc	130km/h (80mph)	100km/h (62mph)
Over 1300cc	140km/h (87mph)	110km/h (68mph)

In built up areas the speed limit is 50km/h (31mph). These limits should be adhered to as there is an on-the-spot fine system for motoring, including parking, offences. Both the fines and their immediate payment are non-negotiable. Besides the fines, which can be as high as £500 ($800) (1987 figures), an offender faces the risk of imprisonment.

It is compulsory while in Italy to have an Italian translation of your driving licence in case you are stopped. Translations are available from national motoring organisations or the Italian State Tourist Authority.

The wearing of seatbelts by front seat passengers is soon to be made compulsory, as is the carrying of the vehicle registration and the owner's written permission for the driving of the vehicle if the driver is not the owner. Left side wing mirrors are compulsory on all vehicles, including those with right-hand drive, and drivers should carry a valid insurance certificate ('Green Cards' are not compulsory, but it is advisable to carry one).

Car Hire
Car hire is available at airports, major stations and in most big towns. The major international companies — Hertz, Avis etc — serve Italy, supplemented by larger domestic companies, eg Maggiore. A large range of (chiefly Italian) cars is offered.

Parking
Can be difficult in many Italian towns, and it is usually advisable to use one of the large car parks, occasionally administered by ACI, as their fee is much less than the fine incurred for illegal parking.

LAKE STEAMERS

Although there are now very few steamers on the lakes, the word is still used to describe the variety of passenger boats that daily crisscross the waters of the larger lakes — Orta, Maggiore, Lugano, Como, Iseo and Garda. The services are mainly modern diesel ferry boats, with a number of the more exciting hydrofoils (*aliscafo*) which reduce crossing times for a price supplement that is generally about 50 per cent. To take advantage of their speed the hydrofoils do not call at all ports, taking more direct lines between the lake ends.

Price reductions are also available for those who buy 'season' tickets, which are available for 1 day, several days, 1 or 2 weeks. The diesel and hydrofoil ferry services, together with the car-ferries that offer limited crossings on the three major lakes, are scheduled services operating every day. In addition the steamer companies run special services in the summer months, offering sight-seeing tours, together with excellent night-time trips on light-bedecked boats with dancing to live music. Some of these trips are by 'old-fashioned' paddle steamer, offering an unforgettable outing, particularly when the trip passes close to some of the floodlit highlights of the lakes, the Rocca d'Angera on Lake Maggiore and Malcesine's castle on Lake Garda for example. The boats for these trips have restaurants and bars, full air-conditioning, and the best of sound systems.

Lake Orta
There is a limited service on the smallest of the big lakes, linking Omegna, Pettenasco, Orta San Giulio and Pella, a full round trip taking about $1^1/_2$ hours.

In addition a boat service links Isola San Giulio with Orta San Giulio in just a few minutes.

Lake Maggiore
There is a full service on Lake Maggiore linking Arona, Angera, Meina, Lesa, Belgirate, Stresa, Carciano, the Borromean Islands, Baveno, Verbania-Pallanza, Villa Taranto, Intra, Laveno, Ghiffa, Porto Valtravaglia, Oggebbio, Cannero, Luino, Maccagno and Cannobio, continuing to Brissago, Porto Ronco, Ranzo, Gerra, Ascona, San Nazzaro, Vira, Magadino and Locarno, all in Switzerland. In addition there are small local services linking Carciano and Verbania-Pallanza with the three Borromean Islands and the Villa Taranto. Because the service crosses the national border between Italy and Switzerland (which zig-zags across the water in curious style in order to stay in the middle of the lake and make right-angles with the shore) the services include customs and border officials, passports must be carried and duty-payable goods must be declared.

The journey from Arona to Locarno and back takes about 6 hours if the outward journey is aboard the normal ferry with its restaurant service, and the return by hydrofoil.

The lake's only car-ferry links Verbania-Intra with Laveno, the crossing taking around 20 minutes.

Lake Lugano
There is a full ferry service on the lake, an end-to-end journey having the delight of numerous crossings into and out of Switzerland. The

formalities noted above for Lake Maggiore also apply here.

The ferry links Ponte Tresa, Lavena, Figino (Switzerland) and Porto Ceresio, crossing into Switzerland to reach Morcote, Brusino Arsizio, Melide, Poiana, Capolago, Bissone, Campione (Italy), Paradiso, Lugano, Castagnola, Caprino and Gandria, and crossing back into Italy to visit Santa Margherita, San Mamete, Claino-Osteno and Porlezza.

Lake Como
Diesel and hydrofoil ferries link a very large number of ports on Como's shores, particularly on the Como arm, and the western shore of the Colico arm. Como itself is a terminus, and from it ferries visit Tavernola, Cernobbio, Blevio, Moltrasio, Torno, Urio, Carate, Laglio, Faggeto Lario, Pognana Lario, Toriggia, Careno, Nesso, Brieno, Argegno, Colonno, Sala Comacina, Lezzeno, Lenno, Tremezzo, Cadenabbia and Bellagio. Continuing to Lake Colico, as the upper arm of Lake Como is sometimes called, the ferries reach Menaggio, Varenna, Bellano, Acquaseria, Rezzonico, Dervio, Cremia, Pianello del Lario, Musso, Dongo, Gravedona, Domaso, Gera Lario, Colico and a terminus at Piona. In the Lecco arm of the lake the ferries leave Bellagio for Lierna, Limonta, Oliveto, Mandello del Lario, Abbadia Lariana and finish at Lecco. In addition boats cross to Isola Comacina from several ports on the mainland close to the island.

A return trip from Como to Piona, via Bellagio, will take about 6 hours, more if Bellagio itself and Piona Abbey are visited. Such a trip can take advantage of the restaurants on the ferries and would be quicker if full advantage was taken of the hydrofoil service.

As an alternative to the ferry for sightseeing, Lake Como also has a flying boat service, regular tourist flights taking off from the lake close to the city of Como. The flights are not cheap, but they guarantee an exciting ride.

Lake Como has four car ferries criss-crossing the waters near Punta Spartivento, beyond Bellagio. They link Menaggio with Bellagio and with Varenna, and Cadenabbia with Bellagio and with Varenna. Each crossing takes from 15 to 30 minutes.

Lake Iseo
On Lake Iseo, ferries leave the Sarnico terminus for Clusane, Predore, Iseo, Sulzano, Tavernola Bergamasca, four ports on Monte Isola — Sensole, Siviano, Carzano and Peschiera Maraglio — Sale Marasino, Marone, Riva di Solto, Castro, Lovere and Pisogne. A full

round trip, including a visit to Monte Isola, takes about 4 hours, which gives some idea of the size of one of the smallest northern lakes.

Lake Garda
On the largest lake there is again a full range of diesel and hydrofoil services with restaurants and bars, and additional steamers offering day and night-time cruises.

Desenzano is the terminus for Garda steamers, and from it the ferries visit Sirmione, Peschiera del Garda, Lazise, Bardolino, Garda, Salo, Gardone Riviera, Fasano, Maderno, Torri del Benaco, Gargnano, Brenzone, Assenza, Malcesine, Limone sul Garda, Torbole and Riva del Garda, with occasional boats calling at Manerba and Moniga, south of Salo, from Sirmione. A round trip from Desenzano to Riva would take around 6 hours. In addition, there is a single car ferry service from Maderno to Torri del Benaco, which takes about 30 minutes.

Note: telephone contact numbers for the ferry services can be found in the Further Information section.

Food

A recently published poll suggested that only about 1 per cent of foreign tourists listed food as a contributing reason for travelling, so any mention of food may be redundant, but few tourists ever pass up the opportunity to sample a local speciality.

It will come as no surprise to discover that the local specialities are fish dishes. The lakes and rivers hold a variety of coarse fish which are served in many different ways. The most popular fish are trout and perch, which are usually served with herbs or soused. For something very different try the *missoltini,* sun-dried fish.

Away from the lakes, the mountain areas specialise in the serving of salted meats — try the spit-roasted salted mutton, perhaps with a few slices from a big, round, dark brown rye loaf — sausages and dairy products. The sausages are chiefly *polenta,* a maize-based pudding, often served flavoured with rabbit or the mountain fungi for which the areas are also famous, or with the Italian delicacy currently under fire from conservationists — song birds. The Ossola valley near Lake Maggiore is famous for its *viulin*, leg of goat salted and stuffed with herbs and spices. Nearby, in Val Vegezzo, Santa Maria Maggiore is famous for its smoked ham. The Valtellina, near Sondrio, is more famous for its dried salted beef, while the Valganna, near Varese, has its own *risotto*. Try too, the *gnocchi*, a pasta of white and chestnut flour, mashed potato and pumpkin, with breadcrumbs and egg yolk, seasoned with nutmeg and the local area's secret spice recipe.

Many of the valleys have their own cheese specialities, the best known being Taleggio from the valley of the same name that links the Val Brembana and the Valsassina, to the north of Bergamo, but try also the goat's cheese of the Brianza, south of Lake Como. Many also have honey in numerous flavours, assisted by the profusion of alpine flowers, azaleas and rhododendrons.

To wash the local dishes down there are the local wines. Italy has a huge number of wines, usually drunk locally since they do not travel well. Since there is no very specific naming system some caution must be exercised, because occasionally quite disparate wines have the same names. It is usually best to look for labels that refer to the government's grading system. The lowest grade — DS (*Denominazione Semplice*) — has no quality standard. DOC (*Denominazione di Origine Controllata*) wines meet defined quality standards and come from officially recognised production areas. DCG (*Denominazione Controllata & Garanzia*) wines are of the highest standards.

Well known wines from Novara, the region that includes the western shore of Lake Maggiore, are Barolo and Barbaresco, dry, full-bodied red wines, and Asti Spumante, the sparkling white. Lombardian wines tend to be white from the plains — Moscato and Reisling dell' Oltepro Pavese, and red from the mountains — the famous Valtellina wines, Sassella, Grumello and Inferno. Lake Garda is famous for three wines, the full-bodied red Valpolicella, the lighter red, dry Bardolino , and the dry white Soave.

In addition, there are many distilled spirit drinks. The most famous are those sold at Como's Piona Abbey, but there are also those from other mountain areas, which are distilled from alpine herbs and wild fruits such as strawberries and bilberries.

1 MILAN

This will necessarily be a short introduction to the city of Milan. Italy's second city, with 2 million inhabitants, is its undoubted economic capital and has enough points of interest to fill a sizeable book of its own. Here the emphasis is on the city centre, with its real treasures that no day-tripper should miss, and on outlining where the more determined traveller can find the museums and galleries which deserve more time.

Milan derives its name from *mediolanum*, the middle land, after the area's capital founded by the Gauls in the fifth century BC in the centre of the Lombardy plain, which was strategically positioned near the rivers Po, Ticino and Adda. The Romans captured the city from the Gauls in 222BC and it grew rapidly in importance. In AD286 Diocletian made the city capital of the western empire, a position it held until the barbarian invasions of AD402. Between these two dates, in the Edict of Milan in AD313, the Emperor Constantine gave Christians freedom of religion.

In AD539 the city was completely destroyed in the war between the Goths and the Byzantines, recovering only when it was taken by the Lombards. For defying Barbarossa the city was partially destroyed in 1157, but rose to organise the Lombard League, the army of which defeated Barbarossa at Legnano in 1176. Then followed the rise of the city as one of Italy's city states under the chiefly benevolent control of firstly the Viscontis, and latterly the Sforzas. This period lasted until 1499 when the French took control of the city. Thereafter it was held by the Spanish for almost 200 years before being taken by the Austrians. Napoléon made the city capital of the Cisalpine Republic in 1797, and then capital of his kingdom of Italy when he was crowned in 1805. Following Napoléon's fall, Milan returned to the Austrians, becoming part of the new Italy after the wars of the Risorgimento. In these the city fought bravely, most notably during the Five Days of Milan (18–23 March 1848) when the citizens threw the Austrians out of the city and barricaded its street. The rebellion was short-lived — the Austrians regained total control by early August.

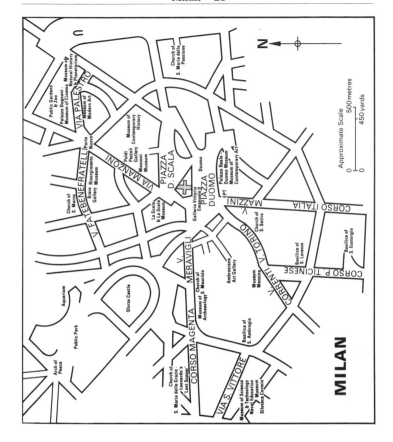

As Italy's richest city, Milan can readily satisfy the needs of the most discerning shopper or gourmet. In every respect, it offers services more usually associated with capital cities. The shopper should visit the area bounded by Via Manzoni and Corso Vittorio Emanuele that lies north of the Piazza Duomo. The gourmet can go there too, and also to countless other areas for fine restaurants, some specialising in fish and some in provincial cuisine, not only of Lombardy but also of all the other Italian regions. Local specialities include *risotto allo zafferano*, rice broth with saffron and *costolletta allo Milanese*, breaded veal cutlets. Try also *panettone*, a light cake with sultanas, now popular throughout Italy but having long been a Milanese speciality.

The tour of Milan, which can use the city's trams and metro to cut down on walking, starts at the city's heart, in Piazza Duomo. At the centre of the square is a bronze statue of Vittorio Emanuele II, but the *piazza* is dominated by the **Duomo** (cathedral) which was started in 1386 but took centuries to complete, such is its complexity. It is the third largest church in the world (only St Peter's in the Vatican and Seville Cathedral are bigger) covering almost 12,000sq m (125,000sq ft). It is 157m (515ft) long, 92m (302ft) wide at its widest, and 108m (356ft) to the top of the gold Madonna on its highest spire. To add to this array of amazing statistics, the cathedral has 2,245 external statues and a further 914 inside. Those who climb to the terrace near the top of the façade will walk among a forest of spires, 135 in all. It all coalesces into a fairy-tale church, romantic, almost bewilderingly ornate, but having some quite beautiful component parts. The exquisite central bronze door is by Ludovico Pogliaghi, and there is a monument to Il Medeghino (see Como chapter). Inside, the cathedral is huge, and beautifully lit by the large windows. A treasury of artwork is illuminated, some pieces of which are priceless.

On the southern side of the Piazza Duomo is **Palazzo Reale**, the Royal Palace, parts of which date from the twelfth century, though it has been remodelled by the Viscontis, the Sforzas, the Spanish, the Austrians and, sadly, following bombing in World War II. Today it houses the Duomo Museum, a must for all who found the cathedral itself of interest, as it explains the history of its building and decorating. The museum occupies the ground floor of the *palazzo*, the second floor holding the museum of contemporary art, dedicated to Italian work from this century and, specifically, to the work of living artists. Beside the *palazzo* is the church of **San Gottardo**, a fine fourteenth-century building with an elegant campanile. On the opposite side from the Royal Palace is the Galleria Vittorio Emanuele II, the Victor Emmanuel Arcade, begun only in 1865 and housing an array of elegant shops and coffee houses. Note too the mosaics, high up near the wrought-iron and glass roofs.

North-west from the Piazza Duomo, Via dei Mercanti leads to Piazza Cordusio. In this street, the **Palazzo della Ragione**, to the left, dates from 1233, the last remaining building, and a beautiful Romanesque one, from the era of the city-state. The **Palazzo dei Giureconsulti** opposite is three centuries older. From Piazza Cordusio, go west along Via Meravigli to Corso Magenta. To the left, is the church of **San Maurizio**, also known as Monastero Maggiore, the largest monastic house in the city, built in the early sixteenth century for

Milan Cathedral

Benedictine nuns. The church is famous for its frescoes by Bernardino Luini and for its mid-sixteenth-century organ. Beside the church is the city's **Archaeological Museum** with items from the city's Roman and pre-Roman eras, and from Greece and Egypt.

At the other end of Corso Magenta is the church of **Santa Maria delle Grazie**, a magnificent church in Lombard Gothic style, built by Donato Bramante in the last half of the fifteenth century, and well worth exploring. Many who visit the church unfortunately fail to go inside, being drawn instead to the small building beside it, the refectory of a Dominican convent, where, between the years 1495 and 1498, Leonardo painted *The Last Supper*. The painting, though almost miraculously surviving the bombings of 1943, has not withstood the ravages of time, and has deteriorated despite extensive restoration. But it remains a masterpiece of subtle colouration and dynamic realism suffused with formidable emotions. It is not to be missed, though time should also be given to the Donato di Montorfano *Crucifixion*, a fresco from 1499, which stands opposite the Leonardo and is too often casually bypassed.

South from Piazza delle Grazie, in Via San Vittore, lies an interesting series of museums. The largest is the **Science and Technology Museum** dedicated to Leonardo and holding a large collection of records on the great man's work in science. In addition, there are galleries for railways, planes and physics. The **Naval**

The entrance to the Victor Emmanuel Arcade

 Education Museum covers ships and shipping, and the **Siloteca Cormio** is devoted to wood and trees.

 East from the museum complex is the basilica of **San Ambrogio**, perhaps the most notable building in Lombardy. It was begun in AD379 and consecrated by San Ambrogio himself in AD386. In AD739 a Benedictine monastery was added, and, in the ninth and twelfth centuries, the campaniles. The porticoed building is magnificent, and the interior art-work equally so. The work of the goldsmith Volvinio is breathtaking.

 South-east from the basilica of San Ambrogio, in Corso di Porta Ticinese, is another, dedicated to **San Lorenzo**, which has a row of columns from a third-century Roman temple, as well as work from a fourth-century Christian church. North again is a museum showing the work of the sculptor Francesco Messina, set up in his studio.

South again, it is worth visiting the basilica of **San Eustorgio**, built in the fourth century, which was a place of pilgrimage for its relics of the Magi until these were removed by Barbarossa, who all but destroyed the church. Today it is more famous for the Portinari chapel, a marvel of Renaissance architecture, and the frescoes by Vincenzo Foppa.

 Return towards the Piazza Duomo to find the church of **San Satiro**, another masterpiece by Donato Bramante, and the **Ambrosiana Art Gallery**. This gallery, set up by a member of the Borromeo

The church of Santa Maria delle Grazie

family in the early seventeenth century, includes work by Raphael, Titian, Botticelli and Caravaggio.

East from Piazza Duomo is the church of **Santa Maria della Passione**, an impressive church with a museum of seventeenth-century Lombardian artwork attached.

Alternatively, walk through the Victor Emmanuel Arcade from Piazzo Duomo to reach Piazza della Scala, and the most famous **opera house** in the world. The opera house was built in 1776 on the site of a church dedicated to Santa Maria della Scala, which had been named after Beatrice della Scala, wife of a fourteenth-century Visconti, but it had to be rebuilt exactly following its devastation in 1943. Today it is revered as *the* opera house, but it was not always so. It was once considered a den of vice for having gambling tables — and that on once consecrated ground. Its reputation was born with the coming of Verdi, whose arrival coincided with the Risorgimento, and whose initials spelled out Vittorio Emanuele Re d'Italia. Everywhere 'Viva Verdi' appeared on walls, an association that did no harm to composer or theatre. The visitor who cannot see a performance in the house, which holds 2,800, can visit the museum with its collection of operatic memorabilia.

In front of the theatre stands a monument to Leonardo, while another famous Italian, writer Alessandro Manzoni, has a monument in front of the nearby church of San Fedele. Near here, in Via Morone,

PLACES OF INTEREST IN MILAN

Duomo Museum
Palazzo Reale
Fascinating insight into the 600-year-old building and art history of the cathedral.

Museum of Contemporary Art
Palazzo Reale
Museum to the work of Italian artists of this century.

Church of San Maurizio
15 Corso Magenta
Frescoes by Bernardino Luini, and fine mid-sixteenth-century organ, in old convent with beautiful woodwork.

Archaeological Museum
15 Corso Magenta
Fine collections on pre-history and Roman history of city and area, as well as from further afield.

Leonardo's *Last Supper*
Piazza delle Grazie
Leonardo da Vinci's famous fresco.
Not to be missed.

Museum of Science and Technology
21 Via San Vittore
Galleries on rail, air and motor transport, on physics, and on the work of Leonardo da Vinci.

Museum of Naval Education
21 Via San Vittore
History of ships, shipping and sea exploration. Includes the tent used by Nobile during his North Pole expedition.

Siloteca Cormio
21 Via San Vittore
Museum to wood and trees. Has 7,000 wood samples including a 3m (10ft) sequoia trunk.

Basilica of San Ambrogio
Piazza San Ambrogio
Beautiful porticoed church with 1,600-year history. Contains notable pulpit and shrines and magnificent gold work by Volvino.

Francesco Messina Museum
10 Via San Sisto
Museum of the sculptor set up in his studio.

Ambrosiana Art Gallery
Piazza Pio XI
Many fine works of art, including Raphael, Titian Botticelli and Caravaggio.

Basilica of San Eustorgio
Piazza San Eustorgio
Beautiful old church with magnificent Renaissance chapel and fine frescoes by Foppa.

Church of Santa Maria della Passione
2 Via Vincenzo Bellini
Museum of seventeenth-century Lombardian art in impressive Renaissance church.

PLACES OF INTEREST IN MILAN - continued

Scala Museum
Piazza della Scala
Collection of operatic
memorabilia in world's most
famous opera house.

Manzoni Museum
1 Via Morone
Collection of memorabilia of the
writer Alessandro Manzoni.

Poldi Pezzoli Gallery
12 Via Manzoni
Private collection of nineteenth-
century Milanese aristocrat.
Contains many fine items
including works by Bellini and
Botticelli, and the Pollaiolo
masterpiece *Portrait of a Young
Woman*. Also collections of lace,
porcelain, clocks and sculptures.

Brera Gallery
28 Via Brera
Nearly forty rooms of work from
pre-Renaissance to twentieth
century. Numerous great
masters.
Not to be missed.

Risorgimento Museum
23 Via Borgonuovo
Fascinating collection on the
history of the struggle for Italian
unity and independence.

Natural History Museum
55 Corso Venezia
Good collections on world, as
well as local, wildlife. Especially
fine bird collection.

Planetarium
57 Corso Venezia
One of the world's finest.

**Cinema Museum, Palazzo
Dugnani**
2 Via Manin
Collection on the showing of
moving pictures, from magic
lanterns to modern times.

Museum of Modern Art
16 Via Palestro
Fine collection of work by both
Italian and international modern
artists.

**Museum of Contemporary
History**
6 Via San Andrea
Covering the years 1914 to 1945
in newspapers, photographs etc.

Church of San Marco
Piazza San Marco
Fine Lombardian church with
good artwork.

Sforzesco (Sforza) Castle
Magnificent Renaissance castle
with excellent art museum which
includes unfinished sculpture by
Michelangelo.
Not to be missed.

Public Gardens and Zoo
Via Manzoni
Excellent gardens in English
style with children's amusement
area and city zoo.

Aquarium
2 Viale Gadio
Interesting collection of fish,
crustaceans and reptiles.

La Scala opera house

is a museum dedicated to the writer, in the house he occupied for almost 60 years until his˙ death in 1873. It contains numerous personal items and his library.

In nearby Via Manzoni, named after the writer, is one of Milan's most famous art galleries, the **Poldi Pezzoli**, named after its nine-teenth-century aristocratic collector and one of the most interesting private collections ever established. Here can be seen Mantegna's *Madonna and Child*, and a Botticelli of the same title, an agonising *Pietà* by Bellini and the famous *Portrait of a Young Woman* by Antonio Pollaiolo.

North-west from the Poldi Pezzoli gallery is the **Brera Gallery**. Here is a series of frescoes by Bernardino Luini and the *Christ Dead* of Andreas Mantegna that cannot fail to move the visitor. There are also works by Rubens, Rembrandt, El Greco and Raphael, as well as a huge collection of Italian Renaissance work. Near the Brera is the **Risorgimento Museum**, with a fascinating collection on the history of Italian nationalism from Napoléon's campaign (1796) to final success in Rome (1870).

At the top of Via Manzoni is the Porta Nuova, which was part of the city's defences when Barbarossa attacked in 1156, and beyond which are the **Public Gardens,** in English style. Here, in addition to the flowers, trees and shrubs, there is a lake, plenty of amusements for children, a zoo, and the city's **Museum of Natural History** with

Market in Via Brera, Milan

2 million insects, 100,000 fossils, 30,000 birds, and 25,000 mineral specimens. The collection also includes a lifesize dinosaur. Next to the museum is the city planetarium, reputedly the best in the world. Also, backing onto the gardens, is **Palazzo Dugnani**, a seventeenth-century building with good frescoes, which houses the **Museum of the Cinema**, with a fine collection from magic lanterns to modern equipment.

South of the gardens, in Via Palestro, is the **Museum of Modern Art**, housed in the eighteenth-century Villa Comunale. Here is a fine collection of Italian work, together with work by many leading modern artists — Renoir, Gauguin, Corot, Monet, Cézanne and others. South again is Milan's **Museum of Contemporary History**, covering 1914–45 in newspapers, posters, photographs etc.

Going westward along Via Fatebenefratelli, observe on the right the church of **San Marco**, in fine Lombardian style and containing excellent frescoes and canvases. Further on again, to the right in Via San Semplicano, is a basilica of the same name built in the fourth century, though much restored and altered since then.

Sforza Castle

Ahead now are the **Sforza Castle** and the parkland that surrounds it. The original castle was built by Galeazzo Visconti in the late fourteenth century, but this was partially destroyed in the mid-fifteenth century. What can be seen today is largely from the late fifteenth century, built under the direction of Francesco Sforza. The central tower, the Filarete Tower, was destroyed in 1521 when lightning struck it and detonated a considerable quantity of gunpowder stored inside. Its rebuilding was part of several restorations carried out as Milan's rulers changed, but eventually warfare outstripped the need for castles and it fell into disrepair. Thankfully, when it was threatened with demolition in 1880, a good sense of history prevailed and it was restored. Today it is seen as one of the great Renaissance castles, and rightly so: the Filarete Tower is an expanded, Russian-doll-like delight of architectural styles; the round towers are beautifully constructed; the entrance gateway is massively functional. In addition, the castle houses an excellent art

*Michelangelo's unfin-
ished Pietà in the
Sforza Castle*

museum in the fine rooms of the Ducal Court and the Roccheta wing.
In the museum, pride of place must go to the *Pietà Rondonni* by
Michelangelo and a frescoed room by Leonardo. The *pietà* is an
unfinished sculpture, almost the more brilliant for being so, the work
seeming to climb out of the stone like a half-emerged butterfly from
a chrysalis. Elsewhere, the museum also has much of interest.

The parkland behind the castle offers excellent walking. At its
eastern corner is the **City Aquarium** with reptiles as well as fish,
while beyond its north-western edge is the **Arch of Peace**. This was
started in 1807 to celebrate Napoléon's victories, but was only about
half finished when the battle of Waterloo rendered the monument
inappropriate. It was finally completed in 1838 and dedicated to
peace. The spectacular bronze chariot and horses on the arch was
sculptured by Sangiorgio. North from here is the **Monumentale
Cemetery**, with a most impressive façade. Manzoni and Toscanini
are buried here, as well as other famous Milanese citizens.

2 LAKE ORTA ✳

T he first lake visited is, by comparison with the main lakes to the east, a mere splash of water in a mountain cauldron. But despite that description Lake Orta is, in fact, 13$^1/_2$km (8$^1/_2$ miles) long, and 2$^1/_2$ km (1$^1/_2$ miles) wide at it widest point. It sits at 290m (950ft) high, nearly 100m (328ft) above Lake Maggiore, and is, at its deepest, 143m (469ft) deep. The whole of the lake lies in Novara province in Piemonte. The region's name means foot on the mountain, and nowhere is the name more appropriate than at Lake Orta. It is filled by numerous streams draining down from the mountains that make the bowl in which it sits, and is itself drained by the Strona river that flows into the Toce at Gravellona Toce, and from there into Lake Maggiore. It is the only lake that drains northward, since the Alps are to the north and the rivers generally must go south into the Po valley.

The Romans called the lake Cusius, which later became Cusio, this also being the name given to the part of Novara province that surrounds the lake. To add to the confusion, the lake was at one time — between being Cusius and being Orta — known as Lago San Giulio, after its most famous saint.

The lake can be reached from Gravellona in the north, from Gozzano in the south, or, by the very intrepid, over the Mottarone massif on a lane that links Gignese (which will be visited in the next chapter), and Armeno, which stands on the hill above Pettenasco. This tour will take take the easiest way, a straightforward drive beside the river Strona from Gravellona to Omegna at the northern end of the lake.

Omegna is a pleasant enough place, a small industrial town with part of its medieval walls still standing, and the ruins of an old bridge that once spanned the river still visible. Some experts think the bridge is also medieval, but others think the ruins are much older, perhaps even Roman. The old part of the town, particularly part of the lake front, is excellent, having beautiful old houses, some with balconies and outside staircases, and with a fine array of shutters and wrought ironwork. The view lakewards is beautiful, the gentle curve taking the

Omegna

lake out of sight to the left as the mountains tumble in from the right. Equally good are the views to the valleys of the inflowing and outflowing Strona, each with mountain peaks like the posts of some giant gateway. The inhabitants of the town are proud of these gateways, particularly that through which the Strona flows out. The northward flowing stream that links the lake and the Strona is La Nigoglia, and the townspeople of Omegna say that 'La Nigoglia goes up, and we make the laws', a firm stance for independence beside this most independent of lakes.

From Omegna the lake can be circled in either direction, but it is a good idea to go first along the western shore, to keep the best until last. A road up and away from the lake leads to **Quarna Sotto** and **Quarna Sopra**, good villages set among chestnut woods. The first has a very interesting museum of musical instruments.

Stay close to the lake, pass Cesara, again set among woodland, and reach **Pella**. Here there is a medieval tower and an equally old bridge, picturesquely set over the Torrente Pellino pouring into the lake. There is also a fine collection of houses from the eighteenth and nineteenth centuries, with open galleries and porches.

Above Pella is **Madonna del Sasso**, the name given to a small collection of villages and hamlets. A visit to the area is very worthwhile and offers fine views of the lake, but the chief reason for a visit is to see the church of that name, set on a rock above the village of Boleto. It is beautiful, both in construction and setting, and contains some very interesting frescoes of the eighteenth century and some fine earlier artwork: a sixteenth-century painting and seventeenth-century wooden crucifix.

The road from the church has to be retraced to the lakeside road, which continues southward with exciting views across the water to Isola San Giulio and the promontory of Orta behind it. **San Maurizio d'Opaglio** is a good holiday resort and is one of Europe's leading centres for the manufacture of bathroom fittings. That sort of information always raises a smile and an eyebrow, but there is, after all, no reason why Italian towns should not make taps. Perhaps it is a surprise that, amid so much scenic splendour, something as mundane as real life should intrude.

Next head for Gozzano, passing, at Luzzara, the Villa Jucker standing in an English-style park — not open to the public — and a fine Romanesque church, the Nativita di Maria. **Gozzano** is another light industrial town, but in a good position, with a building complex known as the 'castle', even though there are no castle remains. The complex includes the church of San Lorenzo, rebuilt in baroque style with a Roman marble font and a sarcophagus, reputedly that of San Giuliano. Beside the church the Palazzo Vescovile is thirteenth century, and there are other fine houses from the seventeenth century. The parish church of San Giuliano has a Romanesque campanile, while the church of Santa Maria has a seventeenth-century wooden altar. The whole complex offers an extremely interesting visit. Also within the town, but set at the lakeside on a wooded headland, is the medieval tower of Buccione built by the Lombards. From the tower it is only a short journey to Orta and the chief interests of the lake.

In the fourth century AD two brothers, Giulio and Giuliano, were sent from Rome to preach the gospel to the inhabitants of the wild area around the lake, then known as Cusius. Giuliano founded his church at Gozzano and died there — some say he was murdered — his body being laid to rest in the sarcophagus in a church on whose remains the present church stands.

Giulio pressed on and reached the anvil-shaped headland opposite the lake's little island. The island attracted him immediately. It was gently wooded, quiet and remote and he wanted to be taken there to live as a hermit and teacher. The locals would not take him,

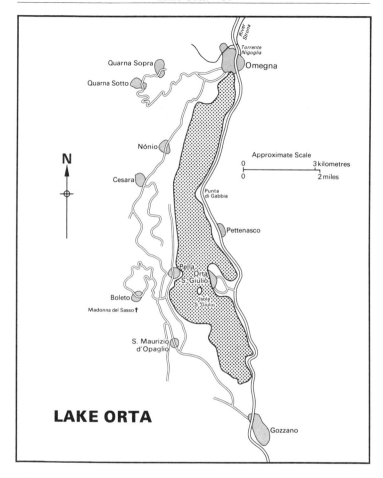

telling him that it was inhabited by dragons and serpents, and was in the possession of the powers of darkness. Undeterred, Giulio flung his cloak on the water and stepped onto it. Then, to the astonishment of the locals, a wind picked up, blowing the cloak across the water, Giulio steering by using his staff as a rudder. By the time he reached the island the monsters had fled, overawed by the sight of him and not daring to fight. Giulio landed and built his hermit's cell, where he lived for the rest of his life converting and teaching the lake-dwellers. Today the island is jammed tight with buildings: there can be very few patches of soil that have not been or are not built on. This is due in

A quiet corner of Orta San Giulio

part to the island's religious past, and to its having been, until earlier this century, capital of the lake district. But some of the building work was for fortification — various ownership struggles — and a heroic defence by Willa, the wife of Berengar, against the forces of Otto the Great.

 Isola San Giulio is reached from Orta San Giulio as the town is known. It still seems to have an 'other-worldliness', many visitors talking of the dreamy atmosphere of its narrow lanes, churches and *piazze*. On the island the basilica of San Giulio is now recognised as the most important Romanesque church in Novara province. It was built in the ninth century on the site of the hermit's cell, but was altered and restored in the eleventh and seventeenth centuries. Much of what remains dates from the first period of alterations, when the campanile was also built. Within the basilica there is a treasure house of artwork and architecture, but pride of place is given to an *ambo* (pulpit) in black Oira marble which dates from the eleventh or twelfth century. The three carved lecterns and the pulpit stand, which are supported on four columns, are also masterpieces. Note too, the interplay of Christian and pagan symbols. The walnut choir stalls are very good, as are some of the painted wooden sculptures. The church preserves a 'monster's bone' said to be from the time of San Giulio (but which is probably a more recent whale bone) and in the crypt holds a silver urn which contains the remains of the saint.

Orta San Giulio

Beside the church, the Palazzo dei Vescovi is fourteenth century and today houses a Benedictine monastery. Elsewhere the island is worth all the time that can be given to its exploration. Its elegant, arcaded houses, narrow alleys and sudden lake views are treasures beyond words. And on the return journey to the mainland, if the lake is flat calm, and especially if there is a light mist that obscures the western lake shore and softens the focus of the island, just stand and stare. The island seems to float in mid-air, magically suspended, unsure of its position between heaven and earth.

The mainland town of **Orta San Giulio** is also an excellent place, not least for its view of the island. At night, when both island and the church of Madonna del Sasso high above it are lit, this is a magical spot. Here too, there are narrow lanes whose curves and breaks give sudden views of mountains, lakes and occasionally the island. The town square, Piazza Motta, at the quay, is open and airy, coolly shaded by trees and with a side dominated by the town hall, a sixteenth-century building with frescoed walls, an outside stairway and a tiny campanile breaking through the grey roof like a chimney. Elsewhere, find more frescoes at Casa Morgarani, called the 'House of Dwarves', though the reason for the name has been lost in time. In searching for that house the visitor will also pass many others which are of interest.

But the treasure of the town is the Sacre Monte, which dominates the headland. The hill is delightfully wooded and has excellent views of the lake. Through the beech and pine woods a single path threads its way, passing twenty-one chapels, chiefly from the early seventeenth century, but one that has only recently been completed. Inside these are a total of 376 lifesize terracotta statues by a number of sculptors, illustrating incidents from the life of St Francis of Assisi to whom the Sacre Monte is dedicated. At the top of the hill is a building comprising two small oratories and the remains of a monastery, which contains a Gothic wooden Madonna. Expert opinion differs slightly about which of the chapels are the best, but all agree that numbers eleven and sixteen are excellent. Chapel number fifteen is on a terrace from which the view is expansive. Beside the Sacre Monte, the secular is represented in sumptious style by the Villa Crespi — sadly not open to the public.

On the hillsides above Orta San Giulio are some good villages: **Miasino** with fine seventeenth- and eighteenth-century buildings and a really good baroque church; **Armeno**, also with a good church, and **Ameno**, a village clustered around a Romanesque campanile.

PLACES OF INTEREST AROUND LAKE ORTA

**Museum of Musical
Instruments**
Quarna Sotto
Collection of old musical instru-
ments and photos of their use in
local music.

Church of Madonna del Sasso
Above Boleto
Beautifully positioned eighteenth-
century church with frescoes and
early artwork.

Isola San Giulio
Reached from Orta San Giulio
Magical island with basilica to
founding saint which contains
many treasures including black
marble pulpit.

Sacre Monte di Orta
Orta San Giulio
Wooded hill with twenty-one
chapels containing life-size
terracotta figures illustrating
episodes from life of St Francis
of Assisi.

Calderara Collection
Vicciago (near Ameno)
Paintings and sculptures, chiefly
by Antonio Calderara, but with
work from all over the world.

Viewpoints
From Madonna del Sasso,
above Pella
From Punta di Crabbia,
Pettenasco/Omegna

In the nearby hamlet of **Vicciago** is a collection of paintings and
sculpture, chiefly by the artist Antonio Calderara who died here in
1978, but including European, American and oriental work. The
collection is in a superb house with triple tiers of porticoed balconies.

On the lakeside the last village is **Pettenasco**, with a pretty lake
front and a very impressive viaduct taking the lake-edge railway line
over the Torrente Pescone. Beyond is the Punta di Crabbia, a small
headland so positioned that virtually the whole of the lake can be
seen from it, the gentle curves in both directions melting into the
enclosing mountains. From this point, the lake road goes back again
to Omegna.

3 LAKE MAGGIORE ✳

M aggiore is a squiggle of a lake, its northern region (about 15 per cent) lying in the Swiss canton of Ticino, its western shore lying in Piemonte, its eastern shore in Lombardy. The lake covers 215sq km (84sq miles). It is approached from the south by anyone entering Italy through Milan's airports or railway stations, or driving in from France via the Mont Blanc tunnel. Those entering from Switzerland, via the Simplon Pass, Domodossola and the Val d'Ossola reach the Borromean Bay, and although this is a wonderful entrance to the land of the lakes, the high gorges of the Simplon making it one of the finest alpine passes, it is an unsatisfactory place to join the lake. Those crossing the St Gotthard or the San Bernardino Passes arrive in Italian Swiss Bellinzona and can choose to go down either the west or east side of the lake. This tour will go through Locarno. There, as a digression, it is worth mentioning that one of the finest short rail journeys in Europe links the town with Domodossola, via Val Vigezzo. Those who take the lake steamer from, say, Stresa to Locarno, the Vigezzo train to Domodossola and a return train to Stresa have a really magnificent day

The Piemontian Shore

After Locarno the visitor crosses into Italy at Piaggio di Valmara, though there is not enough of a village there for him to feel he has really arrived. **Cannobio** is the first town, a fine place, but not as popular as it should be, mainly because it is a long way up the western side of the lake. Its old quarter, with its narrow winding streets (note especially Via Marconi and Via Umberto I) and towers (the campanile is twelfth century) is typically Italian, speaking of ancient trades and allegiances. Cannobio was fortified by the Romans — there is evidence of pre-Roman occupation — and in 1859 the people of the town attacked an Austrian fleet over a period of two days. This is commemorated by a memorial stone.

The northern end of Lake Maggiore

The town harbour, where there is a market each Sunday, is excellent, as is the walk along it which passes the Santuario della Pietà. In 1522 a picture — a *pietà*, that is the dead Christ removed from the cross, with Christ between the Virgin Mary and St John — hung in a house near the lake shore and bled real blood from Christ's wounds. This was miraculous in itself, but soon Cannobio escaped unscathed from a plague that devastated the area around. To enshrine the painting the house was demolished and a small chapel was built. Other miracles followed, and about 50 years later San Carlo Borromeo ordered that a church should be built to do justice to the painting, which should itself be given a silver frame, as befitted its status. Almost immediately, in 1575, Cannobio was spared when plague again devastated the area. Today, the ornately framed picture is kept at the high altar, in a church interior that is almost equally ornate.

Elsewhere in the town there is another church, beside which is the fine thirteenth-century Palazzo della Ragione also known as the Palazzo Paradiso, with a fine, column-supported barrel roof at ground floor level. The *palazzo* holds the Museum for the Promotion of Culture, a small collection on the heritage of the area.

From Cannobio a road leads up the Val Cannobino, and at about $2\frac{1}{2}$ km (1 $\frac{1}{2}$ miles) from the town is the gorge (*orrido*) of Santa Anna, with a church dedicated to the same saint beside it. Here the Torrente Cannobino falls through a narrow gorge before emerging into a wide, calm pool. The gorge can be viewed from either of two bridges, one reputedly Roman, or from the pool in a hired boat.

Continue along the road to the Val Vigezzo, already mentioned in connection with the Domodossola to Locarno railway. Val Vigezzo has been a favourite with artists since its 'discovery' in the eighteenth century because of the variety of shades and tints of greens, browns and greys, and the pure quality of the light. Today it is equally famous for winter sports, for walking, and for its art and crafts. For a really unusual trip try the Chimney Sweep's Museum at **Santa Maria Maggiore** or the museum at **Gurro**, a small village with Scottish connections (Scots settled there after the Battle of Pavia in 1537) — these being two of several small but interesting museums. The lover of food and drink, should try the smoked ham at Santa Maria Maggiore, the valley honey, and spirit drinks distilled from alpine herbs. The church at **Re** is magnificent, and the grey roofs contrast with the red tiles usually seen on the lake shore.There is also an interesting museum here.

Back at Lake Maggiore, take the lake hugging road to **Carmine**, a small village near an elbow in the lake. The village is divided into two, as are several on the sloped lakeside, Inferiore, the lower lake village, and Superiore, the higher cliff village. In this case the upper village really does cling to the cliff, and in that cliff is a *ricetto*, a medieval hermitage. Maintaining the religious theme, the church of San Gottardo, a fourteenth-century building with beautiful fifteenth-century frescoes and paintings, is well worth visiting.

Beyond Carmine the road rounds the elbow headland, and the Cannero, or Malpaga, castles come into view. There were two castles, one on each of two islands, which were originally connected by a drawbridge built during the twelfth to fourteenth centuries, but what is mainly seen today are the ruins of a fifteenth-century Borromean fortified villa. The ruins are not open to the public, but boat trips around them are available from Cannero.

Cannero was once described as a 'Genoese Riviera in miniature... a pearl in a necklace of vineyards and villas'. The vineyards have largely gone now, but the villas remain and Cannero is now Cannero Riviera, claiming the title of the 'Nice of Maggiore' because of its very mild winter climate. At one of the villas, Villa Sabbioncella, Garibaldi stayed after the battle at Luino.

The town has fine old houses in narrow streets, a delightful tiny

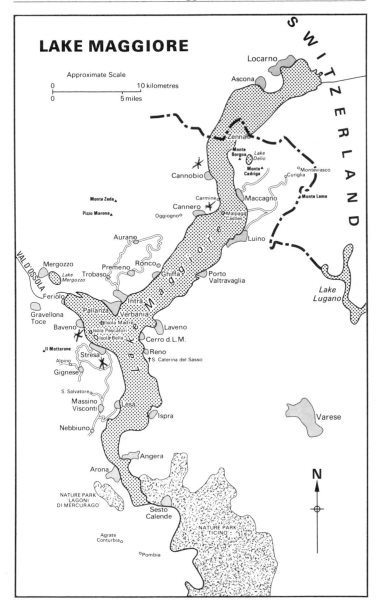

LAKE MAGGIORE

Approximate Scale

0   10 kilometres

0   5 miles

SWITZERLAND

Locarno
Ascona
Zenna
Monte Borgna
Lake Delio
Monte Cadriga
Cannobio
Monteviasco
Curiglia
Carmine
Maccagno
Cannero
Oggiogno
Malpaga Castles
Monte Lema
Monte Zeda
Pizzo Marona
Luino
Aurano
Premeno
Ronco
Mergozzo
Lake Mergozzo
Trobaso
Ghiffa
Porto Valtravaglia
VAL D'OSSOLA
Feriolo
Intra
Lake Lugano
Gravellona Toce
Pallanza
Verbania
Baveno
Isola Madre
Isola Pescatori
Isola Bella
Laveno
Il Mottarone
Cerro d.L.M.
Stresa
Alpino
Reno
S. Caterina del Sasso
Gignese
S. Salvatore
Massino Visconti
Lesa
Varese
Nebbiuno
Ispra
Angera
Arona
N
NATURE PARK 'LAGONI DI MERCURAGO'
Sesto Calende
NATURE PARK TICINO
Agrate Conturbia
Pombia

harbour, and the beautiful gorge of the Torrente Cannero which rushes under a picturesque old bridge. At **Oggiogno**, a village above the town, there is a fine view of town, lake and castles which can be considerably improved by a climb of some 850m (2,990ft) to the top of the Cima di Morissolo.

Drive on along the shore of the lake. Now, round the lake elbow, the view is expansive. Stresa, ahead across the Borromean Bay, nestles below the Mottarone, while to the right the Piemonte Alps are green cascades.

Next pass through a succession of tiny villages, each with its own special charm, and reach **Ghiffa**, perhaps the best of them, with its elegant array of villas and fine gardens grouped around castle ruins. An interesting church is found here, the Santuario della Trinitá, from which there are excellent views, and from a small headland at Ghiffa the view is the most expansive of any from the lakeside.

Beyond Ghiffa, at a sharp angle in the lake as it cuts back into the Borromean Bay, is the largest stretch of habitation on the lake, the towns of **Intra**, **Verbania** and **Pallanza** They are now so close that they virtually merge into one, and usually take the name of the smallest — Verbania. This choice of name can cause confusion as the lake's only car ferry links the village complex to Laveno and is called the Laveno-Intra ferry.

Intra is the most industrialised town on the lake, but the industry is powered by electricity not smoke-stained chimneys, and is light, keeping to the back of the town, to leave the lakeside area fresh and airy. The area between the two streams, the San Giovanni and the San Bernardino — the town's name derives from this position — was certainly settled by the Romans and may even be older, but what is seen today is all many centuries newer, and the town is still being developed as a tourist centre. The basilica of San Vittore is a good example of the comparative newness, for there, though the site is very ancient, the present church is of eighteenth-century origin. The town has older sections, however, and the more modern buildings were designed with an eye to architectural wholeness, and have been satisfactorily integrated into the town.

The lakeside villas make an elegant back-drop, viewed through the chestnuts and oleanders, to the walk along towards the ferry harbour, though the better ones, Villa Poss, Villa Adda and that of the Intra sculptor Paul Troubetzkoy, are closer to the mouth of the San Giovanni and are, sadly, not open to the public. The harbour itself is an elegant arc of masonry, its entrance guarded by a tall light with an

Intra from the car ferry

external spiral staircase. Beyond, cross over the San Bernardino to Verbania-Pallanza, and soon reach one of the highlights of a trip to Maggiore, the Villa Taranto, which has one of the world's finest botanical gardens. The garden covers 16 hectares (about 50 acres) and is criss-crossed by almost 8km (5 miles) of pathway, so that every aspect of its delights can be explored. Those who visit the garden can see about 20,000 varieties of trees, shrubs and flowers, some very rare and some uniquely represented in Europe. The villa itself is used by the Italian government and is not open to visitors.

Further along the lakeside, before the headland of the Verbanian spur, is the Romanesque church of San Remigio, an eleventh-century building with good fifteenth-century frescoes. Beside it stands the Villa San Remigio, with excellent gardens that, sadly, are no longer open to the public. From the headland itself there are fine views of the lake, extending into most of the crevices it fills, and including the little island (the *isolino*) of San Giovanni, on which is a villa that was long the home of Toscanini. Beyond, the old town is dominated by the campanile of the church of San Leonardo, a much restored sixteenth-century building.

At the water's edge near the harbour is a memorial to Marshal Carlo Cadorna, commander-in-chief of Italian forces in World War I and a native of the town. It dominates the view of the lakeside from here onwards. Just offshore here is a line of fountains that are illuminated at night — a spectacular show.

Now go inland, first to Piazza Garibaldi at the heart of old Pallanza, with the maze of interesting narrow streets that lead from it. Strike northward for Piazza Cavour, where, in Palazzo Dugnani, is Pallanza's interesting Museo del Paesaggio, the Landscape Museum. Here there is a collection of paintings, including many landscapes, items from local Celtic and Roman history, and a collection of the work of Paul Troubetzkoy, the Intran sculptor. From Piazza Cavour follow Via Azari and at the top of it (about $1^1/_2$ km — 1 mile) find the church of Madonna di Campagna, the finest piece of Renaissance architecture in the town. The church was built in the early sixteenth century, on the site of another church from which the campanile (mid-eleventh century), has survived. Inside, the church has some fine frescoes, a baroque wooden choir and some good wrought ironwork.

From Pallanza, head not for Gravellone Toce and the head of the Borromean Bay, but upwards into the hills. The best route is to follow the eastern side of the Torrente San Giovanni up, and the western bank back, going from Intra to Campasca, then climbing steadily through a number of excellent hill villages, any or all worth allowing time to explore, to the delightfully named Bee, and on again to **Premeno**, the most famous of the villages in this area. On a fine day it is a spectacularly beautiful village, with its array of white and cream, mostly red roofed houses. The village is high (about 800m, 2,600ft) and the air a little cooler, better for enjoying a mountain stroll with fine views of the surrounding scenery. The best views of the lake, and of Premeno, are obtained from Pollino, a short distance away, or from the Albergo Belvedere just beyond Pollino.

Beyond Premeno is the Pian di Sole where you can play golf in summer and ski in winter, and then the road winds round the Cresta della Cereso for Pian Cavallo and another spectacular view. From here the intrepid can follow a mountain track, drivable only to Colle, about 2km (1 mile), that leads after about 16km (10 miles) to Monte Vada at 1,800m (5,900ft). From there the even more intrepid can walk the high mountains of the Reserva Naturale della Val Grande, set aside for mid-alpine animals and birds. Such an expedition is for experienced walkers/climbers only and should not be undertaken lightly. An adventurous alternative is to descend from Colle to Cannero, the journey getting easier the further you go, which offers the possibility of visiting either Trarego or Viggiona, each with good views over the northern end of Maggiore.

The return route leads down to **Aurano**, which, with the nearby villages of Scareno and Intragna, is beautifully sited, and then descends to **Cambiasca** where there is a fine Romanesque church. From here a road goes up to Pala, offering a fine drive into the mountains and good views of them from the village. A drive can then be made to the memorial to the Alpini (the Italian Alpine Brigade), or it is possible to walk the 3km (2 miles) to Pian Cavallone, 600m (2,000ft) high, and from the refuge hut there to climb Pizzo Marona, a further 2km (1 mile) away and 500m (1,650ft) high. Such a trip will necessitate setting aside an entire half day at least.

From Trobaso, on the return to Verbania, a road leads off up the Val Grande, the valley of the Torrente San Bernardino, to **Cicogne**, a remote village set high up under the peaks and a good centre for walking. The less energetic can drive from Verbania to the summit of Monte Rosso, 613m (2,010ft) with excellent views over the Borromean Bay and islands.

Back on the lakeside, continue to Fondotoce, beyond which a quick route to Stresa crosses the bridge over the Toce. Alternatively, leave the main road in favour of one circling Lake Mergozzo for the village of the same name. The lake is nicely positioned at the mouth of the Val d'Ossola, and the village is very picturesque with its medieval towers. From the village a road traverses the gap between Monte Orfano and the village of that name, with a church dedicated to San Giovanni which is one of the best examples of Lombard Romanesque architecture in the area. It is eleventh century, made from granite blocks, with an octagonal dome. Here too, is a small museum with items from the area's history.

The main road reaches **Gravellona Toce**, where it meets the road from Switzerland and from where a road goes to Lake Orta. Gravellona is a small industrial town, grown up because of its position at the mouth of the Val d'Ossola.

From Gravellona Toce the main road can be followed to **Domodossola**, and some of the most spectacular mid-alpine scenery in Italy. The Val d'Ossola is excellent itself, but from it lead the Val Anzasca with Macugnaga, a famous winter sports centre; Val Antrona; Val di Vedro that leads through high-cliffed gorges to the Simplon Pass; the valleys of Antigorio and Formazza and Val Vigezzo. Remember if you drive up the Val d'Ossola, to watch out for Candoglia, for from the quarries behind it came the marble for Milan Cathedral.

Baveno

Baveno, the first holiday resort on this side of the bay, sits below a mountain of pink granite, the quarrying of which helped the town to prosper. It is an ancient site, with Roman finds from the first century, and has a proud history in the fight for Italian freedom, first from the Austrians and later from the Fascists. Today it is an elegant holiday resort, with a line of villas opposite the excellent flower-gardened lakeside testifying to a long and prosperous history in its newest industry. Villa Branca, the pink villa high up on the hillside on the way out of the town, is mid-nineteenth century and very English looking.

Within the town there are some beautiful old houses, none more so than Casa Morandi which is an Italian national monument. A four-storey building, the floors are reached by interwoven outside stairways. The house is Baveno's most photographed spot, and rightly so. Also much photographed is the church square, the church at Baveno being set slightly apart from the rest of the village, though still in a central position. Dedicated to San Gervaso and San Protaso, it has a twelfth-century Romanesque façade and a Romanesque campanile, the rest having been almost completely rebuilt in the seventeenth and eighteenth centuries in baroque style. Beside the church is a baptistry of great artistic importance. It is an octagonal building under a conical roof, with fifteenth-century frescoes on the domed ceiling which are of considerable historical interest. In the church square, along the roadside, is an elegant arcade, completing

The church, Baveno

the building in this dignified quiet spot.

Next after Baveno is **Stresa** without doubt the most elegant of all Maggiore's towns, and probably the most famous of all the Italian lake resorts. The lakeside speaks of prosperity, with its walks through fine gardens and its trees. On the other side of the lakeside road is an array of fine hotels, some of top international standard, especially the Grand Hotel et des Iles Borromées, a truly sumptious building both inside and out. There is an old part to the town which is worth a visit. Piazza Cadorna is a little square filled with café seats where you can sit and watch, and sniff in the scent from the flowers that seem to grow

The Borromean islands from Stresa

everywhere. But the lake soon draws the visitor back to its elegant walkways.

At the Baveno end of Stresa is a *funivia* that goes up to Il Mottarone. The lake terminus is easily reached, though at the top there is a short walk to the mountain summit, at 1,491m (4,890ft). From here the view extends to Monte Rosa, the valleys around Domodossola, the lakes near Varese, and the Lombardy plain, and on a very clear day as far as Milan and Switzerland's Jungfrau.

From Carciano, the tiny harbour near the lower terminus of the cable car, boats cross the lake for the three Borromean islands. Closest is **Isola Bella,** which is also the most famous. When, in about 1630, Count Carlo III Borromeo first laid plans for the transformation of the closest island to Stresa, the island was flat and rocky with a few fisherfolk's houses and a chapel or two that they used. Count Carlo

Stresa

wanted to change this island into his dream of a palatial ship anchored close to the shore. He started by shipping boatloads of soil to the island which his landscape architects used to create a ten-terraced garden, 40m (130ft) high, sloping back from the island's southern tip to produce the effect of a snub-nosed boat. The result is an elaborate statement of the aims of Italian gardening, an architectural form in which man transforms nature into his own design. This is in sharp contrast to the English garden, where man aids nature in creating a naturalistic design. To the gardens Count Carlo and his sons — for the work outlived the designer, indeed the island was not finally completed until 1958, three centuries after Borromeo died — added a baroque *palazzo*, positively subdued externally in comparison to the gardens, but inside echoing the extravagance. The island was also transformed in name, Count Carlo calling it Isola Isabella

Isola Bella and Isola Pescatori from the air

after his wife. The now familiar, shorter form flows more gracefully from the tongue, and means 'beautiful island'.

The *palazzo* (palace) has a wealth of rooms, some of great beauty, some of great lavishness, almost invariably lit by chandeliers of Murano glass. The Arms Room displays the Borromeo coat of arms, while the Medals Room has carved wooden medallions depicting scenes from the life of San Carlo Borromeo, of the same family as the designer. The Music Room has antique instruments and some very fine paintings, while Napoléon's Room, where he and Josephine slept in August 1797, is wonderfully elegant. Better still is the Great Hall, the last to be completed, with walls the colour of blue Wedgwood china, a geometrically patterned floor and a delightful balcony. The Library contains rare volumes and some good paintings, while the Luca Giordano Room contains fine works by the seventeenth-century Neapolitan master.

The Antechamber has some good paintings, and an excellent ceiling by Tiepolo, and from it the family chapel can be viewed, though permission for entry must be requested. It contains memorials to the Borromeo family. The Tapestry Room has a series of sixteenth-century Flemish tapestries in silk and gold depicting fantastic animals. They are really very good, as are some of the paintings in the room. Finally, visit the grottoes, six cool rooms decorated in light and dark stones to produce, not wholly successfully, a marine

Isola Bella

cave appearance. Here there are some interesting historical items and some unusual curios — all well worth seeing.

And be sure not to miss the Borromean family puppet theatre. This flourished, chiefly for the amusement of the family, during the eighteenth and early nineteenth centuries, but was abandoned during the struggles of the Risorgimento, only coming to light again fairly recently. To a generation brought up on a television diet of instant action, the puppets seem a bit dull, even boring, but the faces are exquisitely carved, and the skill with which a mummy is brought out of its case (pre-dating the horror movie by more than a century!), a sedan chair turns into a woman, or elves appear from a giant, is very impressive.

The second island is **Isola Pescatori**, sometimes known as Isola Superiori, which, by constrast to Isola Bella, is almost drab. The island takes its popular name from the chief trade of the islanders (fishing), and was the first of the group to be inhabited. It seems to have changed very little over the centuries. The visitor can wander freely in narrow, sun-starved alleys, past drying fishing nets, and visit the delightful, though much altered, eleventh-century church. The little island has for long been a favourite with artists, particularly writers.

The third island lies right across the Borromean Bay, **Isola Madre** actually being closer to Pallanza, from where it can also be reached,

PLACES OF INTEREST ON THE PIEMONTE SHORE OF LAKE MAGGIORE

Museum
Cannobio
Small museum on the heritage of the area.

Santuario della Pietà
Cannobio
Sixteenth-century church with miraculous painting of the *pietà*.

Orrido Santa Anna
Cannobio
Narrow gorge of the Torrente Cannobino. Viewed from ancient bridges or from hired boats.

Chimney Sweep's Museum
Santa Maria Maggiore
Statues, paintings and equipment from the history of chimney sweeping. Shades of *The Water Babies*.

Museum
Craveggia
Small museum of local interest.

Museum
Gurro
Museum of local history, showing the Scottish connection.

Museum
Santuario, Re
Collection of beautiful art and decorative work from the history of the church.

Church of San Gottardo
Carmine Superiore
Excellent fourteenth-century church with fifteenth-century frescoes and paintings.

Malpaga Castle
Cannero Riviera
Romantic island castles off Cannero. Boat trip to view from the town.

Villa Taranto ✗
Pallanza-Verbania
Beautiful landscaped gardens in grounds of fine villa, the work of Captain Neil McEacharn, a Scotsman.
Not to be missed.

**Paesaggio
(Landscape Museum)**
Pallanza-Verbania
Small museum of landscape and other paintings, and of statuary, in sixteenth-century Palazzo Dugnani.

Museum
Mergozzo
Local finds from Celtic and Roman history.

Funivia
Stresa
To summit of Monte Mottarone. View to Monte Rosa, lakes and Lombardy Plain.

than it is to Stresa. Though the biggest of the three islands, Isola ✗ Madre is occupied only by a single villa, and its gardens compete with those of Isola Bella on a botanical basis, though not at all in terms of

PLACES OF INTEREST ON THE PIEMONTE SHORE OF LAKE MAGGIORE -continued

Isola Bella
Stresa
World-famous baroque villa and gardens.
Not to be missed.

Isola Pescatori
Stresa
Delightful fishing island with array of old houses in narrow alleys.

Isola Madre
Stresa/Verbania
Magnificent garden island, gardens set around eighteenth-century villa.
Not to be missed.

Villa Pallavicino
Stresa
Parkland of nineteenth-century villa turned into a small zoo with mainly free roaming animals. Parkland is excellent.

Umbrella Museum
Gignese
Fascinating history of umbrella and parasol industry in which the area around the village played a leading role.

The Pope's Stone
Gignese
Huge erratic monolith weighing over 8,000 tons.

Alpine Garden
Alpino
Garden with over 2,000 species of plants in wonderful position.

Museum
Lesa
Collection of Alessandro Manzoni memorabilia in fine villa.

Church and Monk's Cells
San Salvatore
Thirteenth-century monk's cells with original frescoes, beside a late fifteenth-century church.

Museum
Arona
Small collections on history and mineralogy of local area.

Statue of San Carlo Borromeo
Arona
Colossal copper statue of saint, on granite plinth. Ladders inside allow ascent to viewing points in the head.

Zoo Safari del Lago Maggiore
Pombia
Safari Park, including an aquarium.

La Torbiera Safari Park
Agrate Conturbia Safari Park.

Viewpoints
Oggiogno or Cima di Morissolo, above Cannero —
Church of the Trinity, Ronco
Pollino/Albergo Belvedere, near Premeno
Pian Cavallo, near Premeno
Mottarone above Stresa —
Belgirate
San Salvatore, near Massino Visconti
Monte Cornaggia, above Nebbiuno

lavishness. The island has been landscaped into five terraces, though this fact is frequently lost to the visitor, as the northern end appears totally natural and even the southern end has terraces so

Isola Pescatori ✳

wide that they get lost in the distance.

The eighteenth-century villa is simple but charming, and stands beside its own chapel where there are tombs of the Borromeo family. Inside, it is again simple and elegant, a great contrast to the villa on Isola Bella.

Back on the mainland, stroll along Stresa's waterfront again, this time towards the southern end of the town. The larger harbour where the lake steamers put in is a busy spot with yet more public gardens beside it. Carry on, and reach the entrance to Villa Pallavicino. The nineteenth-century villa is not open to the public, but its parkland is — there is car park opposite the entrance. The park extends to about 12 hectares (40 acres) and is largely natural: sweeping grass, tall trees, flowers and a natural stream. At several points there are more formal gardens, but even these, perhaps because of the setting, do not detract from the naturalness. And the park is teeming with wild animals! But it is all quite safe. It has been turned into a small zoo with the minimum of caging. It really is rather pleasant to just amble about between the llamas and the antelopes and it is very good for children.

Stresa is famous now for its international congresses, and the town also arranges an international music festival annually, during the last week of August and the first 3 weeks of September. Other events are frequent in the town but do not generally follow a fixed pattern, so it is wisest to ask for details at the Tourist Office.

Isola Pescatori

From Stresa, and also from Baveno, roads lead up into the mountains that border Lake Maggiore and separate it from Lake Orta, the area known as the Verganate. This area was once mysterious, its people secretive, and there was little interchange between them and

 Isola Madre

the lake dwellers. Today it is still a little-visited area, but a drive through it is worthwhile, the mountain villages having great charm and offering excellent views over the lake. On the slopes of the Mottarone and Monte Zuchero, the neighbouring peak, a series of marked walks have been laid out, varying in duration from about $1^1/_2$ to $5^1/_2$ hours. A leaflet on them is available from the Baveno Tourist Office.

On the road beyond Levo there is an excellent view down into the Borromean Bay, though the best is obtained from Motta Rossa 689m (2,260ft) reached by a not-too-arduous climb from Carpugnino. The summit of the Mottarone can also be reached (well, very nearly — the car park is just below the top) by car, though the last stretch of the road is privately owned and a toll is levied. The road to the Mottarone starts from **Gignese** where there is a most curious museum. The local industry in this hillside area was umbrella-making. The finest umbrellas, parasols and umbrella-makers came from around here, both products being exported around the world. The museum is devoted to the industry and to the history of the umbrella. Near the village is the Pope's Stone, an erratic monolith (ie, a glacier-deposited single stone) of 1,550cu m (55,000cu ft) which must weigh about 8,500 tons. Quite a size for a boulder.

Also near Gignese, on the road to Alpino (the road that leads on to the Mottarone), are the Giardino Alpino (the Alpine Gardens), with many species of plant. Ambrosini, the founder of the garden, produced a small book in which he gave a poem, folklore tale, or story about each species he had planted. After the delights of Isola Madre and Isola Bella, the gardens here can seem a bit uninspiring, but in truth they are very good, and the views from them provide some very inspiring backdrops.

From Gignese it is possible to follow a road around Monte del Falo and down to Lake Orta, and also to take a road southward to Massino Visconti, above Lesa, but first, back to the lake.

South of Stresa is **Belgirate** with a mixture of old houses and newer, elegant villas, some with historical connections from the time of the Risorgimento: Garibaldi stayed here, as a guest of Giovanni Cairoli, in the broad fronted Villa Bono Cairoli. The Belgirate Sailing Club is the oldest on Maggiore.

At **Lesa** there are the ruins of a medieval castle, and Villa Cavallini, which has superb gardens though not open to the public. Villa Stampa is open, and holds a small museum of memorabilia of the author Alessandro Manzoni who spent many holidays here. Lesa is an old port, and a walk along its lake front is very pleasant.

On the way to Solcio the road crosses the back of a headland, emerging beside the lake again near the small bay named after the village. From the bay, travel to **Meina** along a road tightly held between the blue of Maggiore and the greens and multi-colours of the trees and flowers in the roadside villas. Meina is a pretty village with a large number of elegant villas, one of which, the neo-classical Villa Feraggiana, is quite superb. It is set in its own park, and from it a road leads up into the mountains allowing access to **Massino Visconti**, which can also be reached from Lesa. It was from here that the Visconti family came and their 'home' castle can still be seen, though little now remains of the original twelfth-century building following a fairly thorough dismantling and rebuilding in the fourteenth century. Massino is a village of great charm, some of its older parts being a great joy to wander through. There is a monument to the area's *lusciatti*, the umbrella-makers, and just north of Massino Visconti a track leads off to **San Salvatore** high up on the hillside. There, at the track end, is a welcome restaurant, expansive views, and the church of Madonna della Cintura, built in 1499 on the remains of a Romanesque church, some of which survives in the campanile. The church itself is not outstanding, but all around it are cells for monks, constructed in the thirteenth century, some still with their original frescoes. Not surprisingly, this spot is listed as one of Novara province's principal architectural treasures.

In the opposite direction from San Salvatore is **Nebbiuno**, a pleasant village from where a road leads up Monte Cornaggia to Poggio Radioso at 620m (2,035ft). From here there are good views, but they are much improved if Monte Cornaggia, 922m (3,025ft) is climbed. The ascent, $1^1/_2$km distant, 300m high (1 mile, 980ft) takes about $1^1/_4$ hours, but is worth the effort.

From Nebbiuno the mountain road continues through Pisano to **Invorio**, where there are the remains of a Visconti castle of the fifteenth century. From there it is only a short distance to Gozzano and Lake Orta, or back to Arona.

Arona is the next place on the lakeside from Meina. It is the largest town on the Piemonte side of Maggiore, a size in part due to its important position at the point where the railway from Switzerland via the Simplon Tunnel meets railways from Turin, Milan and Genoa. Its prosperity has resulted in a lot of modern building which has not added substantially to the town's elegance, but some of the older parts of the town, while not being of great interest, make up for this lack of character.

Arona

On the right coming into the town, is the *rocca*, a natural fortress which makes an elegant backdrop to harbour views, topped by the ruins of a medieval Borromean family castle. The Borromean family history is tied up with the history of the town (and with that of Angera which lies just across the lake at one of its narrowest points), the family having been lords of the town from the late fifteenth century, taking over from the Viscontis. The Borromean family produced several great men, and also a saint. San Carlo Borromeo was born in Arona Castle in 1538. He was a cardinal at 22 and archbishop of Milan by 26, though these appointments were as much to do with his uncle being Pope Pius IV as anything he had accomplished in his life up to those times. But from his appointment to Milan onwards he was a diligent worker for the Christian faith. It was said that he was too ugly to be anything but a saint, and those who would like to check on this could view a portrait of him in the church of the martyrs, San Gratiniano and San Felino, which stands in Piazza San Graziano.

In 1679 a later Borromeo, Federico, himself archbishop of Milan, decided that a statue should be erected to the saint, and it can be seen a short way back towards Meina, on a road off to the left. In the original concept it was to be of marble, and to include fifteen chapels dedicated to the saint. It is in fact copper, and there are three chapels, only one completed. It is certainly impressive, for sheer size alone — the statue itself is 23^1/$_2$m (76ft) tall and stands on a granite plinth 12m (39ft) high. It is well constructed, and has a patina of venerability. But it is not fine sculpture and the patina is mostly of doubtful origin.

 In the town itself, in the Palazzo de Filippi, is the Civic Museum, with an interesting collection on the town's history, and the mineralogy of the local area.

 From Arona the short trip to **Paruzzaro** is worthwhile, to see the church of San Marcello, an eleventh-century Romanseque building with an excellent campanile and a fine series of fifteenth- and sixteenth-century frescoes. The road to the village touches one bound-ary of the Parco Naturale i Lagoni di Mercuragio, a nature reserve set up around the wooded slopes that surround a tiny lake.

The road that leaves Arona southward passes through **Dormelletto**, famous with sailors for its boat-yards and with lovers of the turf for its race-horse stud farms, and then branches left, as the lake ends, for Sesto Calende. The right fork goes to Novara, capital of the Piemontian province in which both Lake Orta and western Lake Maggiore lie. Also along this road at **Pombia**, is a safari park with an aquarium. Another similar park, La Torbiera, can be found a short distance from the first, at **Agrate Conturbia**. Nearing Sesto Calende, a road off right leads to **Castellato Sopra Ticino**, which has quite recently yielded very interesting Bronze Age tombs. Finds are in the Novara City Museum and in Turin's Archaeological Museum.

The Lombardian Shore

Crossing the Ticino river which drains Lake Maggiore into the Po, the route crosses into Lombardy, Italy's fourth biggest region, and the name most synonymous with the Italian Lakes.

The first Lombardian town is **Sesto Calende** (Sesto C is how it is termed on the *autostrada* signs going north from Milan). The name is thought to derive from Roman times when the town had a market on the sixth day after Kalends (the first day of a new month). Even in Roman times the town was old, numerous finds having been made here of the so called Golasecca culture (named after a village a little way south of Sesto Calende), a people in transition from the Bronze to the Iron Age. Some of the finds are held in the town museum, in Piazza Mazzini.

Northward is **Angera**, a pleasant town with one of the finest castles on any of the lakes. Today Angera is a commercial town, but under the Romans it was not only commercial, a busy trading port, but also a military town of importance. When the barbarian hordes streamed down the valley of the Ticino the town was destroyed, but the strategic importance of the site, with its huge natural fortress, the *rocca*, led the Lombards to make it the centre of their Verbano province which included Maggiore and much else besides. Such was its importance that it was involved in battles for supremacy successively by the Franks, the Torrianis, the Viscontis and, finally, the Borromeo family. The latter, who gained possession in 1450, survived the rule of Spaniards and Austrians, and the upheaval of the Risorgimento. Today the Borromeo family still own the castle that stands on the *rocca*.

The road to the castle is steep and passes a natural cave the 'Cava del Lupo' (the wolf's den), which was inhabited prehistorically, and was the site of a Roman temple to Mithras. The castle itself has a fortified gateway that is probably partly a Roman watch tower, though modified by the Lombards. The Lombards made other additions, as did the Viscontis and the Borromeos, so it combines a mixture of ages. The Maschio tower dominates the first courtyard, beyond which is the 'noble' courtyard and the Borromean residential *palazzo*. Here the Ceremony Room contains frescoes detached from the Palazzo Borromeo in Milan, including a series on *Aesop's Fables*, painted in the late fourteenth and early fifteenth centuries. The Justice Room is fifteenth century and is architecturally of great interest, with its elegantly vaulted ceiling and mullioned windows. This room also has fifteenth-century frescoes commissioned by Giovanni Visconti, Archbishop of Milan, and depicting in part, battles of the Visconti family. The ceiling bays are mainly of geometric design, the vault bases once having been decorated with the signs of the zodiac. Sadly only two signs, as one pair, survive. There is no furniture in either room and, strangely, that improves the appearance, allowing the mind to concentrate on the architecture.

From the castle the views are superb, and it is easy to see why the *rocca* was so sought after as a defensive position. On the far side of the lake the statue of San Carlo can be seen (a mixed blessing — the view from statue to castle is superior). At night the castle and *rocca* are illuminated and that is a sight worth travelling many a mile to see. When the lake is calm go around to Arona — the sight of the *rocca* reflected in the mirror of the lake, is worth the drive.

Angera was the birthplace of Pietro Martire, the chief contempo-

Angera castle

rary documenter of Columbus' expedition to the New World, and on the tiny Isolino Portegora in its bay, the monk Arialdo was murdered for daring to defend Christianity against the excesses of an archbishop of Milan. That happened in 1066, as the Normans were invading England. Some items of these, and other aspects of the town's history, can be seen at the Town Museum in Via Marconi. Elsewhere in the town a walk will be well rewarded, particularly in the shade of the double row of chestnut trees on the lake front.

From the town, Monte San Quirico, 412m (1,350ft) can be climbed in about 45 minutes. The mountain is the summit of the ridge on which the castle stands, on a lower plateau. From the top the views to the lake and castle are excellent. The peak stands above the headland of Ronco, a village that can be reached from Angera by taking a minor road rather than the main road that goes directly to Ispra. **Ispra** is a small town still growing on the prosperity brought by the Euratom centre that lies behind it, on the road to Lake Monate. Also behind the town, on the slopes of the Motto di Cisano, are the scars of quarries, white in the sun.

Beyond Ispra the road gives a pleasant drive through small villages to **Reno**, from where the famous church of Santa Caterina del Sasso can be reached. Reno is a beautiful village set on a small bay formed by two headlands, one on which the church stands, and one at Cerro further north.

The church of Santa Caterina del Sasso, near Reno

PLACES OF INTEREST ON THE LOMBARDIAN SHORE OF LAKE MAGGIORE

Museum
Sesto Calende
Small museum of finds from local pre-Roman Golasecca culture, and of town's important Roman era.

Borromeo Castle
Angera
Famed Rocca di Angera. Well preserved castle, chiefly from the fifteenth century with fine frescoes in the attached *palazzo*. Small museum of modern art.

Museum
Angera
Small museum with items chiefly from the town's early and Roman eras.

Sanctuary of Santa Caterina del Sasso
Near Reno
Monastery and chapel on site of former hermitage. Magnificent position. Re-opened in 1987. Will be served by lake steamers. Not to be missed.

Ceramics Museum
Cerro del Lago Maggiore
Small museum with items from the local ceramics industry, from eighteenth century to present day.

Studio of Sergio Tapia Radic
177 Via Labiena, Laveno
Studio of Spanish-born sculptor, whose work can also be seen in exhibitions throughout the area during the summer months.

Funivia
Laveno
Bucket ride to Sasso del Ferro from where the views are expansive.

Museum
Luino
Historical items, and a collection of local fossils.

Monteviasco
Near Curiglia
Unspoilt, beautifully positioned village that can only be reached on foot from Curiglia.

Viewpoints
Monte San Quirico, Angera
Agra, above Luino
Monte Borgna, above Maccagno

In the twelfth century a man from Besozzo (inland from here), known as Alberto Bessozi made a living locally by a variety of unlawful means — for example, smuggling and high-interest money lending. One day while out alone in a boat on the lake he was surprised by a sudden storm, his boat capsized, and he was in imminent danger of drowning when he promised God that if his life was spared he would dedicate it to prayer and penance for his sins. Miraculously he was thrown onto a ledge of the steep cliff near Reno and there he spent the rest of his life — almost 40 years — being kept alive by food local folk gave him (lowering it to him in a basket), or which he raised from boats, and by water from a spring. When plague threatened the local community Alberto prayed for them and they were spared, showing their gratitude by building, on the hermit's ledge, a chapel to Santa Caterina who had answered his prayers. There, later, Alberto was buried. In the fourteenth century a Dominican monastery was added to the chapel. Further evidence of the miraculous nature of the spot was given in the mid-seventeenth century when a substantial rock fall from the cliff above the sanctuary was prevented from crushing the hermit's tomb by three bricks which, when the dust had cleared, were found to be holding the weight of numerous huge blocks, all jammed into a stable position. Not until many years later were the blocks finally removed. The highlight of the 1987 tourist season was the re-opening of the sanctuary. Now the visitor can enjoy the peace of the site, marvel at the frescoes, some of which are very well preserved, see the remains of the Blessed Alberto's winch, and also view his body, miraculously preserved from decay, though not surprisingly looking a little mummified.

It should be noted that descent to the sanctuary is via a long series of sometimes tricky steps, with only the shady views and the lizards for company. The climb back up is, of course, no easier. However, the site is to be added to the list of stops of the lake steamers, so access will be easier for those who find climbing difficult. But at all costs do visit it.

Inland from Reno, at **Leggiuno**, there is an interesting Romanesque church which incorporates parts of a Roman temple, including two columns supporting the portal.

Cerro del Lago Maggiore was a favourite resort of the writer Manzoni. It is a pretty village with an excellent view into the Borromean Bay across the lake. Within the village there is a very interesting museum, dedicated to the local ceramics industry.

⚔ **Laveno** is a small lakeside town with an industrial area — known as Mombello — behind it, beside the Torrente Boesio. It was here that many of the potteries represented at the museum in Cerro were located. Legend has it that the town is named after a Roman general, Titus Labienus, who either led an expedition against the Gauls from the town, or alternatively, fought the decisive battle of the campaign here at the Boesio crossing. During the Risorgimento there was action here again when the forces of Garibaldi fought the Austrians, who were in control of the castle whose ruins can still be seen in the

 Laveno

park laid out on the Punta San Michele, on the northern headland of the small bay in which Laveno lies. A memorial to those who died stands at the lakeside.

At Christmas in Laveno a most unusual nativity is set up, not in the church as might be expected, but beneath the waters of the lake. Marble figures are set up on the lake floor by divers, and on the night of Christmas Eve the statue of the baby Jesus is lowered. The reason for this event is not well understood, but the floodlight nativity attracts many visitors.

The car ferry from Intra docks at Laveno, which makes the town a busy place in summer, but also ensures that there are always sufficient places in the roadside cafés. The best way to see the town is to ride up almost to the top of the Sasso del Ferro, 1,062m (3,485ft) on the *funivia*. This is quite an experience, the ride being in cylindrical buckets that hold two people and are open to the air to get the best of the views and an equal sense of exposure. The ride up the hill is spectacular at the right time, because the grassy swathe cut through the woods below the cables — presumably to aid maintenance — is a haven for butterflies. The *funivia* top station is at 959m (3,145ft), and from there a path goes to the actual summit — allow about half an hour. There is little point in the walk however, as it does not improve the view substantially. Monte Rosa is visible, beyond the Mottarone, and a substantial part of the lake can also be seen.

Luino

Laveno, as viewed from the buckets, is dominated by the church of San Giacomo and San Filippo, a very recent church built on a grand scale with a fine dome. In the town a visit to the studio of Sergio Tapia Radic, a Spanish sculptor specialising in devotional work, is worthwhile. Exhibitions of his work can be seen throughout the area during the summer months.

Beyond Laveno the road is galleried for some distance, and when the visitor emerges from the gallery the view ahead is dominated by the Rocca di Calde, one of the most distinctive and impressive sights on the eastern shore. The *rocca* was once topped by a castle, built in the tenth century and defended against Otto I when he came this way. It was destroyed by the Swiss in 1513, and it is easy to see why any invading army would be concerned about leaving a castle in such a position. Away from the lake, the *rocca* is more gently sloped down to **Castelvecanna** where the campanile of the church of San Pietro points sharply skyward. The church has a rare marble altar.

To reach Luino, either continue along the lake road — the quick way — or go inland via Musadino and Brezzo di Bedero. At this last village there is a fine lake view and a church of some interest. From Brezzo the inland road goes back down to the main road at Germignaga which is now almost continuous with Luino, from which it is divided by the river Tresa which drains Lake Lugano into Maggiore.

Luino is the chief town of the Lombardian shore of Maggiore, with a large railway complex in keeping with its light-industrial status. The town is believed to have been the birthplace of Bernardino Luini the painter. An *Adoration of the Magi* widely attributed to him can be seen in the church of San Pietro, beside the town cemetery in the eastern, uphill, section of the town. Another son of the town was the Blessed Giacobino Luinese, a Carmelite who founded a monastery and to whom miracles are attributed. In his birthplace he founded the church of Madonna del Carmine, which stands beside the lake road on entering the town. In the church there are frescoes attributed to scholars of Luini.

At the town's centre is Piazza Garibaldi with a monument to the great man — the first ever erected to him in Italy, and completed before his death. After his defeat at Custozza, Garibaldi raised a small army here to continue the struggle against Austria. The enthusiasm of local men for this renewal of the struggle, and the erection of this first Garibaldian monument, are deeds of which the town is justly proud. Many aspects of the town's history, and a fossil collection, can be seen in the Town Museum in Palazzo Verbania.

From Luino it is just a few kilometres eastwards to Switzerland. The frontier follows the Tresa river to a point just short of the village of Fornasette and so gives a fascinating drive from Luino to Ponte Tresa, the road following the river all the way. From the second tunnel onwards, Switzerland is on the other side of the river from the road.

Alternatively, go from Luino to **Dumenza** or **Runo**, each nicely placed villages, and climb the peaks of the Clivio or the Lema to stand on a ridge with one foot in either country. From the summit of Monte Lema, 1,621m (5,320ft), a chair-lift descends to Miglieglia in Switzerland. The climb, however, is long and fairly strenuous — leave aside half a day. From Due Cossani — where there is a good view of Monte Lema for potential walkers — a road leads to **Agra**, a beautiful mountain village well worth a visit. From just beyond the village there is a most beautiful view of northern Lake Maggiore.

The alternative road from Due Cossani leads to **Curiglia**, an interesting road, occasionally too narrow, occasionally too tightly curved. On the way is a more life-like, but no more handsome statue of San Carlo Borromeo. The reward for the journey is the scenery *en route*, in the Val Veddasca. Curiglia is very picturesque, and from it **Monteviasco** can be reached but only on foot. It is said to be 1,000 steps to Monteviasco, though it feels much further, but the reward is a completely unspoilt village in magnificent surroundings.

The lake road from Luino goes to **Maccagno**, the last lake village with probably the best camp site on the lake. The upper part of the village is very pretty, and from it the Val Veddasca can be followed to the Swiss border at Indemini. From there a short walk — only about 130m (425ft) — leads to the summit of Monte Cadriga, 1,300m (4,265ft) with good panoramic views, including northern Lake Maggiore and little Lake Delio below (in the pass between Monte Cadriga and Monte Borgna, 1,158m (3,800ft). The latter peak does limit the view from Cadriga, and a better view of Maggiore is obtained by climbing Borgna from Lake Delio, reached by branching off the Val Veddasca road. The climb is longer than that to Monte Cadriga, but very worthwhile. On the road to Lake Delio the sanctuary of San Rocca also offers a fine view of the lake.

Maccagno was one of the earliest inhabited places on Maggiore, and it was there that Count Mandelli, the feudal lord, gave food and shelter to Otto I when he arrived in 962 to fight Berengar. In return for this, Otto made the village a self-governing fief, with the power to mint its own money. The village is divided into two, Inferiore which is reached first, and Superiore with its quiet square, and there are remains of a tower from a later period of history.

Beyond Maccagno there is only one more village before Zenna and the Swiss border. That village is **Pino sulla sponda del Lago Maggiore**, which has the longest place name in Italy.

4 AROUND VARESE

T he large, modern city of Varese is built on flat land below Monte Campo dei Fiori. It is of ancient origin, probably Celtic, though little that remains outside the Town Museum is older than the sixteenth century. Today the city prospers as a provincial capital, with a large amount of light industry and manufacturing — especially shoe making — and a range of good restaurants and fine shops to attract the visitor. Varese is known as the 'garden city', a name that derives as much from the public gardens within the city boundary as from its position at the mouths of some very green and fertile valleys.

The heart of the city was also the heart of the old city, dominated by the 72m-high (236ft) campanile known as Del Bernascove, after its architect. The campanile, whose attractiveness lies in the ever-changing design patterns as it rises, is thought to be among the finest examples in Lombardy. Work on it started in the early seventeenth century, but it was not finally completed for 150 years. The ironwork bell-wheel mechanisms peeping out from the stone pillars of the bell cell are particularly interesting.

Beside the campanile is the basilica of **San Vittore**, built as the sixteenth century was becoming the seventeenth, to a plan by Pelligrini. The façade is much newer, a late eighteenth-century neo-classical addition. Inside there is a fine collection of artwork: paintings, sculpture and some very elaborate woodcarving. The work in the Chapel of the Rosary is by Morazzone, from the early seventeenth century, while the frescoes in the chapel of Santa Marta are, mostly, a century older.

Beside the basilica is the baptistry of **San Giovanni**, an Italian national monument, which is the oldest building in the town. It is a fine, simple, but dignified stone building. The present structure dates from the twelfth and thirteenth centuries, though it stands on the site of a previous church. Inside there is an interesting eighth-century immersion font, with a single-stone basin carved in the thirteenth century. Also from that time is the series of frescoes, one of the finest Lombardian series in existence.

Villa Ponti, Varese

Close to the complex beneath the campanile is the old town with its arcaded buildings, now mostly converted to shops and cafés. This area once housed the *Broletto*, (town hall), but now the city's municipal centre has been transferred to the magnificent **Palazzo Estense**, another national monument, which stands at the head of the equally magnificent Estense Gardens. The palace, built in baroque style in the mid-eighteenth century, was the summer and autumn home of Francesco II of Este, the Duke of Modena. It now houses the city fathers in grand style, but the visitor is allowed the freedom of the façade and the Italian style gardens to its front.

Within the gardens, on the opposite side from the palace, is **Villa Mirabello**, in less sumptious style, and housing the town's museum. Here there are several quite different collections — archaeological items, including some from the Lake Varese site; a picture gallery, including detached frescoes from Castelseprio; a Risorgimento collection (Varese was an important centre — Garibaldi defeated the Austrians at Biumo, now within the city boundaries, in May 1859); and the butterfly collection of Francesco Tomagno, the tenor, who was born here.

To the north, in Biumo, are the two **Villas Ponti**, now used as a congress centre. The larger villa is late nineteenth century, built in what is termed 'eclectic' style, ie bits from everything; the smaller is neo-classic. The villas stand in a large park that is open to the public.

PLACES OF INTEREST
IN AND AROUND THE CITY OF VARESE

Town Museum
Villa Mirabello
Many differing collections —
archaeology/history; art gallery
with detached frescoes;
Risorgimento; butterflies.

Villas Ponti
Biumo
Fine gardens of two villas now
used as a congress centre.

Sacre Monte
Fourteen chapels with paintings
and sculptures laid out along a
Via Crucis, to the church and
village of Santa Maria del Monte
from which there are magnificent
views.

Baroffio Museum
Sacre Monte
Paintings, sculptures and
vestments from Sacre Monte,
and the art collection of Baron
Baroffio.

Pogliaghi Museum
Sacre Monte
Greek, Roman and oriental art
collection, and work of Ludovico
Pogliaghi including plaster cast of
bronze door of Milan Cathedral.

Tre Croci
Monte Campo dei Fiori
The 'Panoramic Balcony of
Lombardy' with nearby excellent,
but sadly neglected, art nouveau
buildings.

Observatory
Monte Campo dei Fiori
Guided tours, for individuals and
groups, of observatory and alpine
flowers under glass.

The old village of Biumo, to the south of the park, is also worth visiting, its ancient heart looking much as it must have done when Garibaldi came this way. Across the city to the south, at Bosto, the eleventh-century church of San Imerio is worth a look on the way to the Milan *autostrada*.

 Of considerably more interest are the Varese **Sacre Monte** and **Campo dei Fiori**, reached by going north from the Palazzo Estense for about 10km (6 miles). A document exists from AD922 noting the existence of a church to Santa Maria on Monte Vellate, although both before and after that time the site was of considerable strategic importance and was fortified. In the early fifteenth century San Ambrogia came, bringing to the spot an ancient wooden statue of the Virgin — known as the 'Black Virgin' — which legend ascribes to the apostle Luke. Pilgrimages were made to the Sacre Monte following this, and a nunnery was set up. The pilgrimages declined until San Carlo Borromeo renewed them, bringing a fresh impetus to the

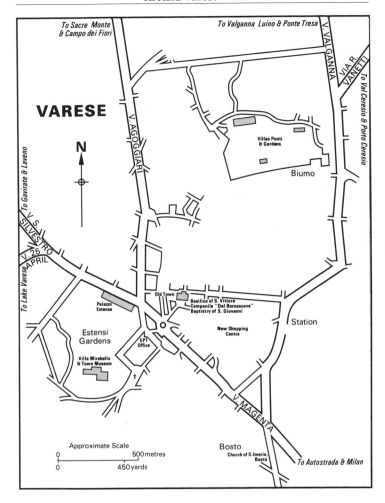

VARESE

N

To Sacre Monte & Campo dei Fiori

To Valganna Luino & Ponte Tresa

V. VALGANNA

VIA R. VANETTI

To Val Ceresio & Porto Ceresio

Villas Ponti & Gardens

Biumo

To Gavirate & Laveno

V. S. SILVESTRO

V. 25 APRIL

To Lake Varese

V. AGOGGIARI

Old Town

Basilica of S. Vittore
Campanile "Del Bernascove"
Baptistry of S. Giovanni

Palazzo Estense

Estensi Gardens

EPT Office

Villa Mirabello & Town Museum

New Shopping Centre

Station

V. MAGENTA

Bosto
Church of S. Imerio, Bosto

To Autostrada & Milan

Approximate Scale

0   500 metres

0   450 yards

sacred site. In the seventeenth century fourteen chapels were erected along a Via Crucis leading to the church of Santa Maria del Monte, which illustrated Christ's life in painting and statuary. All the chapels are interesting, but general opinion holds that the seventh, with frescoes by Morazzone, is the finest.

At the top of the Via Crucis, beside the church, is the little village of Sacre Monte, from which the views are magnificent. The church still holds the 'Black Virgin' and has a silver altar rail by the sculptor

Estense gardens and palace

Ludovico Pogliaghi who died in the village in 1950. His villa is now a museum devoted to his work, and contains a plaster cast of the central door of Milan Cathedral for which he was also responsible, and his own art collection. Also in the village is the **Baroffio Museum**, with artwork which, anciently, was in the church, and the art collection of the founder, Baron Baroffio.

Beyond the village the road continues up Monte Campo dei Fiori, the hill of the fields of flowers, which has several peaks. Near the first summit, Monte Tre Croci (1,098m, 3,600ft) is the Grand Hotel, built in the early years of this century in fine art nouveau style. Sadly it is now closed and neglected. From the hotel, the summit is easily reached (about 70m (230ft) of ascent). The three crosses are now dedicated to those who have fallen in all wars. From the summit known as the 'Panoramic Balcony of Lombardy' the view is magnificent, stretching to Monte Rosa and the Bernese Oberland as well as Varese town and the local lakes. A higher summit can also be easily reached, and here there is an observatory which is open for guided tours, but these must be booked in advance.

Lake Varese

The Lakes of Varese

To the west of Varese is a trio of small lakes that can be seen in one circular outing. Travelling west from Varese the main road, the N394, bound for Laveno, goes through **Gavirate**. *En route*, at Luvinate, is the Varese golf course, with a club house that started life in the eleventh century as a Benedictine monastery — surely one of the most romantic club houses in the world; Barasso, whose church has a fine painting by a pupil of Luini; and Camerio, famous in caving circles for the caves in Monte Campo dei Fiori behind the town, and with a fine Romanesque church.

At Gavirate the visitor reaches **Lake Varese**, the largest of the trio of lakes but sadly the most polluted of them too, so badly polluted that swimming is banned and a full-scale ecological rescue exercise is under way. The lake is 9km (5$^1/_2$ miles) long, and at its broadest, into the bay beside Cazzago Brabbia, is 3$^1/_2$km (2$^1/_4$ miles) wide. Those dimensions mean the lake is about the same size as Lake Orta, and so has considerable scope as a tourist attraction once it has been 'restored'.

Gavirate was once famous for its fishing, but this has now declined. It is an interesting town with a local museum in Via Voltorre dedicated to pipes. Continue along the same road to arrive at **Voltorre** itself, where, beside the church of San Michele whose

PLACES OF INTEREST AROUND THE VARESE LAKES

Pipe Museum
Gavirate
Small museum dedicated to
history of local pipe making.

San Michele
Voltorre
Fine eleventh-century cloister
beside newer church whose
campanile holds Italy's biggest
bell.

Gliding Club
Calcinate del Pasce
Demonstration flights available.

Villa Ponti
Isolino Virginia, near Biandronno
Very interesting and important
site for the study of Neolithic and
Bronze Age lake dwellings.

Museum
Golasecca
Museum of the Golasecca
Culture of the Bronze/Iron Age.

Salvini Gallery
Cocquio-Trevisago
Work of the artist Innocente
Salvini.

massive campanile boasts one of the biggest bells in Italy, there is a most interesting eleventh-century brick cloister of an old Cluniac monastery. At **Calcinate del Pasce** there is a gliding club that offers demonstration flights, an excellent, though not cheap, way of seeing the local geography. Beyond Schiranna, the site of the lake's rowing club, a large sports complex has been built, including two swimming pools, and from which boats can be hired.

On the southern side of the lake, the views across the water to Monte Campo dei Fiori are excellent as we make for **Biandronno**, behind which is a fourth lake, tiny and almost overgrown with weed. From the village, boats cross to Isolino Virginia, a national monument site of enormous importance to the study of the Neolithic and Bronze Ages. The island is, in part, built up on the remains of pile-built lake dwellings, which have been constructed over a period of centuries. Many of the items discovered here, together with displays on the dwellings and the cultures which created them, are on display in Varese. In the summer months, on Saturday and Sunday afternoons, the Varese Museum organises tours to the island. The museum and Tourist Offices have details.

South from Biandronno the emerald green **Lake Comabbio** (no swimming here either), is reached. The lake is 3km long and 1km wide (2 miles x $\frac{1}{2}$ mile). Vareno Berghi on its eastern shore is an industrial centre, but does have one splendid building, the Villa

Berghi. On the road that leads south from the town to Cargeno, the visitor enters the huge Ticino Nature Park, which, in its southern section around Pavia, is very good. In the northern section, which touches Lake Comabbio and Sesto Calende and extends almost to Lake Monate, the park is less well defined and less interesting. South from here is **Golasecca**, a name already familiar in the context of the prehistoric remains in Novara province. The name of the ancient culture derives from the village, and a museum there houses some of the better finds.

Reach **Lake Monate** by the main road along the western shore of Comabbio. It is the smallest of the lakes, ($2^3/_4$km ($1^3/_4$miles) long, 1km ($^1/_2$ mile) wide) and in it there have been found a number of important pile dwellings from the Bronze Age. At the lake's western tip is Cadrezzate, from where there are fine views towards Maggiore as well as over the small lake. At Travedonna, at the lake's northern end, the thirteenth-century Romanesque church has a fine series of frescoes.

Northward is Besozzo where a medieval tower has been incorporated into a more modern villa, though this is not open to the public, and the combined villages of **Cocquio-Trevisago** where there is a museum dedicated to the work of the artist Innocente Salvini, a local Impressionist.

Valcuvia

The Valcuvia is one of the greenest, most unspoilt valleys near any of the large lakes, and though it is very short, approximately 12km ($7^1/_2$ miles) long, it is worth the effort to visit. It begins at Cittiglio (a road the other side of the valley starting at Gemenio is not as good, though **Gemenio** itself is, having an eleventh-century Romanesque church, with fourteenth- and sixteenth-century frescoes, which is a national monument), and the first spot in the valley from there is **Casalzuigno** where the small but very pleasant gardens of the Villa Bozzolo are open to visitors.

From Casalzuigno a narrow, windy lane leads up through some magnificent woodland to **Arcumeggia**, one of the most remarkable of local villages. Here contemporary artists have painted frescoes on the outside walls of the village houses. Each year new paintings are added, so that the village is an open-air exhibition of contemporary Italian art. The artists have also produced panels for a Via Crucis on the grassed churchyard.

Arcumeggia

    The road to Arcumeggia can be followed further, to **Sant' Antonio**, where there is a good view across Lake Maggiore, and from there down to the lake. To regain Valcuvia, go back down the winding lane. The tightness of the curves does at least allow the driver to look down the hillside to see what is coming up.

    Back in the valley the scenery remains attractive as the road reaches **Cuvio**, with an old Visconti *palazzo*; **Cuveglio**, with a crenellated Romanesque bell-tower; and, above Cuveglio, **Duno** with a small church dedicated to Italy's doctors. Beyond these Valcuvia ends, roads going right for the Valganna or left to follow Val Travaglia to Luino.

Valganna

The Valganna is followed by the main road, the N233, which goes northward from Varese towards Ponte Tresa and Switzerland. From Varese the road runs at first through open country, until the valley is joined. Valganna here is narrow, with steep, verdant walls. At one point a grotto has been carved out from the cliff top, and a moss blanket covers it, constantly dripping.

    The road passes two small lakes, **Ganna** and **Ghirla**, each named for its neighbouring village and both very popular with the

Fresco at Arcumeggia

locals for winter skating. Lake Ghirla, the larger of the two, is also a summer resort, with swimming and windsurfing. In **Ganna**, the first village reached, the excellent frescoed remains of the eleventh-century monastery of San Gemolo now house a small museum to the history of the monastery and the area.

From Ganna a side road leads uphill to **Boarezzo**, from where the views are excellent, and which, like Arcumeggia, has contemporary frescoes.Though the overall effect is not as impressive as at Arcumeggia, some of the frescoes are very good, particularly the still-life of Aldo Ambrosini and the intricate abstract work of Albino Reggiori.

From Boarezzo it is possible to climb Monte Piambello, 1,129m (3,700ft) for expansive views over Lake Lugano. There is a track to the summit, but it would be a very difficult drive, and those with no time for the walk (2-3 hours are required) can go to **Marzio** where the view across Lake Lugano is equally good.

Beyond Ghirla, a developing holiday resort, the road divides. Going left the visitor passes **Cunardo**, in a fine position, and drops down to Luino. Going straight on the road descends through the equally open and pleasant Val Marchirolo to **Ponte Tresa**. From **Viconago**, above Marchirolo, there are fine views over Lugano and Switzerland. The village is a fine one, with old houses and two very good churches.

PLACES OF INTEREST IN VALCUVIA, VALGANNA AND VALCERESIO

Villa Bozzolo
Casalzuigno
Small but excellent, Italian-style gardens of villa.

Arcumeggia
Outside wall frescoes by contemporary Italian artists. Not to be missed.

Museum
Ganna
Housed in eleventh-century monastery of San Gemolo. Exhibits on history of buildings and area.

Boarezzo
Frescoed village. Work by contemporary artists.

Museum
Induno Olona
Fine collection on mineralogy and natural history of Valceresio.

Butti Gallery
Viggiu
Plaster casts of the work of Enrico Butti, and a collection of the work of local artists.

Villa Cicogna Mozzoni
Bisuschio
Fine sixteenth-century villa with good artwork and furniture, surrounded by equally fine Italian-style gardens.

Museum
Besano
Museum of fossils found locally.

Viewpoints
Valcuvia — Sant' Antonio, near Arcumeggia
Valganna — Marzio

Valceresio

The Valceresio heads north-east from Varese to Porte Ceresio on Lake Lugano, through many interesting places.

At **Induno Olona** there are good paintings in the parish church and fourteenth-century frescoes in the oratory of San Pietro. The town also has a fine museum with exhibits on the natural history of the valley. Here too, or rather at the hamlet of Frascarlo, is the beautiful Villa Medici di Marignano, a Renaissance building sadly not open to the public.

Beyond is Arcisate where, in 1848, a handful of Garibaldi's troops held off 5,000 Austrians for over 4 hours. From the village a fine wooded road leads off to **Viggiu**, a pleasant village with good views of the Valceresio. Here there is a museum to the work of the artist

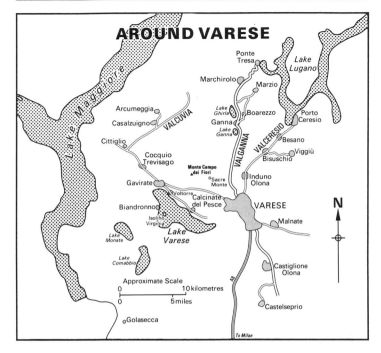

Enrico Butti with a collection of his sculpture plaster casts, and a collection of the work of local artists. The village churches are also worthy of note. Beyond Viggiu, roads lead to the Swiss border.

Back in the main valley the next village is **Bisuschio**, notable for the Villa Cicogna Mozzoni, a sixteenth-century building which is a national monument. The villa is a beautiful building with an arcaded ground floor, elegant rows of square cut windows and a shallow roof.   Inside it has sixteenth-century frescoes by the Campi school, some excellent antique furniture and rare ornaments. The villa is surrounded by fine Italian-style gardens with ponds behind stone balustrades, fountains and a statue-filled, niched wall.

The last town before Valceresio reaches Lake Lugano is **Besano**, a small town famous for the fossils of the Triassic era found locally, some of which can be seen in a small museum in the town. Also noteworthy is the church of San Giovanni with good frescoes and fine views of Lake Lugano.

Castiglione Olona

PLACES OF INTEREST
SOUTH OF VARESE

Transport Museum
Malnate
Fine collection of steam locomotives, stage coaches, bicycles etc.

Museum/Church Complex
Castiglione Olona
Beautiful secular and temporal buildings of fifteenth century, with excellent frescoes.

(Secondhand and antiques fair on first Sunday of the month).

'Archaeological Zone'
Castelseprio
Complex of ruined medieval buildings including castle. Of interest chiefly to the specialist. Village has seventeenth-century church with Byzantine frescoes.

South of Varese

South from Varese the 'Lake Country' is quickly left behind. Two short journeys are worthwhile however.

The first is to **Malnate** on the Como road where, after a drive through country that is parched by comparison to the green valleys, the Villa Rachele-Ogliari houses a fine transport museum with steam locomotives, stage coaches and much more.

The second is on the N233 to Milan. At **Castiglione Olona** is one of Lombardy's finest collections of art treasures. The whole village seems as quiet as it must have been in the early fifteenth century when Cardinal Branda Castiglioni, Papal Legate, Bishop of Piacenza and a local man, constructed the complex of religious buildings which is still largely complete. There is Castiglioni's *palazzo* with his own room and a fine archive; the house he built for his parents; a beautiful, domed church; a baptistry with wonderful frescoes by Masolino da Panicale — *Herod's Feast* is widely renowned as a medieval masterpiece; and a collegiate church, also with frescoes by Masolino. There is also a small museum with items on the building and the cardinal.

In the town there is a fine fifteenth-century town hall and in the streets of the centre, every first Sunday of the month, is the *Fiera del Cardinale*, the Cardinal's Fair, a secondhand and antique fair.

Nearby is **Castelseprio**, a Roman fortress town that became a Lombard stronghold and was destroyed by the Viscontis in 1287. Today an 'Archaeological Zone' contains the remains of the original town and castle walls, and a medieval monastery. The new town also has a beautiful seventh-century church, to Santa Maria 'Foris Porta', with Byzantine frescoes.

5 LAKE LUGANO

L ake Lugano is a fox-shaped piece of water — nose at Ponte Tresa, ear at Agno, paws at Porto Ceresio and Capolago, and a huge tail all the way to Porlezza. From nose to tail the lake is 36km ($22^1/_2$ miles) long. It is always narrow, the maximum width — not measured into the many bays — being only about 2km ($1^1/_4$ miles), just south of the bridge at Melide. The greater part of its shoreline is in Switzerland. The city of Lugano is the lake's largest, and one of the leading cities in the Swiss canton of Ticino, though once it was under the influence of Milan, having been caught up in the wars between Como and Milan in the early Middle Ages. The Swiss took the city and the neighbouring country from Milan in 1512, and have held it ever since, as the land freed from Austrian rule in the Risorgimento was the entire claim by the new Italian state, which never made any serious attempt to annexe Italian-speaking Swiss territories.

Italy holds the north-western shoreline and the eastern tip of the lake together with the enclosure of Campione. However, to deal solely with the Italian territory is, despite the title of the book, unnecessarily pedantic, so Swiss Ticino will be briefly explored, with reference made to other places of interest there in the Further Information section.

Swiss Lake Lugano

From Porto Ceresio the eye is drawn northward to **Morcote**, the village at the very point of a large finger of land that points southward into the lake from Lugano city. From across the lake the village, reflected in the water and held against the cone of Monte Arbostera, is very picturesque, an impression that is amplified when the village — known as the 'pearl of the lake'— is reached. It is a glorious place, a mass of narrow, interweaving alleyways between houses of great character, a fine old church, a cemetery heavily guarded by cypress trees, an open park with trees and shrubs, the harbour, the lake

The model of Switzerland at Melide

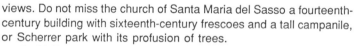

views. Do not miss the church of Santa Maria del Sasso a fourteenth-century building with sixteenth-century frescoes and a tall campanile, or Scherrer park with its profusion of trees.

At **Melide** those with insufficient time can see Switzerland in miniature, all the essential features modelled at 1:25 scale. From the village a *funivia* takes the visitor to **Carona** where there is a fine park.

Nearby, the summit of Monte San Salvatore (912m, 2,990ft) can be reached via a cable car from Lugano. From the summit the views are magnificent, taking in — if the weather has been kind — the Matterhorn and the Apennines, and the local lakes. Elsewhere on the peninsula **Gentilino** can be visited where, in the cemetery of the church of San Abbondio, the grave of Hermann Hesse can be seen.

Lugano, at the foot of the Monte San Salvatore, lies at the back of a small lake bay, an elegant place, vying with Como as the finest lake city. Within the city there are fine buildings. The *Duomo*, the cathedral church of San Lorenzo, has fine fourteenth-century frescoes, but is best known for its fine façade in Lombard-Venetian style, with three portals that some say are by the Rodaris and others say are by local sculptors. From the cathedral narrrow streets lead to the central square, Piazza della Riforma, close to which giant plastic chess pieces offer a game on a grand scale for visitors.

South-west from here the church of Santa Maria degli Angioli stands in Piazza Bernardino Luini. It is a simple, plain church built in

Lugano

the late fifteenth century for Franciscan friars, but now famous for its frescoes. These were executed by Bernardino Luini, for whom the square is named, at the end of his life when he was a guest of the friars. Luini was Leonardo's best student, and the *Passion* here, a huge work, is thought to be his masterpiece, almost the equal of that of Leonardo himself. The other two works are also excellent, one being a clear tribute by student to teacher.

South-east from the chess pieces, the tree-lined lake front road leads to the Parco Ciani, a public park in which stands the Villa Ciani, holding the city's very good art collection. A century ago the villa, built on the site of the city's medieval castle, was the headquarters of Guiseppe Mazzini, one of the main political leaders of the Risorgimento. From here propaganda pamphlets were issued, and in the park (at that time the villa's private garden) a statue by Vincenzo Vela, of a mourning woman — called *La Desolazione* — was said to have had great significance when erected, representing occupied Italy.

On from the park (a good way by foot), in **Castagnola**, is Villa Favorita, set in fine grounds and with one of the finest private art collections in Europe. Beyond Castagnola is **Gandria**, the last Swiss village on the lake's eastern reach and the equal of Morcote for picturesque setting and unspoilt appearance. There is nothing to rival Morcote's park and the church is not quite as good, but there is more character here. There are also excellent fish restaurants and an

PLACES OF INTEREST AROUND SWISS LAKE LUGANO

Villa Favorita
Castagnola, Lugano city
One of the finest private art
collections in Europe by Baron
Heinrich Thyssen-Bornemisza.
Includes work of Caravaggio,
Titian, Hals, Vermeer, Bosch and
Durer; El Greco, Velasquez and
Goya; Gainsborough and
Reynolds.

Villa Ciani
City Park, Lugano city
City art gallery. Works include
Monet, Renoir, Picasso and
many Ticino artists.

Natural History Museum
Via Cattaneo, Lugano city
Museum of wildlife, geology and
mineralogy.

Archives Museum
Strada di Gondria, Lugano city
One room dedicated to work of

the Italian writer Carlo Cattaneo;
the second to Latvian poets.

**Church of Santa Maria degli
Angioli**, Lugano city
Piazza Bernardino Luini
Plain church with magnificent
frescoes by Bernardino Luini.

Scherrer Park
Morcote
Good collection of local trees
and shrubs, and of statuary.

Swissminiatur
Melide
1:25 scale models of Switzerland. Lit at night.

Funivia
Melide to Carona

Botanical Park
Carona
Fine collection of trees and
shrubs.

 interesting Customs Museum that has to be reached by boat. The
'Customs' here relates to smuggling, as the village's position on the
frontier and on the lake meant that the customs officials were once
kept very busy.

 Above Gandria towers Monte Bre (925m, 3,035ft), a peak that is
climbed by *funivia* from the village that names the mountain — Bre.
From the summit the views — both those of the lake and of the
Bernese Oberland and Valais Alps — are breathtaking. The village
 of Bre has a museum with some interesting paintings.

South of Lake Lugano there are two distinct regions of Switzerland, the Mendrisiotto, and Val Muggio. The former is an interesting
 area with a fine peasant culture that finds voice in a series of
museums dedicated to its lore and art, while the latter is a gentle
mountain valley. But first comes **Bissone**, a village just yards away

PLACES OF INTEREST AROUND SWISS LAKE LUGANO - continued

Funivia
Lugano to Monte San Salvatore
Magnificent views from summit.

Customs Museum
Gandria
A museum of anti-smuggling!

Funivia
Bre to Monte Bre
Terrific viewpoint for lake and
Bernese Oberland/Valais Alps.

Wilhelm Schmid Museum
Bre
Collections of paintings and
objets d'art.

Casa Tencalla
Bissone
Seventeenth-century Ticino
house complete with period
furnishings.

Cog Railway
Capolago to Monte Generoso

Excellent journey and expansive
views.

Museum
Stabio
Museum to the area's peasant
culture.

Museum
Meride
Ancient history of the area.

Vela Museum
Ligornetto
Paintings and sculptures of
Vincenzo and Lorenzo Vela.

Gallery Ziist
Rancate
Work of Ticino artists.

Gallery
Mendrisio
Work of Ticino artists and also
some Italian and German
paintings.

from Italian Campione, with a preserved seventeenth-century Ticino house (Casa Tencalla), and **Capolago** from where a cog railway runs up Monte Generoso (1,701m, 5,680ft).

Italian Lake Lugano

At the south-west corner of Lake Lugano there is a 12km (7$^1/_2$ miles) section of the lake shore that lies in the Varese province of Italy, from Ponte Tresa (opposite Luino on Lake Maggiore), to Porto Ceresio. **Ponte Tresa** is a frontier town, and another Ponte Tresa lies across the river Tresa, flowing out of Lake Lugano, in Switzerland. Between the two towns is a five-arched red granite bridge straddling the river.

Porto Ceresio is a pleasant little port, tucked into a sheltered,

Ponte Tresa

square-cut bay of Lugano with excellent views along the dog-legged lake and across to Morcote. From here it is necessary to cross into Switzerland in order to reach the next part of Italian Lugano. Indeed it is necessary to cross from Switzerland whichever way you travel to **Campione d'Italia**, for it is a small enclave of Italy totally surrounded by Switzerland, a political-geographical freak. This situation arose from a gift of the town to the church of San Ambrogio in Milan in the eighth century, from which time the town shared the fate of the northern Italian cities, being annexed first into the Cisalpine Republic and then into Austria, fighting in the wars of the Risorgimento and emerging triumphantly Italian. Since relationships between the Swiss and the Italians have never been bad, Campione remains Italian, though it uses Swiss currency and the Swiss postal service.

There is an air of prosperity about the place which is nowhere more obvious than at the casino, a well frequented spot — not least by the Swiss — built in wealthy style amid pleasant gardens. It is well sited, the view across to Lugano being very good. That view will be enhanced considerably, however, by a trip on the *funivia* up to Sighignola, on the outskirts of Val d'Intelvi in Italy, when the cableway has been completed. Then it will, at last, be possible to travel from Italy into Campione.

The town is famous historically as the home of the Maestri Campione, the Master Builders of Campione, who were a part of the

Porto Ceresio

Maestri Comacina who will be mentioned again in connection with Como. The Maestri were architects, builders and sculptors, most renowned for their work on Modena Cathedral and the church of San Ambrogio in Milan, but whose work can be appreciated here in the church of San Pietro which dates from the early fourteenth century. More interesting still is the Madonna dei Ghirli at the western end of the town, a fine medieval building best seen from the lake, with work in both Gothic and baroque styles. It is to the Gothic period (the fourteenth century), that the internal and external frescoes for which the church is famous, belong.

From Lugano (on the other side of the lake), Italy is reached beyond the village of Gandria. The first Italians are met at the frontier hamlet of Oria, though the first village is San Mamete, beautifully placed at the mouth of the unfrequented Valsolda. The valley can be penetrated for a short distance by car, but soon becomes land for the

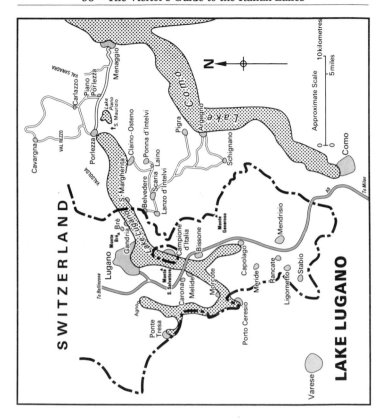

walker, superb hill country. **Oria** is famous in Italy for being the birthplace of Antonio Fogazzaro, an author not well known to the English speaking world. In **Castello**, above San Mamete, a small museum to the art and history of the Valsolda is being prepared which should be very interesting when complete. Across the lake the Val d'Intelvi can be seen, opening through the ridge of mountains separating Lugano and Como, and to the side of the road driving on to Porlezza, Monte del Pizzoni dominates the view.

   Porlezza is a pretty town and seems very Italian to those who have arrived from Switzerland. The name is derived from its Roman origins when it was *Portus Retiae*, the gateway to the *Retiae* (the people of the country beyond), and it was famous as a centre for artists in the Middle Ages: one, Guglielmo della Porta, was the favourite pupil of Michelangelo. It is worth exploring, but do not fail to visit the ruins of the church of San Maurizio, lonely beside the road to the Val d'Intelvi. Here are campaniles and some ruined walls.

From Porlezza, continue along one of three roads. Going north to Corrido the road enters the Val Rezzo, climbing up through vineyards to meadows, beech woods and rocks. At Buggiolo a side road leads to Seghebbia, at 1,149m (3,770ft) the highest of the mountain hamlets and a convenient starting point for walks along the ridge from Cime di Fiorina to Monte Garzirola that forms the border between Italy and Switzerland. The first peak is the better one to climb, the top being only at 1,809m (5,935ft), which offers a reasonable afternoon's walk and magnificent views from the top.

Beyond Buggiolo the road rises further and then drops down into Val Cavargna, a beautiful, rugged, but heavily wooded, valley — certainly the best in this area near the Swiss border. **Cavargna** itself is a picturesque village and has a church built in 1970, with contemporary artwork. The campanile is seventeenth century however. Above Cavargna is the 'Holy Wood', so called because it protects the village from winter avalanches. Cavargna is the seat of the Museo della Valle, the Museum of Val Cavargna, opened only recently and still expanding. There are four rooms: in the first the work of a valley blacksmith is illustrated; the second has items from the sanctuary of San Lucio which stands 457m (1,500ft) above the village on the Italian-Swiss border; the third room deals with the agriculture of the valley; the fourth with the local trade of woodworking.

From Cavargna, travel down the valley, a somewhat winding journey with occasional very windy sections, but one where each turn brings new scenic delights. There are several villages in the valley: **San Nazzaro Val Cavargna** with the best of the views; **San Bartolomeo Val Cavargna**, the biggest village with a rebuilt church that still contains some fine medieval art work; and **Cusino**, where the campanile seems to be held up by faith alone.

Leave the valley at Carlazzo at the valley's entrance, once fortified and still with a farmhouse called 'The Castle'. The peak behind the village, Monte Pidaggia (1,528m, 5,010ft) is reached by a straightforward, but very long climb to a good panoramic position. From Carlazzo either return to Porlezza, or join the second road from the town that passes Lake Piano, originally attached to Lake Lugano but separated from it by landslides and silting. The lake has abundant fish and a quiet air, with blue mountains reflected in its blue waters. The road is joined by the one from Carlazzo and Val Cavargna at Piano, from where it leads on through several pleasant hamlets to Menaggio and Lake Como. At **Cardano** on this road, is the very fine

Lugano from Campione d'Italia

Villa Beagatti Valsecchi, from the early part of this century, set in beautiful gardens, though sadly not open to the public. From Cardano the road enters Val Sanagra and the pretty mountain hamlets that comprise **Grandola ed Uniti**. Here there are some excellent villas and, in the upper reaches of the valley, some fine walking.

The third road from Porlezza rounds the northern tip of Lake Lugano to reach **Claino-Osteno**, a joined pair of villages and the only ones on the road on the southern shore of this reach of the lake. Claino-Osteno stands at the mouth of Val d'Intelvi.

Val d'Intelvi is a fine, airy series of valleys with delightful villages, many with superb churches by the Maestri Comacini, the medieval builders and sculptors. As an important link between the lakes of Lugano and Como it was heavily fortified, surviving almost unscathed when it sided with Como in the Ten Years' War. During the wars of the Risorgimento its position was again important and it was active against the Austrians. Today the valley takes advantage of its position and its beauty and is an important tourist area. In winter there is skiing on the Piano della Noci above Pellio d'Intelvi and near the villages of Lanzo d'Intelvi and Casasco d'Intelvi.

This exploration starts at Claino-Osteno. The second village (Osteno), was the birthplace of the Bregnos, sculptors well known for their work in Venice. There is a marble Madonna and Child in Osteno's church of San Pietro and San Paolo by Andrea Bregno.

Campione d'Italia

Also at Osteno is a fine *orrido*, which is best viewed by boat, and an interesting natural cave, the Grotte di Rescia.

Above Claino-Osteno is Laino from where **Ponna** can be reached, two small hamlets with excellent views. At the upper hamlet, Superiore, is a museum in the form of a house furnished as a valley house would have been in the late nineteenth century, and including the first electric lights used in the valley, dating from 1910.

Laino itself lays claim to the most elegant church in Val d'Intelvi, a sixteenth-century building with local artwork. Near Laino are the two villages, Inferiore and Superiore, of Pellio d'Intelvi, from which the road to Lanzo d'Intelvi is followed, passing through **Scaria** with a fine frescoed church to San Nazaro and San Celso and, below it, the museum of the valley, with exhibits on valley life and the history of art and crafts.

Lanzo d'Intelvi lies beyond Scaria, a beautifully sited, rightly popular village with multi-green meadows and conifer forests. In the village there is a fine square and a range of interesting houses, one of which — in Via Mascheroni — has a fine eighteenth-century fresco over an ancient doorway. From Lanzo, Sighignola can be reached with a view to Campione — and soon, as already noted, there will be a cable car too. The better view is from Belvedere to the north, from where Monte Rosa, the Matterhorn and the Jungfrau can be seen, together with Varese's Campo dei Fiori, and much of Lake Lugano.

PLACES OF INTEREST AROUND ITALIAN LAKE LUGANO

Casino
Campione d'Italia
Restaurant open from 12noon.
Gaming rooms open from 3pm.
Dancing and floor shows nightly.

Church of Madonna dei Ghirli
Campione d'Italia
Fine church with excellent
fourteenth-century frescoes.

Museum
Valsolda
Small museum of art and history
in process of preparation.

Church of San Maurizio
Porlezza
Campanile and ruined church
beside excavated remains of
landslide-destroyed hamlet.
Legendary, lonely, evocative
site.

Museum
Cavargna
Fascinating new museum to life
and work in the Cavargna

Grotte di Rescia
Claino-Osteno
Natural cave.

Orrido
Osteno
Fine chasm that is best viewed
by boat.

Museum
Scaria
Museum of local life and history,
arts and crafts.

Museum
Ponna d'Intelvi Superiore
Valley house furnished in the
style of the late nineteenth
century.

Viewpoints
Belvedere, near Lanzo d'Intelvi
— Lake Lugano and the Alps
Pigra — Lake Como
Schignano — Lake Como

A round trip from Lanzo to Pellio can be made over the Pian della Noci, which is a golf course in summer, as well as being used for winter skiing. From Pellio, go towards Argegno, reaching a tangled mass of roads and hamlets, all of them worthy of note, but through which no straightforward itinerary can be devised. **San Fedele d'Intelvi** has the best Romanesque church in the valley; **Pigra** has one of the best panoramas of Lake Como; from **Casasco d'Intelvi** roads lead up into the mountains offering fine walks; **Schignano** is beautifully sited and has fine views over Lake Como.

From Schignano a road follows one side of the river Telo out of Val d'Intelvi to Argegno, but the main valley road is now on the other bank, from Castiglione d'Intelvi, a fine place with ancient ruins and old houses. That road too drops into Argegno.

6 LAKE COMO

L ake Como is the third biggest of the northern lakes, with an area of 148sq km (55sq miles) and has the longest perimeter, a shore line of over 170km (106 miles). The glacier that cut out its hollow, the Adda, divided around the promontory ridge south of Bellagio, forming two arms. These arms, extending to the towns of Como and Lecco, give the lake an inverted Y-shape, and explain the lengthy perimeter. It is the most enclosed of the major lakes, and many think it is the finest, its northern reaches showing to perfection the V-cut hollow of its glacial birth.

The City of Como

Como is situated at the southern end of the western arm of the lake's upturned Y. There is no outflowing river from this arm, which helps to maintain a wholeness to a city whose first founding was probably at the end of the Bronze Age, around 1,000BC. Little is known of the early town, recorded history starting when the Romans took it, probably from the Gauls, in 196BC. Como was then rebuilt by Julius Caesar, who re-populated it with about 5,000 settlers, including 500 Greek noblemen whose influence can still be detected in the names of some lakeside places.

The site was already strategically important before the Romans, the lake being navigable and offering easy access to Val Bregaglia and Val San Giacomo, both of which offered passes over the Alps to northern Europe. Recognising this importance, the Romans linked the city with Milan, building the Royal Road, Via Regia, that continued northward to Chiavenna. At a later stage, probably when the city was ruled by Queen Theodolinda, the name was corrupted to Via Regina (Queen's Way), a name that lives on in Strada Regina to this day.

Later in its history the town was an important centre in the growth of Christianity, and its churches commemorate important martyrs and bishops — Fedele, Carpoforo, Abbondio and Felice. But the

Como from Baradello Castle

town also saw its share of the strife from which this border country suffered so much. It was almost destroyed in the Ten Years' War with Milan, recovering thanks to the efforts of Barbarossa, but being plagued by civil wars after the death of his grandson, Frederik II. At one point in its history it was actually sold to the Visconti family who held it for a century. At this time, and later under the Sforzas, the city was very prosperous, a prosperity based on silk and woollen industries. The prosperity did not last however, the city falling under Spanish rule in 1535 following the Franco-Spanish Wars. Spanish rule, which lasted almost two centuries, was harsh — this was the time of the Inquisition. The silk and woollen industries declined drastically, barely surviving until relief came in 1714 with the arrival of the Austrians. The city's fortunes improved immediately, an improvement which was maintained through the Napoleonic period, and which gave the city the self-confidence to battle courageously during the Risorgimento. Como rose up with Milan in 1848, setting the scene for the battle of San Fermo, fought just to the west of the city in 1859, when the forces of Garibaldi defeated those of the Austrian Marshal Urban. When Garibaldi's troops marched in triumph following their great victory, it was through the Porta Vittoria in the old town walls that they came. With the coming of the Italian kingdom, Como's prosperity increased again. Today it is a flourishing city, with around 90–100,000 inhabitants. The city's prosperity, tourism apart, is still

Como

based on the silk and textile industries, together with some light engineering and manufacturing. Como is also the provincial capital of the Lombardian province that bears its name.

There is much of interest in the city, and it is well worth an exploration. Those with sufficient experience can borrow a bicycle-made-for-two, welded line-abreast (not a tandem), from the lake shore. It is just a few pedal pushes to the *Duomo*. Approaching from Piazza Cavour, probably by way of Via Plinio, Piazza del Duomo is reached at the western end of the building to which is attached the *Broletto*, the old court of justice, and attached to that is the campanile. Each of these buildings is excellent, the unfaced stone of the tower with its delightful eyebrow roof over the one-eye-clock, and the smooth faced, arched *Broletto* with its especially elegant balcony, but they do interrupt the splendour of the cathedral building itself. It has to be said, of course, that both tower and *Broletto* pre-date the building whose symmetry they obscure. But as a comparison, walk the *Duomo*'s length to view the eastern end, where the apses and dome can come as a great surprise.

The difference between the two ends of the building is not wholly due to the attached buildings, however, Como's *Duomo* having been built over four centuries, and representing one of the most important examples of architecture in transition. The western façade is late Gothic, with elegant sweeps of polished marble between equally

PLACES OF INTEREST IN COMO CITY

Civic Museum
Palazzo Giovio and Palazzo Olginati
Really two museums, the first to local history and including an art gallery; the second dealing with the Risorgimento.

Baradello Castle
Remains of twelfth-century castle of Frederik I Barbarossa

Villa dell' Olmo
Sumptious villa in fine style with formal garden to front and wooded parkland to rear.

Temple Voltiano
Museum to the life of Alessandro Volta, pioneer of electricity.

Funivia
To Brunate
Rack railway. Fine views of lake and city.

Temple Sacrarium
On the road to Brunate
Church dedicated to nautical sports.

elegant long windows and fine arrays of statues. In the niches on either side of the doors are statues by the Rodari brothers of the Plinys, Elder and Younger, both of whom found fame in Rome from origins near the city. The Rodaris were also responsible for the sides of the cathedral, including the northern doorway — the Porta della Rana or Frog Door.

The eastern end of the cathedral marks the transition in architectural style from Gothic to Renaissance, the apses being of the later period. Surprisingly, the final dome is later still, not having been completed until the mid-eighteenth century. The whole is breathtaking and it is no surprise to find that it has been described as the most beautiful building in Italy for illustrating the fusion of styles.

The interior maintains the standards of the exterior. The inside of the dome has both beauty and symmetry, and the works of art — paintings and tapestry — would grace the walls of any museum or art gallery.

Continue the walk through Como by going through the Piazza del Duomo and along Via Vittorio Emanuele, followed by a quick right, then left turn, to reach Piazza San Fedele, a highlight of the walk. The *piazza* was the centre of the old walled town of Como, and was, at that time, the corn market. Some of the houses that enclose the square are still supported by pillars, and date back perhaps 500 years. That is an interesting thought as you sit beneath their shade and gaze across the patterned cobble to the basilica of **San Fedele**, which is now thought to be one of the finest examples of the work of the

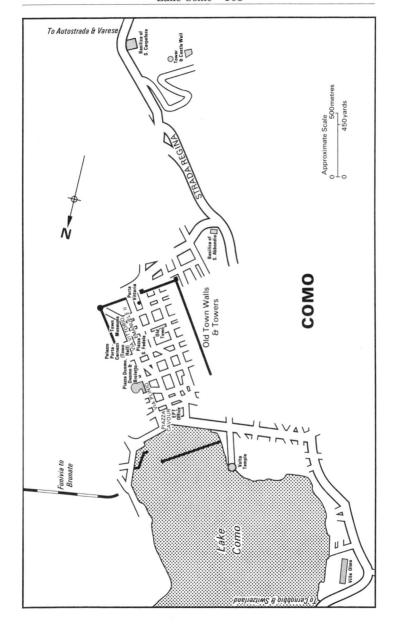

To Autostrada & Varese

Basilica of S. Carpoforo

Tower & Castle Wall

STRADA REGINA

Basilica of S. Abbondio

N

Approximate Scale

0   500 metres
0   450 yards

COMO

Porta Vittoria

Old Town Walls & Towers

Palazzo Cernezzi (Town Hall)

Porta Torre & Museum

VIALE VITTORIO EMANUELE

S. Fedele

Piazza S. Fedele

Old Town

Piazza Duomo, Duomo & Broletto

VIA PLINIO

PIAZZA CAVOUR

EPT Office

Funivia to Brunate

Volta Temple

Lake Como

To Cernobbio & Switzerland

Villa Olmo

Piazza Cavour, Como

Maestri Comacini, though to see the best work it is necessary to continue along Via Vittorio Emanuele to the church which stands opposite the **Palazzo Cernezzi**, a seventeenth-century palace, now the town hall. The Maestri Comacini, literally the Masters of Como, were a collection of tightly knit corporations of architects, stone-masons and decorators who, from the seventh century through to the seventeenth, were renowned throughout Europe as builders of the highest calibre. Their best work is now believed to be represented in the Intelvi valley that runs down to Lake Como at Argegno, around Lake Lugano and in Swiss Ticino as well as here at San Fedele, though examples are known from as far afield as Poland and Russia.

Going left from San Fedele would bring the visitor to the **Civic Museum**, housed in two palaces. The **Palazzo Giovio** is the Archaeological and Art Museum, with many items from pre-historic Como and the surrounding area, including an Iron Age chariot, a boat from Lake Monate, and a fine Roman bronze sword. The art is chiefly from the sixteenth to eighteenth centuries, but there are also some very fine, and much earlier, frescoes. The second palace, **Palazzo Olginati**, holds the Giuseppe Garibaldi Museum of the Risorgimento. The name is hardly surprising in view of Garibaldi's triumphant entry into the city after the battle of San Fermo. The Como area was of considerable importance in this area, and the museum reflects its often heroic contribution to Italian unification.

Tha basilica of San Fedele

Alternatively, turn right and enter old Como, the remaining section of the old walled town. Here there are narrow alleys, held in shadow by tall stone houses with shuttered windows, from which the visitor occasionally emerges into small blindingly sunlit squares. Alessandro Volta, whose museum can be visited, was born in the street that bears his name, while Pope Innocent XI was born in his named street, just the other side of the old town wall. On that wall there are three original towers, none more impressive than that of **Porta Vittoria**, the central one, which stands at the head of the Via Cantu. This is 40m (130ft) high with huge scalloped windows and a most impressive arched entrance. The towers all date from the latter half of the twelfth century.

Not far from the Porta Vittoria is the basilica of **San Abbondio** on a site where the city's first cathedral once stood. The present church was built in the mid-eleventh century and was once the church of a Benedictine monastery, the cloister of which is still visible. Again the church is the work of the Maestri Comacini, building here at a time when their work was influenced by Nordic art, perhaps due to travel of the masters or to northern monks in the monastery. The church is more austere than some of their other work, almost to the point of being severe, but it does have a recognisable apse and, though here as a symmetrical pair, campaniles.

Beyond the church is a hill, and the tower on top of it dominates most views of the city. This is the **Baradello Tower** which, together with a small section of curtain wall, is all that remains of a castle built by Barbarossa in the mid-twelfth century, which was finally slighted by the Spanish in the sixteenth century. From the tower, 35m (115ft) high, the view of Como and the first arm of the lake is excellent.

At the foot of the hill is **San Carpoforo** the last of Como's trio of magnificent basilicas. This one is believed to have been built on the site of a temple to Mercury, and has a Christian history going back 1,500 years. Its style is very early Romanesque, its earliness revealing itself in its irregularities, the poor quality of much of its stone, and the almost complete absence of decoration. But even here there is an apse, and the campanile is clearly of the same style as the pair on San Abbondio.

Near the lake are two buildings of great contrast but equal interest, the sumptious Villa dell'Olmo, first of the great villas that characterise Lake Como, and Tempio Voltiano, built to house a museum to Alessandro Volta, one of Como's greatest sons.

Villa dell' Olmo is named after a forest of elm trees which, according to Pliny the Younger, grew on this spot. The earliest building was in the twelfth century when a monastery was built by the Umiliati Order. The present villa was built in the late seventeenth century by the Odescalchi family, though it was more than a century before it was finally finished. In the late nineteenth century the villa was owned by the Viscontis, who pulled down a pair of much criticised side wings and restored much of the original. Since 1927 the villa has been owned by the city. Today the formal gardens that lie between the villa and the lake, and the wooded parkland to the rear of the villa, are open to the public. The villa itself can also be visited, and is used for concerts, conferences and exhibitions. Its interior has fine stucco and gilt work and a large number of statues. Externally it is solid and formal, though the arched centre section with the colonnade surmounting it is very elegant.

Most people know the name of Alessandro Volta, if only because it has given us the word 'volt'. He was born in Como in 1745, had no scientific training at all, but taught himself to such a degree that he was appointed professor at the University of Padua. After his death in 1827 many of his pieces of apparatus, together with his manuscripts, were gathered together, and they were exhibited in Como in 1899. Sadly a fire destroyed a great number of the exhibits though most of the manuscripts were saved. Over a period of years many of the pieces of apparatus were reproduced and in 1927 these, together

with the surviving material, were housed in the specially built **Temple**
Voltiano. The temple is of almost classical design, the interior having polished marble columns and a mosaic floor, and the exhibits are held in glass cases. There are also books on, and paintings of, the city's great son.

Back in the city there will be time to look at the range of locally made silkwear for which the city is famous, before taking the *funivia* to Brunate. On the journey, and at the top, there are fine views of the city and lake, if you can find a gap between the equally fine and very tall conifers! For the more energetic there is a footpath from the village, or better, from the end of the lane through San Maurizio, to the summit of Monte Boletto, 1,236m (4,055ft). The views from here are wonderfully expansive, taking in on a good day Monte Rosa and Milan, as well as giving a very good view of the glacial valley of Lake Como. Those travelling by road from Como to Brunate pass a Temple Sacrarium dedicated to all nautical sports in the name of the Madonna del Prodigio.

Western Lake Como

Leaving Como on a road that leads, in only 6km (4 miles), to Switzerland, turn off right to follow the western arm of the inverted Y towards Cernobbio. Almost immediately the route begins to pass the villas for which this western arm of Lake Como is so famous, though unfortunately most are not open to the public. Beyond Tavernola the road crosses the Breggia, a *torrente* not a *fiume* (a torrent not a river), draining the Val di Muggio and in spring, heavy with melt-water. Beyond is **Cernobbio**. After Como and Lecco, this is one of the biggest towns on Lake Como, an industrial town, well situated up the hillside between the trees. There is a good beach here, a pleasant, small harbour, and in the old part of the town close to the lakeside square a delightful collection of picturesque houses and narrow alleys grouped around the ancient church.

All walks seem to lead towards the Villa d'Este, one of the most famous of the Lake Como villas and now the grandest of its grand hotels. The villa was built in the late sixteenth century for Cardinal Gallio, Secretary of State to Pope Gregory XIII, and this is what can still be seen, with some minor alterations required by its new use as a hotel. In the eighteenth century the villa was owned by the local Austrian commander-in-chief and so probably played its part in the intrigues of Austrian occupation. Later it was occupied by Caroline of

Lake Como

Brunswick, wife of the British Prince of Wales, George Frederick, later George IV.

The hotel it has now become is possibly the grandest encountered on this tour of the Italian Lakes. With its beautiful gardens and an interior that is a treasure house of art, it would seem to be the absolute height of luxury, though whether it would be possible to shake off the feeling that you were sleeping in a museum is questionable. The swimming pool is worth a mention too. Advertised as unique in Italy, it is a floating swimming pool!

Above Cernobbio rises Monte Bisbino, which at 1,325m (4,350ft) offers truly spectacular views of the lake, and is easy to reach along a winding road through **Rovenna**, a village that clings precariously to a low ridge of the same peak. The summit of Bisbino has a refuge hut and a chapel to which pilgrimages are still made, and offers the possibility of a panoramic view with one foot in Italy and one in Switzerland.

Back at lake level the visitor can now choose an upper road that swiftly bypasses Moltrasio, Carate Urio and Laglio, but makes the most of the lake views before dropping into **Torriggia** where the lake is at its narrowest: a few hundred metres separates it from Careno.

Isola Comacina

But what will be missed? In **Moltrasio**, another fine collection of villas, each with its own historical interest. In particular, the Villa Passalacqua is open to the public — a fine late eighteenth-century building once known as the Palace of Moltrasio, and in which the composer Vicenzo Bellini stayed. Also a delightful little Romanesque church, dedicated to Santa Agata, built towards the end of the eleventh century, with a fine campanile. The chance, too, of excellent walking in the wooded shade of the upper reaches of the town, or near the gorge that splits the town in half and offers a fine show in spring or after heavy rain.

Carate Urio is also split into two, but this time because it was once two separate villages. From the second village, Carate, there is a walk all the way to the top of Colmegnone (1,383m, 4,535ft), though to actually reach the top would take considerable time and effort. **Laglio** also has a good walk, taking about 1¹/₂ hours, up to the 'Bear's Den', a cave from which have been excavated a number of fossil bones, including those of cave bears. Exhibits from the cave can be seen in the museums of Como and Milan, and also in the Laglio village hall.

Beyond Torriggia the new upper road goes on to **Argegno**, where the Intelvi valley (described in the chapter on Lugano) reaches Lake Como. Val d'Intelvi is drained by the river Telo, which flows under an ancient, single-arched bridge in a crowded, but still wooded, part of the town. When approaching from the Intelvi, Argegno is a pretty town, an array of red tiled houses — the half-round tiles so familiar to all visitors to northern Italy (but perhaps best associated with Venice) — in a wooded inlet of the lake. It is worth a tour, a bustling holidaymaker village with a *funivia* to Pigra and fine views of the lake.

Isola Comacina, Como's only island, is quite small, only 800m by 400m (875 by 437yd) and can be reached by a short ferry ride from Sala, Ospedaletto or Spurano. The visitor finds a church dedicated to St John (which explains the occasional alternative name of Isola San Giovanni), an excellent restaurant and a large number of ruins. For the rest, the island is a wilderness of trees and shrubs. It takes a great effort to think of this small island as anything else, but once it was a community so rich it was known as 'Crisopoli', the 'City of Gold' — sometimes, quite wrongly, given as 'Christopoli', the 'City of Christ'. Today the only link with its illustrious past is the festival of St John on the weekend following St John's Day (24 June). On the Saturday there is a night-time firework display on both island and lake, followed by a mass on the island on the Sunday morning in the ruins of the basilica of Santa Eufemia. It is perhaps the most spectacular of all the lake festivals.

On shore, the towns benefit from the island's shelter, the quiet bay between island and mainland once having been known as 'zocca de l'oli', the oil container, because of the growth and importance of the local olive trees.

At **Ospedaletto** is one of the most photographed of all the lakeside campaniles, a late Gothic turret having been grafted onto the Romanesque belfry of the church of Santa Maria Magdalene. The church's annexation to a hospice — a *hospitalis* — by a rich local family gave the village its name. At **Spurano**, if you have enjoyed the Ospadaletto campanile, take a moment to look at the eleventh-century church belfry. The contrast is overwhelming.

At **Ossuccio** the church contains a third-century Romano-Christian altar. The village also has a long avenue climbing the hill past fourteen chapels dedicated to the Madonna of the Rosary, leading to the sanctuary of the Madonna del Soccorso. The whole of it was built between the mid-seventeenth and early eighteenth centuries, and some of the chapels are minor works of art. High above the sanctuary (about 400m (1,310ft) and fairly steep and strenuous — allow 2 hours at least) is the basilica of San Benedetto in **Val Perlana**, generally agreed to be the best preserved Romanesque church in Como province. The church can also be reached from the massive abbey

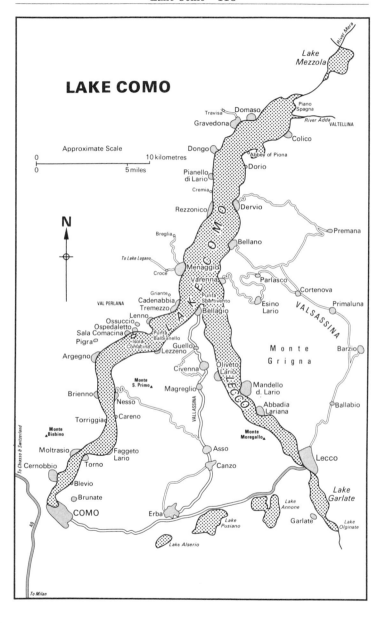

LAKE COMO

Spurano

  at Acquafredda — itself reached by road from Lenno and worth a visit — but again there is a walk of about 2 hours, though in this case a less strenuous one.

From Ossuccio the Balbianello Point, or Back of Lavedo, pokes out into the lake, the Villa Balbianello having been built here to take advantage of the impressive views down towards Como and across to the Bellagio spur. The villa was originally built as a rest home for Franciscan monks and is justly famous for the statue of St Francis offering a welcome to lake-borne visitors. The statue, with the landing stage (the villa can only be reached by boat from Lenno or Campo) and long stone stairway up through an explosion of colour from the flowers and shrubs to its side, is reckoned to be the most photographed spot on Lake Como. The present building, a rebuilding and extension of the original monastic house, is from the late eighteenth century, built for Cardinal Angelo Durini.

Beyond the point, at **Lenno**, is the start of the Tremezzina, the Azalean Riviera, where the fertile soil allows luxuriant growth to a profusion of shrubs and trees. Here there are orange trees, lemons and olives. Magnolias and laurels cover the hill slopes and there are, of course, azaleas. Lenno was the site of Comoedia, a villa belonging to the Elder and Younger Plinys, where, they said, you could 'fish from your very bed'. Some of the excavated remains of the villa are in Como Museum. **Azzano**, the next village, is where, on 28 April

Ossuccio

1945, Mussolini and his mistress Clara Petacci were shot following their capture on the previous day at Dongo, to the north.

At **Tremezzo** is Villa Carlotta, the most famous of all Lake Como's villas. The 'C' above the entrance is not for Carlotta, as many visitors believe, but for Clerici, the family for whom the villa was actually built in the early eighteenth century. The Clerici were not responsible for what we see today however, that claim resting with the Counts Sommariva who owned the villa for the first half of the nineteenth century. The last Sommarivan owner sold the building to Princess Marianna, wife of Adalbert of Prussia, who gave it to her daughter Charlotte (or Carlotta, hence the name) when she married the Prince of Saxe-Meinigen. It has been in the hands of the Italian State since early this century.

Inside, the villa is a shrine to the plaster-workers' and painters' art. Every ceiling is a masterpiece. But in addition to the paintings and the ornamental work, be sure to see the marble table. Also look at the sculpture, particularly that of Antonio Canova. Outside, Sommariva made the most of the area's fertile soil: there are around 150 species of rhododendron and azalea, many grouped in 'Azalea Avenue'. Here too, are a giant sequoia, wisterias, cypresses, camellias, trees and shrubs from Japan and Australia, in all over 500 species. There is 'Great Avenue', with towering specimens of tropical and sub-tropical trees, a fern valley, a rock garden and a host of citrus fruit

SOME PLACES OF INTEREST ON THE WESTERN SHORE OF LAKE COMO

Villa Passalacqua
Moltrasio
Late eighteenth-century villa, associated with Vicenzo Bellini.

Isola Comacina
Reached from Sala, Ospedaletto or Spurano
Numerous excavated ruins from eras throughout the island's history. Festival with fireworks, lake procession and mass during weekend following St John's Day (24 June)

Funivia
Argegno to Pigra
Fine viewpoint (see Lugano chapter).

Basilica of San Benedetto
Val Perlana, near Ossuccio
Best preserved Romanesque church in Como province.

**Villa del Balbianello
(Il Balbianello)**
Lenno
Magnificently sited villa with panoramic views of the lake. Excellent gardens, including most photographed spot on Lake Como.

Villa Carlotta
Tremezzo
Villa with fine art and decoration including sculptures by Canova. Gardens with many species of plants, including large collection of rhododendrons and azaleas. Not to be missed.

Boat Museum
Pianello del Lario
Fascinating museum of the history of Lake Como's boats, including fishing boats and gondolas. Collection of boat building tools.

Palazzo Gallio
Gravedona
Cardinal's palace of the early sixteenth century built around a huge central salon.

Church of Santa Maria del Tiglio
Gravedona
Twelfth-century church on fifth-century Roman church. Some fifth-century mosaic flooring still visible. Crucifix carved from a single piece of wood.

Viewpoints
Monte Bisbino, above Cernobbio
Griante, near Cadenabbia
Croce, above Menaggio
Breglia, above Menaggio
Travisa, above Gravedona

trees and bushes.

Outside the villa, **Tremezzo** is a fine lakeside town, some of its remaining wealth of villas having been converted into regal looking hotels. A tree-lined avenue, celebrated by the visiting Longfellow as a leafy colonnade, links it with **Cadenabbia** where the lake attains its

Villa Carlotta, Tremezzo

maximum width, the two arms linking at last, beyond Bellagio. Cadenabbia is a row of fine hotels, and it has car ferries linking it with Varenna and with Bellagio. Beyond, the Tremezzina ends, though the road is just as pleasant all the way to **Menaggio**, from where it is 12km (about 8 miles) to Lake Lugano, that journey starting with a twisting road to Croce which is a good viewpoint. The nearby golf course must be one of the most romantic courses anywhere. A little higher, and further north, the village of Breglia offers a short walk to the point of San Domenico and an even better view, taking in the whole northern end of the lake. Those with sufficient time and energy can continue to the summit of Monte Bregagno for a tremendous panorama of both lakes — Lugano and Como — and the pre-alpine peaks. But, at a distance of 6km and a height of 1,400m (4 miles and 4,590ft) the walk should not be undertaken lightly.

Menaggio is more of a bustle than the places visited so far. This atmosphere is no doubt due to its position, at a point where access to Lugano and Switzerland is straightforward, and it is doubtless this that contributed to its troubled, as well as prosperous, past. It was fortified, but sieged and taken in the Ten Years' War, and almost

Eros and Psyche *by Antonio Canova at Villa Carlotta*

destroyed a century later, when it was again on the wrong side of a feud. As elsewhere, it also had its problems with both Spaniards and Austrians.

Menaggio is a good place to stroll, the trading influence making window shopping worthwhile, and it is also a good centre for exploration, both of the road to Lugano (dealt with in the chapter on that lake) and also the little villages on the first terrace above the town. As an example, try the walled streets of Laveno. Try also the beautiful valley of the Senagra stream.

Menaggio also has an excellent beach, equipped with a swimming pool, and has a car ferry to Varenna on the eastern side of the lake. Beyond Menaggio the elegant Como villas and garden countryside are left behind for the moment as the lake becomes progressively more confined by higher peaks on the way north. The peaks sweep up to over 2,500m (8,200ft) and are often snow-topped. Indeed, the mountains on each side of the lake are centres for skiing.

The road disappears into a tunnel beyond Menaggio, re-emerging almost opposite Bellano. Ahead now is **Acquaseria**, with a fine old stone harbour, beyond which a road up into the hills reaches **Santa Maria di Rezzonico**, a collection of old hamlets, little touched by the course of time and certainly worth a visit.

At **Cremia** there is another collection of interesting hamlets stretching up the hill from the shore village of San Vito, with a good,

Tremezzo and Lake Como

though small beach, to Vezzedo, almost lost among the streams and hills. Beyond is **Pianello del Lario**, with a most interesting museum. This was opened fairly recently, is housed in a nineteenth-century mill, and is devoted to the history of the boat on Lake Como, with well over a hundred boats in the large number of exhibition halls. Equally fascinating is a collection of boatbuilding tools from across the ages.

It is appropriate, in view of the presence of the museum, that Pianello del Lario should also be home to Como Sailing Club, the lake's oldest club. As with the other lakes, the northern reaches have the best and most dependable winds. Those on northern Como change with a regularity that can almost be used for clock setting, and their steadiness assists anyone learning to sail. The club runs schools of varying length, as well as holding races.

Beyond Pianello is **Musso**, dominated by the Sasso di Musso, a natural fortress, its sides scarred by quarries that have yielded marble for Como Cathedral and Milan's Arch of Peace, among others. On top of this natural barrier there once stood a man-made castle, one-time home to Il Medeghino, a fierce pirate. Gian Giacomo Medici was born in Milan, but exiled here as a youth for the killing of another boy. At the time of Milan's war against the French and Spanish, Il Medeghino, as Medici became known, organised a murder for the city's governor, receiving as reward governorship of Musso's castle. From it he terrorised the lake, his reign coming to an end only when he sold the castle to Milan, choosing just the right moment to escape, both rich and free from retribution. When he died he was even buried in Milan Cathedral, where the visitor can still see his memorial.

Recognising its awesome use to an enemy, its new owners razed the castle when its possession was threatened and today only the *sasso* remains. Elsewhere, the village has a fine villa, the Monzi-Orombelli, not open to the public, and the usual walks and beaches.

At **Dongo** next along the coast, a German motor column was halted by Italian partisans on 27 April 1945, and a search of the lorries revealed a large number of Italy's Fascist leaders, including Benito Mussolini together with his mistress Clara Petacci. At a drumhead trial here the following day thirteen of the leaders were convicted and executed by shooting immediately. Mussolini and Clara Petacci were driven south to meet their fate in Azzano. The Fascist leaders were held at Palazzo Monti, now the Town Hall, which overlooks the town square, a building whose bland exterior is at odds with an interior that is quite regal.

An alpine hut above Dongo

In medieval times Dongo was one-third of the 'Tre Pievi', the three parishes, chief of which was **Gravedona**, the next stop on the route. The Tre Pievi had a warship with a crucifix mounted on it which, it was said, made the ship invincible. It is certainly true that the villages pirated a gold-laden ship of Barbarossa's and later defied him successfully enough to obtain special terms in the Treaty of Constance. The last village of the Tre Pievi, Sorico, can be visited as Lake Como reaches its northern end. Gravedona has the last fine villa on the western shore, Palazzo Gallio, built for Cardinal Tolomeo Gallio about 1500 on the remains of an old castle. The palace was known as Gallio's 'Villa of Delights', but today is the head-office of a local council. It is open to visitors during office hours on an informal, by request basis. Do not miss, either, the church of Santa Maria del Tiglio, built in the twelfth century, but on a fifth-century Roman church. Part of the earlier church's mosaic flooring is still visible, and there is an awesome crucifix carved from a single block of wood.

Behind the Tre Pievi are a number of hamlets strung out along roads that thrust cautiously between the hills to the west. This is summer walking rather than winter skiing country, in the valley of the Albano, or on the flanks of Monte Cortafon (1,688m, 5,540ft) or Monte Duria (2,264m, 7,430ft). The villages too are worthy of note — Garzeno, Dosso del Liro, Livo — old stone houses grouped around interesting churches. On the Gravedona to Travisa road do not fail to

Gravedona

stop for the marvellous panorama of the northern lake.

Beyond **Domaso**, recognised as *the* centre for windsurfing on Lake Como, there are a couple of villages — **Gera Lario**, last stopping point of the lake steamers, and Sorico — before reaching the river Mera inflowing from Lake Mezzola. At Gera Lario another series of roads leads off to ancient villages in the hills, while at **Sorico** there is a church dedicated to St Mirus who landed here after crossing the lake on his cloak — shades of San Giulio and Lake Orta.

Lake Mezzola is 3km by 2km (2 miles by 1$\frac{1}{4}$ miles) and has, at its northern end, an historically interesting church that can only be reached by water. The lake, and the marshes of Pian di Spagna formed between the two inflows (the rivers Adda and Mera) into Lake Como, is an important site for migrating birds. Those interested should not fail to visit Varenna's Museum of Ornithology, which includes many exhibits on the migrations.

Eastern Lake Como

The first town at the northern end of the eastern shore is **Colico**, which is also the first town where the lake steamer stops on its way to its terminus a short distance south at the Abbey of Piona. The town, nestling beneath conical Monte Legnone (2,609m, 8,560ft), is sur-

Sasso Canale above Gera Lario

prisingly new, though there have been settlements here sporadically over the centuries. Only with the partial reclamation of Pian di Spagna, now a nature reserve, and the passes north and east ceasing to be highways of war, did any reasonable chance exist for settled buildings. Beyond, two spits of land, reaching forwards like the pincers of a crab, enclose a small portion of Lake Como, creating Lake Piona, beloved of sailors. On the tip of the southern pincer is the isolated Abbey of Piona. The abbey was founded by the Cluniac order in 1138, though it was built on a site that was already ancient, possibly even pre-Christian. Earlier this century the abbey was taken over by the Cistercians, an order famous for their liking of sites in remote, but scenically beautiful, country. The building has a beauty to match its setting, note especially the cloisters — dating from the mid-thirteenth century — a blend of Romanesque and Gothic architecture in stone and brick. The church is the oldest part of the abbey, though the campanile is eighteenth century, replacing the original.

Returning to the main road southward, pass through Dorio, a well sited village, and reach **Corenno Plinio**. This village is named, it is believed, from Corinth and from Pliny the Elder, who liked this area. The lake is quite narrow here and the castle was important in its day, but the little that remains is in private hands. The church is dedicated to St Thomas à Becket. Elsewhere there is much that is of interest. There are some beautiful old houses, and the town square has three

The gorge at Bellano

fourteenth-century marble tombs — as the outside walls of the church and castle!

Next is **Dervio**, which now shows little of the fortifications that grew around it because of the local headland which makes this the narrowest spot of the lake. Today the town is remarkably industrial-

A quiet backwater in Varenna

ised for a small lake town, but is a good centre for exploring the
northern lake and Val Varrone, and Valsassina through the mountains to the east. These excellent valleys will be explored later, the
present route continuing instead southwards to Bellano.

At **Bellano** do not miss the *orrido*, a gorge cut through the
mountainside by the Pioverna, a stream that brings down melting
snow in spring, and rain in any season. The gorge has been cut deep,

Menaggio from Varenna

but not wide, and is viewed from a collection of ladders and ropeways that allow the visitor to get really close. The gorge holds the sound of rushing water and confines the spray too, making for a really unusual visit that only the Cascata del Varonne near Riva on Lake Garda can match.

Elsewhere, the town (which is, after Mandello, the largest on the eastern lake shore) is an active holiday centre, but with some fine old sections. The lakeside pathway passes two monuments to famous sons — Sigismondo Boldoni, a seventeenth-century scientist, and Tommaso Grossi, a nineteenth-century writer — neither of whom is widely known in the English speaking world. Another Bellano Boldoni, Pietro, was responsible for introducing the silk trade to Como. Be sure also to see the church of San Nazzaro and San Celso, a really beautiful building with a symmetrical façade of contrasting colours and a magnificent circular centrepiece, a rose window with terracotta surround. There are other fine buildings in the town, on some of which the observant may still spot the Visconti emblem, the viper, carved.

On from Bellano the views from the road are excellent, culminating in the first sight of the Bellagio peninsula, and the beautiful car-ferry town of **Varenna** is soon reached. Its houses cling to the foot of a hill on which are the ruins of a castle, said to have been the last home of Theodolinda, Queen of the Lombards, who died in the early

The car ferry at Varenna

seventh century, and which has its own torrent stream, the Esino. Varenna has a long history, the name being, it is thought, of Celtic origin. The old quarter is the most picturesque. Here are steep, narrow lanes, with occasional archways, all of which eventually end at the lake. One of the town's famous sons who walked these lanes was G. Pirelli, who founded the now huge industrial company famous for tyres and calendars. But many visitors come here, not only for the old quarter, but for the more luxurious surroundings of the two famous villas or, perhaps, for the museum devoted to the birdlife of the lake. Those who have come from Colico and Lake Mezzola, particularly during the annual migrations, will certainly want to see the museum where the hundreds of species that have been seen on the lake are displayed, together with other displays on bird migration.

Villa Cipressi, in Via 4 Novembre, is well sited for the best of the views from the Varenna promontory across the lake and to Bellagio. Its terraced gardens go right down to the lake edge to gain maximum benefit from the position, and are a riot of colour in summer. But although Villa Cipressi is well positioned, Villa Monastero is the highlight of Como's eastern shore. It was built in 1208 for Cistercian nuns and was dedicated to Santa Maria Magdalene, but was later sold to a private owner. Following World War I the building was acquired by the Italian Government and housed the Italian Centre for Hydrobiology and Lake Geomorphology. Today it is still a scientific

PLACES OF INTEREST ON THE EASTERN SHORE OF LAKE COMO

Abbey of Piona
Near Colico
Magnificently sited early twelfth-century abbey. Cistercian monks distil a range of spirit drinks sold in abbey shop.

Orrido
Bellano
Gorge of the Torrente Pioverna seen from suspended ropeways.

Ornithological Museum
Varenna
Displays of birdlife of Lake Como, and the annual bird migrations.

Villa Cipressi
Varenna
Villa used for conferences etc. Well sited for fine lake views from terraced gardens.

Villa Monastero
Varenna
Beautiful old monastery con-verted to International Science Centre. Elegant gardens and magnificent views.

Villa Manzoni
Lecco
Eighteenth-century villa furnished to illustrate lifestyle of the period. Collection of Manzoni memorabilia.

Museum (Palazzo Belgioioso)
Lecco
Seventeenth-century palace holding town museum. Sections include development of lake fishing.

Funivia
Versasio, near Lecco, to Piani d'Erna
Expansive views from summit.

Museum
Primaluna
New museum on ethnography of the Valsassina. Covers agricul-ture and iron-making.

Museum
Esino Lario
Items on history of the area, and the geology of the Grigna mountains.

Viewpoint
Parlasco, in Valsassina above Varenna

(chiefly physics) centre, playing host to annual summer schools and meetings that have attracted the best scientists from all over the world. It has stone staircases, with columns and statues, which lead up from elegant shrubberies; an arcaded terrace beside the lake; arched windows and balconies; and a lovely view across the water. Monastero is a beautiful place.

At **Fiumelatte**, a little south of Varenna, is a torrent stream which

Villa Monastero, Varenna

is the shortest in Italy (and surely in Europe), which was noted by Leonardo da Vinci. The village name derives from this stream — milk river — which emerges from a cave on the hillside and disappears 250m (just over 800ft) further on, in the lake. The stream starts quite suddenly in spring as the snows melt, and runs until autumn, occasionally as the torrent of its name, occasionally as a trickle. The village has another stream lower down that runs continuously, the cave stream being, as it were, the overflow.

Below Fiumelatte is Lake Lecco, the eastern arm of Como's inverted Y, as the road passes the Bellagio spur. At **Castello** the ruins of an old castle form part of the village houses; at **Lierna**, Bronze Age remains have been discovered. Then comes **Mandello del Lario**, a fine town which is seen to perfection from across the lake when the rocks of the Grigna make a spectacular backdrop. It is an industrial town, but is increasingly developing its tourist potential. Within the town, the lakeside church of San Lorenzo dates from the ninth century, although since this was a re-building there must have been a Romano-Christian church. Above the town, the village of Maggiana has 'Barbarossa's Tower' — tradition has it that he stayed here in 1158.

South again, the views are increasingly dominated by rocky, as opposed to grass-covered, peaks. Beyond Abbadia Lariana, named for a long gone Benedictine abbey, the western side of the lake is

The Grigna mountains

dominated by the crags of Monte Moregallo, while those of Monte Coltignone, crowd in on the east.

Lecco, at the southern end of the eastern arm of Lake Como, is a large town, second only to Como itself, but still has an old-fishing-port quarter and surroundings of such scenic splendour that its modernity is easily forgiven. Of its particular attractions special note should be made of the Visconti Bridge — the most southern of the two, ie the furthest from Lake Como — that has been renovated to look much as it did when Azzone Visconti had it built over the Adda in 1336. Originally it had drawbridge sections on both ends, but with modern traffic it was not thought reasonable to restore these!

Within the town there are statues of Garibaldi, who liberated the area, and of Lecco's most famous son, Alessandro Manzoni, a writer whose book (translated as *The Betrothed*) deals with the Spanish occupation of Lecco in the seventeenth century and was described by Sir Walter Scott as the best book ever written. The villa, known as 'Il Caleotto,' in which Manzoni spent much of his early, and parts of his later life, is now a shrine to the writer. Known now as Villa Manzoni, it is in Via Amendola, which can be reached by continuing in a straight line after crossing the Visconti Bridge into Lecco.

Due north from Villa Manzoni (follow Via XI Febbraio from Largo Caleotto) is the town's museum, housed in the Palazzo Belgioioso, a palace built by Cardinal Locatelli in the seventeenth century. Apart

The Lepontine Alps above Lake Como

from the building, which is worth the visit in itself, there are items from the town's early history, a hall on the development of fishing in the lake and a natural history section.

An overall picture of town and lake, together with the smaller lakes that crowd in on Lecco, can be gained by riding the cable car from Versasio, above the town, to Piani d'Erna, at 1,329m (4,360ft).

Lecco is a good place from which to explore the Valsassina, the valley which threads its way behind the Grigna, allowing the visitor to reach the lake again at Varenna (via Esino Lario), Bellano (via the Val Muggiasca), or Dervio (via the Val Varrone). All start, however, by leaving Lecco for **Ballabio**, from which a twisting road leads up to Piani Resinelli, a winter sports centre and, with its mountain huts, a centre for summer climbing. Beyond Ballabio the road crosses the Balisio pass and enters Valsassina itself. The valley has been widely described as the finest in the pre-Alps, a continuous mixture of scenic delight from rocky grandeur to pastoral green. It also has a long and important history. Bronze Age man lived here, though the metal which has brought lasting fame is iron. This was mined in the upper reaches of the Val Varrone, but was worked in Valsassina, the trade only having stopped when ore extraction became too expensive. Then the trade went to the more easily reached Lecco, where it flourishes today.

At this rocky end of the valley is **Barzio**, another important winter sports centre and an equally fine summer holiday centre. Cable cars take visitors up to the Piani di Bobbio or the Piani di Artavaggio where, in winter, there are a good number of blue and red ski runs, and in summer fine high-level walking. Down the valley, a road off left leads to Pasturo where one of Manzoni's heroines lived, while further on at **Primaluna**, there is a very fine museum on the ethnography of the valley. Exhibits deal with iron-making, and with the range of farming carried on here. There is also a collection of local minerals.

The valley widens now, the view extends, and all around is a sea of greens to complement the lake's blues. **Cortenova** is set among fields, belying its remaining, though small, interest in the iron industry, and here a side road leads off for Varenna. On this road, at **Parlasco** and several points beyond, are exhilarating views over Lake Como, as the road winds round to **Esino Lario**, the 'Pearl of the Grigna'. In the sixteenth century this village was famously prosperous, and it retains a wealth of architectural beauty. A recent addition, as lately as 1941, is a Via Crucis, with fourteen shrines and sculptures, leading up through firs and larches to the church on its hill. From the church both Como and Lugano lakes can be seen. Also here is a museum with items from local history, and also from the geology and mineralogy of the Grigna group. From Esino Lario a road winds down to Varenna.

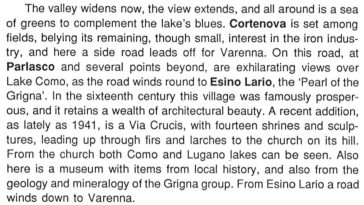

The Valsassina continues from Cortenova, passing the thermal springs of Tartavalle Terme, and reaching Taceno where a left turn follows the Pioverna stream through the Val Muggiasca. The stream drops finally though Bellano's *orrido*, while the visitor endures a more winding but controlled descent to the town.

Going right at Taceno, the road reaches **Margno**, from where a cable car rises to Pian delle Betulle at 1,456m (4,780ft), another winter sports area with good summer walking. Nearby are two tiny villages, Crandola Valsassina and Vegno, in superb positions. The **Val Varrone** is reached near Premana, the archetypal valley village still famous for its iron working, the ladies' costume — an echo of Venetian influence — and its dialect, also a reminder of its Venetian past. From Val Varrone a series of fine villages and tremendous views are laid out along the road that winds down to Dervio.

Southern Lake Como

Because of its shape, Lake Como creates a triangular peninsula of land at its southern end, the point of the triangle being at Bellagio, the base sitting on the road from Como to Lecco. The exploration of this area is awkward, requiring some doubling back if everything is to be seen. Here all the important sites are noted, but in recognition of the difficulty of traversing the area in one tour, the peninsula will be explored by travelling from Como to Bellagio, following the Valsassina to Erba, then the road into Lecco.

The peninsular triangle, sometimes called the High Brianza, has been created by a ridge of hard rock running south from Bellagio. This high land, steep but not rocky and almost continuously wooded, hems in the road on the right, so much so that the road engineers had to tunnel through a couple of times *en route* to **Blevio**, the first village on this western shore of the Como lake arm. Blevio lies opposite Cernobbio, but the sun lies behind the hills here, and there is little similarity. It must be said however, that the position does offer sun in summer and the most beautiful sunsets. There is a row of elegant villas on the lake front, and their gardens are a tribute to the summer sun.

The next village is **Torno** where the shore takes a right-angled bend, the turning of which offers a marvellous view north (which the Villa Pliniana further on was built to capture). In the thirteenth century a monastery here led to the establishment of a woollen industry, and the town became very prosperous. Much of the surviving old town has remained as it was, a wealth of old houses, narrow lanes, archways and two excellent churches. The better is San Giovanni, with an excellent Renaissance doorway in marble. Those who see a resemblance to Como's cathedral doorway are correct, the statuary here being by the Rodari school if not actually by the Rodaris. It is an irony that Como provided both builders and destroyers of the town. Inside, the church has much of interest, including a sixth-century memorial stone and a reliquary — shown only three times each year — that holds a piece of a Holy Nail.

Beyond Torno the road has beautiful tree-laden cliffs to the right, blue water and the villas of the western shore to the left. A road from Faggeto del Lario reaches three villages set among the trees, hanging off the cliffs themselves. **Palanzo**, the last village, has the ruins of an old castle, while at **Molina**, the first, a waterfall drops noisily into a rocky gorge.

North of Pognana Lario, where Roman tombs were discovered, the road climbs a little way up the hill with an improvement in the lake views. Several picturesque villages are now passed before **Nesso** is reached, itself a picturesque, but much larger village. Its castle did not

The view from Monte San Primo

survive a battle between the Sforzas and Il Medeghino, though a single wall with three turrets can still be seen in the oldest, most picturesque, part of the town. Here too is an *orrido* (a gorge), of the Torrente Nesso, best viewed from a bridge over the stream near the lake shore. From Nesso a road climbs into the High Brianza, passing through several well sited villages, reaching the winter sports area of Pian del Tivano, and then descending to Vallassina.

Back on the shore road the lake has an elbow at **Punta della Cavagnola**, beyond which are a series of villages belonging to the commune of **Lezzeno**, the village of that name being the largest and last. The views across the lake to Isola Comacina and Punta del Balbianello are spectacular, and equally spectacular are the light plays in the lake cave, Buco dei Carpi, which can be reached only by boat. The cave is named for the carp which, together with other lake fish, take refuge there, but is more famous for its reflections of the setting sun.

The shore is overhung now by broken cliffs all the way to **Bellagio**, the 'Pearl of the Lake', thought by many to be the loveliest town not only on Como but in Europe. The town stands just behind the tip of the triangle of land. The actual tip is called La Punta Spartivento, 'the point that divides the wind'.

Before the town comes Villa Melzi d'Eryl, which sets the tone for Bellagio itself. The house cannot be visited, but externally it is a

Bellagio from Tremezzo

masterpiece of neo-classical architecture. Even the chimneys are exquisite. The gardens were landscaped by the moving of many tons of earth, though now, as with the best of all landscape gardening, that is not obvious.

The defences which Bellagio's position almost compelled its possessor to build are now gone — indeed they have been dismantled more than once in the town's history. But what still remains is the intricate network of lanes, some steep, some cobbled, that rise from the lake shore. The church of San Giacomo has work from a Romanesque (eleventh century) construction and a later baroque expansion.

Villa Serbelloni, which now belongs to the Rockefeller Foundation, is built on an ancient site. The present building fell into disrepair, even to the extent of having its name transferred to a hotel that stands on the other side of the point from it. It is now restored, though the visitor can only visit its gardens, which are terraced in grand Italian style. But beautiful though the villas are, it is the old, cobbled village of Bellagio, and the views, which haunt the memory.

South from Bellagio the route follows the Vallassina, but an alternative would be the shore road to Lecco. This is dominated by the Grigna across the lake, with some good closer views of the mountains of the High Brianza as Lecco is approached. At **Olivati Lario** the olive groves that give the village its name offer a pleasant,

---

PLACES OF INTEREST ON THE SOUTHERN SHORE OF LAKE COMO

Orrido
Nesso
Gorge of the Torrente Nesso.
Can be seen from lake or road
or, better, from a bridge over the
stream.

Buco dei Carpi (Carp Hole)
Lezzeno
Lake cave, reachable only by
boat, where lake fish congre-
gate. Good reflections of the
setting sun.

Villa Melzi d'Eryl
Bellagio
Magnificent neo-classical villa
with fine landscaped gardens.

Villa Serbelloni
Bellagio
Restored villa, owned by
Rockefeller Foundation, with
terraced Italian style garden.

Town Museum
Erba
Collection on history of the town,
as well as other, more general,
exhibits.

Museum of Silk
Garlate
Museum of the silk industry
established in an old silk mill.

Viewpoint
Monte San Primo, above
Bellagio/Nesso

---

softer contrast.

The uphill route starts by climbing quite steeply to **Guello**, a village sitting on a wooded shelf, from where there are two roads forward. To the right, the western road can be followed for one of the best views of Como, obtained from the summit of Monte San Primo, 1,882m (6,175ft) The summit can be reached from Alpe di Ville, but does involve a climb of around 800m (2,625ft) for which 3 hours should be allowed.

The eastern road from Guello takes the visitor through **Civenna** which was once, with Limonta below it, an independent state, rather as Campione d'Italia is today. This existence, for more than 1,000 years, was only ended 200 years ago. Thereafter the village became a popular holiday resort, as the number and wealth of its villas amply testifies. Beyond Civenna at the high point of the road, is a church dedicated to the patron saint of cyclists, and a monument to cyclists. Those who arrive on cycles must find it a delightful resting spot.

South again, enter the Vallassina, a valley of green meadows and scattered woods of chestnut, birch, beech and various firs and pines, set among which are Magreglio and Barni, justifiably well known as

A side street in old Bellagio

holiday centres. The first has a camp site, and is a reasonable, though not well equipped, winter sports centre.

Before Asso, one of the chief villages of Vallassina, a road off left leads to **Lasnigo** with its beautiful church, while one to the right leads to Sormano and the road that drops steeply into Nesso. **Sormano** itself is beautifully sited, an open sunny village.

Asso, which gives its name to the valley, is an ancient village.

Bellagio

There was a Roman settlement here, as an inscribed stone set into the tower which is itself all that remains of the tenth-century castle, shows. Today Asso is a busy, light-industrial town, worthy of an exploration. From it a road left drops down to the Lecco arm of Como, but the route carries on to **Canzo**, another town with a prosperity based on light industry and tourism. Canzo too was fortified, the remains of the castle now forming part of the Albergo Castello, the Castle Hotel, which also acts as an unofficial museum of the town. High above the town to the east, are the Corni di Canzo, rock masses set in the green alpine meadows, below which is a remote chapel dedicated to San Miro, a twelfth-century hermit who was said to be able to control water, producing the odd spring at the Villa Pliniana and bringing or ending rain.

Two roads lead to **Erba**, one passing the tiny Lago del Segrino, exquisitely set among the trees, the other following the river of the Vallassina. Because of its position this large industrial town was fortified from its earliest history, though its defences have now been dismantled. Those interested in its history, from earliest times to the Risorgimento, should visit the town museum which has some good exhibits, and a walk around the town goes past some fine villas.

South of Erba is **Lago di Alserio**, the first of three lakes on the route back to Lecco. The second lake, **Lago di Pusiano**, has a tiny island, named for the cypress tree and is surrounded by pleasant

Bellagio and the Grigna mountains

villages each with an elegant array of villas. The third lake, **Lago di Annone**, is the largest and has a tongue of land, Isella, extending into it, reminiscent of Sirmione at Lake Garda. At the very tip of Isella is a camp site that must be in the ultimate position for the water lover. The view from here of the village of Annone with its tall campanile is superb. At one time a bridge linked Isella and the shore at Annone, but this was never rebuilt following its destruction by the Spaniards in the seventeenth century. Today, traces of it can still be seen below the water.

Beyond Lago di Annone are two more lakes, south of Lecco, **Garlate** and **Olginate**, each worthy of a visit. The village of Garlate at the southern end of the lake bearing its name is interesting for its museum of silk, the only one in Lombardy devoted to this most important provincial industry.

7 BERGAMO AND THE SURROUNDING VALLEYS

The city of Bergamo (or rather the cities of Bergamo, since there are two distinct cities, the upper and lower), stands at the junctions of the Val Seriana and the Val Brembana — though neither of the two valley rivers actually runs through the cities. It is an ancient place — there was a Celtic settlement here even before the establishment, around 200BC, of the Roman *Bergomum*.

From any position that offers a view of Bergamo, it is the upper city — Bergamo Alta — that attracts the eye. This is true even from the lower city — Bergamo Bassa — but it is there that the tour will begin. Bergamo Bassa is a spacious city, with broad avenues and open *piazze*. At its centre is Piazza Matteotti, with gardens and memorials, and running parallel to it, the Sentierone, linking Piazza Cavour and Piazza Vittorio Veneto. In Piazza Cavour is a monument to Donizetti, the eighteenth-century composer who was born in the city, while the Teatro Donizetti stands on the Sentierone. The monument has the composer listening to Melopea, on her lyre; the theatre, built at the end of the eighteenth century was named for the composer in 1898, the centenary of his birth. It holds 1,300 people. Also in the Sentierone is the church of **San Bartolomeo** with a large altarpiece by Lorenzo Lotto, one of his major works. Other works by the painter can be seen in the churches of **San Spirito** — in Via Torquato Tasso next to San Bartolomeo, and in **San Bernardino**, a small church in the steep Via Pignolo to the north. East of Piazza Matteotti is the church of **Sant' Alessandro in Colonna**, outside of which a column made of ancient stone fragments marks the spot where St Alexander is said to have been martyred in AD297.

The upper city is fully walled (the walls having been completed by the Venetians in the late sixteenth century when the city was the Venetian Republic's western bastion) and so entry to it can only be made through the ancient gates and cars are, to all intents and purposes, excluded. Four gates exist, two on the Bergamo Bassa side, two towards the open country to the north. In addition a *funivia* runs up from the lower city — follow Via Vittorio Emanuele II from

BERGAMO

To Val Brembana

Botanical Gardens

Porta S. Lorenzo

Porta S. Alessandro

Old Town Walls

Donizetti's Birthplace

Museum of Archaeology & Natural History

Seminary

Piazza Vecchia
Palazzo della Regione
Venetian Mayor's Mansion
Campanile
Biblioteca Angelo Mai

Church of S. Agostino

Accademia Carrara

Rocca-Risorgimento Museum

Donizetti Museum
Piazza Duomo
Duomo
S. Maria Maggiore
Colleoni Chapel
Baptistry
Church of S. Croce

Gombito Tower

Diocesan Museum

Palazzo Terzi

Porta S. Agostino

Porta S. Giacomo

EPT Office

VIA PIGNOLO

Church of S. Spirito

VITTORIO EMANUELE

VIA TORQUATO TASSO

Church of S. Bartolomeo

Donizetti Monument
PIAZZA CAVOUR
Donizetti Theatre

Church of S. Alessandro in Colonna

PIAZZA MATTEOTI

Approximate Scale

0 — 500 metres
0 — 450 yards

To Autostrada

To Val Seriana

N

Piazza Vittorio Veneto and it is on the left after the road has curved rightward. This is an excellent way to approach the upper city. You climb on board the rack railway and when you get out you are several metres higher, and 400 years further back in time.

Porta San Giacomo lies to the left of the *funivia*, while further along Via Vittorio Emanuele II is Porta Sant' Agostino. Using this last gate has the advantage of taking the visitor close to the **Palazzo dell' Accademia Carrara**, which no art lover will want to miss. Here are works by Raphael, Titian, Botticelli, and Rubens as well as paintings by local artists Maroni and Lotto, and by artists of the Venetian school. The gallery was founded in the late eighteenth century by Count Giacomo Carrara.

Beyond the Porta Sant' Agostino is a church to the same saint built in the thirteenth century, but deconsecrated following extensive damage in a fire. The Gothic façade is superb, though little else remains of the original. Today the church is used for occasional exhibitions.

(above) *A portrait by Maroni in the Accademia Carrara, Bergamo*
(top left) *The city walls, Bergamo*
(bottom left) *San Giacomo gate, Bergamo*

The centre of the upper city is Piazza Vecchia, the Old Square, a wonderful place, thought by many to be without any equal anywhere. The square, at first sight, is tiled on a grand scale, but closer examination shows that each large 'tile' is of brick, the bricks going diagonally across the square 'tile'. A simple yet brilliant idea. In the centre of the square is the Contarini fountain, presented to the city in 1780 by the Venetian mayor Alvese Contarini. Its lions, symbol of the Venetian Republic, demurely hold chains in their mouths. When on St Stephen's Day in 1796 the citizens of Bergamo tore the Venetian

PLACES OF INTEREST IN AND AROUND BERGAMO CITY

Accademia Carrara
Piazza dell' Accademia
Fine collection of paintings
including works by Raphael,
Botticelli, and local artists.

Church of Santa Maria Maggiore
Piazza Duomo
Magnificent twelfth-century
church with monument to
Donizetti.
Not to be missed.

Colleoni Chapel
Piazza Duomo
Remarkable fifteenth-century
chapel attached to Santa Maria
Maggiore.

Campanile
Piazza Vecchia
Bell tower, mainly from sixteenth
century. Lift climbs to top for
superb views.

Archaeology Museum
Piazza Cittadella
Pre-history and Roman history of
city and area. Includes many fine
pieces of sculpture and excellent
mosaic floor.

Natural History Museum
Piazza Cittadella
On same site as Archaeology

Museum. Exhibits covering
zoology, geology and mineralogy
of the area.

Botanical Gardens
Porta Sant' Alessandro
City botanical gardens in north-
west corner of old city.

Risorgimento Museum
Rocca
Collection of memorabilia of city's
part in Risorgimento. Includes
the piano on which Garibaldi's
Hymn was first played, in Genoa,
in 1858.

Donizetti's Birthplace
14 Via Borgo Canale
The house where the composer
was born.

Donizetti Museum
9 Via Are
Remarkably comprehensive
collection of memorabilia of the
composer's life and death.

Diocesan Museum
3 Via Donizetti
Beautifully sited in sixteenth-
century *palazzo*. Fine collection
of sacred documents and deco-
rations.

Sotto il Monte
Near Bergamo
Birthplace of Angelo Roncalli,
Pope John XXIII, whose house
can be visited.

lion from the façade of the **Palazzo della Ragione** and smashed it,
they had decided that the chains were those of slavery, and that they
would bear them no longer. Today the *palazzo* has another lion.

The *palazzo* was rebuilt in the mid-sixteenth century following a
fire. It is a dark, brilliantly conceived building with a statue of the poet

Torquato Tasso on a plinth to the side of its central portico. In the room above the statue there is a collection of detached frescoes, some from the original building and some from the Venetian Mayor's mansion, rebuilt in the fifteenth century, which also stands on a side of the *piazza*. The mansion is now part of the university. To the side of the *palazzo* is the city's campanile, begun in the twelfth century, but not completed until the sixteenth. A lift climbs the tower and from the top there are superb views over the old city. Each evening the largest bell tolls a 180 chime curfew. In front of the campanile, access to the Palazzo della Ragione is up a beautiful covered stairway.

At the opposite end of the *piazza* from the *palazzo* is the library, the **Biblioteca Angelo Mai**, built in the seventeenth century as a new town hall, and only completed when the façade above the portico was added in 1928.

The Palazzo della Ragione separates the Piazza Vecchia from the Piazza del Duomo, its arcades providing a perfect frame for a view of the church of Santa Maria Maggiore and the Colleoni chapel. Also in the square, not surprisingly in view of the name, is the city **Cathedral**, seemingly jammed in between its surrounding buildings. Externally — though it is very difficult to see the whole of the outside, even from the campanile — the cathedral is simple, a fine dome overtopping red tiled roofs and a dignified white front. The building was started in the mid-fifteenth century on the site of the old cathedral, but additions were made until the seventeenth century, and the dome and frontage were added only last century. Inside, the cathedral is magnificent, with many fine artworks. Chief of these are a painting by Maroni, to the left after entering, one by Tiepolo at the far end, and the two altars, the northern with bas-reliefs of the seventeenth century, the southern with sculptured saints, of the eighteenth century.

Opposite the Palazzo della Ragione is the church of **Santa Maria Maggiore** built in the late twelfth century by the citizens when they were exhausted by war, famine, drought and plague, and in need of spiritual assistance. It is a simple building, the elaborate red and white marble porch over the entrance having been added 150 years later. Inside, the church is massively and sumptuously decorated, with so much to look at that it is beyond reasonable description. But do look out for the sixteenth-century Florentine and Flemish tapestries, the wooden choir and the monument to the composer Donizetti.

Built into the side of Santa Maria Maggiore is the **Colleoni Chapel**. Bartolomeo Colleoni, who died in 1476, was a remarkable

Piazza Vecchia, Bergamo

man, a son of Bergamo, who twice captained Venetian forces against Milan, and twice captained Milanese forces against Venice, managing during the whole time not only to maintain his head but to make a small fortune besides. Colleoni gave money for a statue of himself in Venice, specifying a position in front of San Marco. He meant the basilica of San Marco but was given instead the school of that name, a play on words he was never to be aware of, as the statue was positioned after his death. It is now considered one of the finest equestrian statues in the world. Another, also finished after his death,

Bergamo Cathedral

can be seen in the chapel that Colleoni had built here in Bergamo. The chapel was begun in 1470, designed by Amadeo, the most famous architect and sculptor of the day, and is a masterwork of intricate design and craftsmanship. Inside are the tombs of Colleoni, and of his daughter Medea, both of which are also by Amadeo.

 On the fourth side of the Piazza del Duomo is a delightful polygonal **baptistry** built in the fourteenth century, which originally stood inside Santa Maria Maggiore, but which was taken down and accurately reconstructed here in the last years of the nineteenth century. Inside, it is a minor treasure house of bas-relief and sculpture by Campione masters.

 Surrounding the two *piazze* is a large number of equally fascinating buildings, the oddly shaped and squat eleventh-century church of **San Croce**; the **Ateneo** built over an early water supply cistern which, a still-extant memorial tablet tells us, was completed in 1342; and the **Bishop's Court**.

Beyond is still more of interest, old Bergamo being virtually an open-air museum. An exhaustive tour is beyond the scope of this book, but some general pointers are worthwhile. Inside the old walls a tree-lined road circles the city, and taking this from Porta Sant' Agostino leads to Porta San Giacomo and then on past the **Palazzo** **Terzi**, the most magnificent private palace in the city.

Beyond the seminary that dominates the south-western corner of the city is the **Citadel**, built around a closed *piazza*. The buildings here are of the thirteenth century, with fine cloisters, and one houses the **Archaeological and Natural History Museum**. The thirteenth-century tower near the *piazza* is 'di Adalberto', the tower of hunger. Ahead now is a green valley, a surprising, but delightful, discovery, beyond which is Porta San Lorenzo, through which Garibaldi passed in 1859. To the left is the final gate, Porta Sant' Alessandro, and the city's **Botanical Gardens**.

From Piazza Cittadella, Via Colleoni leads back to the old square, a magnificent, narrow, enclosed street of old houses and fine churches. Past the old square is Via Gambito, with the **Gambito Tower**, square cut and unadorned, marking the entrance to the beautiful Piazza Mercato del Fieno with its strange medieval tower- houses. At the back of the square is the thirteenth-century convent of San Francesco, and to the side of it, the *rocca*, with the **Museum** **of the Risorgimento**.

Elsewhere in the city the visitor can see the birthplace of Gaetano Donizetti in Borgo Canale, just outside Porta Sant' Alessandro, while a museum devoted to the composer is in Via Arena. Donizetti died in old Bergamo in 1848, and a monument to him can be seen in the church of Santa Maria Maggiore, a remarkable work with seven distraught children representing the seven musical notes, and the muse of music hanging her head.

In a road named for the composer, Via Donizetti, running from close to the Piazza del Duomo towards the *rocca*, is a fine Renaissance mansion, the **Casa dell'Arciprete** which houses a small diocesan museum.

Another famous man who came from Bergamo province, though not actually from the city, was Angelo Roncalli, who found fame as Pope John XXIII, one of the most universally loved popes of modern times, who died in 1963. His birthplace at Sotto il Monte lies a few kilometres west of the city, and the house of his birth has become a place of pilgrimage and homage.

Val Seriana

Val Seriana, the valley of the river Serio, has one of the longest histories of any of the local valleys and is, as a result, one of the best to visit for a glimpse of Italy's architectural and artistic heritage. The valley's place in history is due to its metal mines, and to its wide bottom and gently sloping sides that allowed easy farming on fertile soil. Today the lower valley, that closest to Bergamo, is industrial, mainly the light industry of silk and cotton milling, but with the heavier activity of a cement works occasionally visible. Higher up, the valley is still beautifully unspoilt, and there agriculture is still the mainstay, though tourism is now a major industry, especially in winter as the valley's winter sports facilities improve. In summer the alpine pastures offer excellent walking in cool surroundings — just the thing for relaxation after long hot days at the lake's edge — with wonderful views, occasionally to jagged ridges of peaks.

Nembro and **Albino**, the first valley villages reached from Bergamo, are a little industrial, but do not be put off and so miss the painting of the Crucifixion by Maroni in the church of San Giuliano, Albino. Maroni was born near the village, in the hamlet of Bondo Petello on the slopes above it. The hamlet can be seen by those who take the *funivia* from the top of Albino to the hill village of **Selvino**, a pretty, well sited village, rightly popular both in summer and now, more frequently, in winter.

Colleoni Chapel,
Bergamo

By crossing the river at Albino a road can be reached that links the Val Seriana with the Val Cavallina at Lake Endine. This road passes **Abbazia** where there is a delightful twelfth-century Cistercian monastery. The half-cone apses with stone-tiled roofs are especially attractive. Another road out of the valley, but here into a side valley, can be taken at Gazzaniga to reach **Gandino**, a very old, very pretty village with a fine artistic history, which was the birthplace of Bartolomeo Bon, the sculptor, and the painter Castello. The town's past is well represented in its preserved medieval gateway and in its excellent early fifteenth-century basilica, with a baroque interior that includes a sixteenth-century bronze balustrade. The basilica's campanile is topped by a very eastern-looking spire. The town museum has exhibits which include items from the historically important local textile industry, while the basilica's own museum holds a collection of important documents and vestments. From Gandino a chair lift can be taken to a high plateau that offers good

The Dance of Death, *Clusone*

skiing in winter and good walking in summer.

Vertova, in the valley, and **Casnigo**, on a road that branches off right after yet another bridge over the Serio is crossed, are each worth visiting for their churches. The one at Vertova is surrounded by a remarkable arcade that gives it a curious 'hen and chickens' look which belies its great interest, while that at Casnigo is a simple, elegantly arcaded, fourteenth-century building.

In the main valley, at Ponte Nossa, a very winding road links (eventually!) Val Seriana and Val Brembana, and a little further up the valley, **Clusone**, a major centre, can be reached by a short detour. The Oratorio dei Disciplini, beside the church, has fifteenth-century frescoes of the *Triumph of Death* and the *Dance of Death*, the latter a mixture of people and skeletons hand in hand. Also here is a fine astronomical clock by Pietro Fanzago, a local man, dating from the late sixteenth century. The nearby village of **Rovetta** has a museum to the work of the Fantoni family, sixteenth-century sculptors.

Beyond the Clusone turn off, the valley is dotted with pretty villages in beautiful positions and outlooks increasingly dominated by big mountains. **Gromo** has a fine medieval tower and an equally good Palazzo Communale with three tiers of arcades, and from the village there is what must be the most corkscrew road in the province up to the winter sports centre of Spiazzi.

PLACES OF INTEREST IN VAL SERIANA

Funivia
Albino to Selvino
Cableway to well known plateau.

Museums
Gandino
Small museum of history of town and area including its textile manufacturing. Museo della Chiesa with precious tapestries and frescoes.

Oratorio dei Disciplini
Clusone
Frescoes of *Triumph of Death* and *Dance of Death*.

Astronomical Clock
Clusone
Beautiful clock by Pietro Fanzago, a local man, dating from 1583.

Fantoni Foundation
Rovetta
Museum of the work of local medieval sculptors.

Cascata del Serio
Reached from Valbondione.
One of Europe's highest waterfalls.

The last village is **Valbondione**, where the valley is rugged, and from there it is possible to walk to the Cascata del Serio, one of Europe's highest waterfalls — 315m (1,035ft) — set in very rugged, almost inhospitable, country. The water is now used to power a hydro-electric station, so that at most times the waterfall is dry! In the past the station has 'opened' the fall at set weekends in summer and when the station plant was being overhauled, but there is now a rumour that it will no longer be doing this. Ask the Tourist Office for up-to-date information.

Val Brembana

The valley of the Brembo has a curious geography which, before the advent of modern road engineering, meant that it was virtually cut off from the outside world. To the north, at its head, there are high peaks without passes, and the ridges of these peaks run down not only the east and west sides of the valley, but weave east and west at the southern end as well, to produce a difficult exit for the river through the 'straits' as they are called. As a consequence, until about 1600 there were only two passes into the valley, and neither of them was particularly easy. Not surprisingly the valley folk evolved a rich mixture of dialect, culture and architecture which, while it has not survived intact into the modern era, does at least colour the land-

(PLACES OF INTEREST IN VAL BREMBANA)

Church of San Tome
Almenno
Beautiful twelfth-century circular
church on site of Roman temple.

Grotte delle Meraviglie
Sedrina
Limestone cave.

Museum
Zogna

Museum showing history and
development of valley.

Funivia
San Pellegrino Terme
To fine viewpoint at Vetta.

Grotte del Sogna
San Pellegrino Terme
Limestone cave.

scape, making a trip up the valley very worthwhile.

From Bergamo the road reaches the valley at Villa d'Alme where
the river ends its sinuous curves through the straits. Over the river
from here, at **Almenno**, the twelfth-century circular church of San
Tome stands on the ruins of a Roman temple. Its unusual shape and
its isolation make it a captivating building. Beyond, **Sedrina** is most
famous for its series of bridges high above the river, linking the steep
cliffs that form the banks in the straits. Over the river the tourist can
visit the Grotte delle Meraviglie, one of the limestone caves for which
the valley is famous among speleologists. One cave hereabouts, the
Buca del Castello, is one of the deepest in Italy.

Zogna is a commercial and industrial centre, but does have the
Museo della Valle, a museum showing the history and development
of the valley. Beyond is **San Pellegrino Terme**, the most famous of
the valley's towns, and one of Italy's most famous spas, specialising
in the treatment of kidney disorders. The history of the thermal
springs at the village goes back to the thirteenth century, but it is really
only in this century that they have become famous and have brought
the prosperity that allowed the Grand Hotel and the casino, for
example, to be built. The casino, with its square but elegant lines and
its backdrop of trees, is a very fine building. In the town a *funivia* goes
up to Vetta where there are fine views of both town and valley.
Nearby, the Grotte del Sogna, another cave, can also be visited.

From San Pellegrino Terme, a side valley can be followed to
Serina, a beautiful village with frescoed, arcaded houses and a huge
church with many works by Palma il Vecchio, who was born here. In
the main valley is **San Giovanni Bianco**, with an equally magnificent

A winter scene at Foppolo

 church — an imposing collection of cylinders, half cylinders and squares with a pencil-thin campanile. The village sits at the mouth of the Taleggio valley, famous for its cheese, and has slim, elegant bridges over the rivers of both valleys as they meet.

Next in the main valley comes **Cornello dei Tasso**, just a huddle of houses around a fine campanile, hardly credible as a birthplace for household words. The Tasso family came from this village, a family that started a Europe-wide postal service in the late thirteenth century and who have given us the name of the Russian news agency (Tass), and the word 'taxi', deriving from their exclusive, private vehicle service when they were postmasters to the Holy Roman Empire in the sixteenth century. Torquato Tasso, the poet whose statue is in old Bergamo, was from this family.

 At **Piazza Brembana**, a beautiful spot with expansive views over green meadows and blue mountains, the valley splits. The western fork goes over the San Marco Pass and down into the Valtellina, while the eastern fork, the Val Brembana proper, goes on through a series of fine mountain villages, to end at **Foppolo**, the most developed of all Bergamo province's winter sports centres and fast becoming one of the leading centres in Italy. Using the village's chairlifts as a start, it is possible to climb the Corno Stella — (2,620m, 8,595ft). The climb is about 1,000m (3,280ft) and 3km (2 miles) in distance and should not be undertaken lightly, but the summit does offer one of the finest alpine panoramas of the whole region, from the Bernese Oberland peaks across to the Ortler Alps.

Sondrio and Valtellina

Sondrio

The Valtellina has always been important in Italian history, for while most of the alpine valleys, and all of the passes, run north–south, the Valtellina — the valley of the river Adda — lies predominantly east–west. As a consequence many of the alpine passes end in the Valtellina, so that control of the valley gave control of many passes. In addition, the Adda flows into Lake Como which gave the defenders of the valley quick access to the Lombardy plain.

Sondrio, half way along the Valtellina, is capital of a Lombardian province that bears its name, a mountainous province sharing a long border with Switzerland and including, arguably, the best of Italy's skiing resorts. The town lies each side of the Torrente Mallero (now enclosed in a trench that signifies its potential destructive force) which seems to cut the town in half. Above one bank is the **Masegra Castle**, last of a long line of castles on the site, all destroyed by various warring factions. Today the castle is in government hands and is not open to visitors.

The centre of the town is Piazza Campello, where the Town Hall, the **Palazzo Communale**, stands — a square cut sixteenth-century building, its lower façade interestingly textured. Also here is the parish church of **San Gerasio and San Protasio**. The site is ancient, but the eleventh-century church that stood here was demolished in the eighteenth century, and the present building was erected. The fine campanile was built at the same time.

North of the square is the oldest part of the town, well worth investigating, though many of the finest buildings date only from the eighteenth century, which is rather new by Italian standards. The **Palazzo Lavizzari** in Via Parravicini is an exception, a fine building with a white marble doorway from the sixteenth century.

To the east is **Palazzo Quadrio**, a neo-classical building that houses one of the town's two museums, that devoted to a history of the Valtellina. It has some good exhibits: Etruscan and Roman finds, and paintings by local artists. A diocesan section has some fine religious works including a rare seventeenth-century copper cross. The second museum is in Via Ragazzi del' 99, a natural history

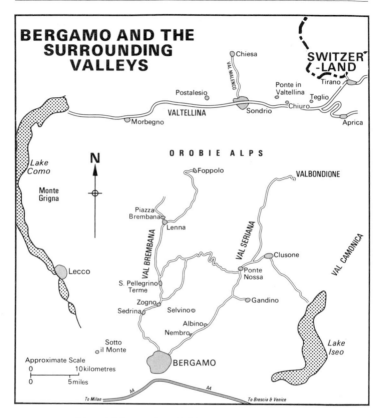

BERGAMO AND THE SURROUNDING VALLEYS

museum, with exhibits on the wildlife, geology and mineralogy of the valley. Just outside the town the church of the **Madonna della Sassella** is set among the vineyards that grow the grapes for Sassella wine. It is a fine fifteenth-century church with some good paintings.

Valtellina

Visitors will have already glimpsed the Valtellina as they crossed the Piano di Spagna which separates the lakes of Como and Mezzola. The valley is famous for its wines — Grumello and Sassella to name just two — the vines for which are frame grown and are to be seen everywhere. It also has great scenic beauty, the lower alpine slopes bearing woods of oak and chestnut, while higher there are rhododen-

PLACES OF INTEREST IN SONDRIO

Valley Museum
Villa Quadrio
Via 4 Novembre
Exhibits on history of the valley.
Paintings by local artists, and
collection of religious art.

Natural History Museum
Via Ragazzi del' 99
Exhibits on wildlife, particularly
birdlife, and geology of the
valley.

dron, fir and larch, and everywhere the usual rich and diverse alpine flora. It is also an area rich in minerals and has attracted crystal hunters for many years.

From the western end of the valley, after a side road heads north for Chiavenna and Switzerland, the first call is at **Morbegno**, a very pleasant town from which two alpine side valleys — the Val Gerola going south towards Monte Ponteronica and a valley leading to the San Marco Pass and Bergamo's Val Brembana — can be reached. Each of these valleys is delightful, with rugged hamlets set among some magnificent unspoilt scenery. In the town the eighteenth-century bridge, the Ponte di Ganda, is elegantly constructed, with a semi-circular arch. Also worth noting is the natural history museum with exhibits on valley birdlife and mineralogy.

Beyond Morbegno (and before it also, though it is of less importance there) the main road, the N38, carves a fast route through the valley, avoiding all the valley villages on its way to Sondrio, Tirano and Bormio. Many of the villages which are avoided are worth seeing if time permits, though none is of really exceptional note.

In the **Val Masino**, going north from the main valley, is **Bagno del Masino** with thermal springs used for therapeutic purposes, and a centre for excellent walking on rough alpine terrain among massive granite peaks. At **Postalesio** in the main valley there are earth pillars — pyramids of erosion — the same odd, other-worldly pillars each capped with a boulder, that are seen again near Cislano, above Iseo.

From Sondrio the **Val Malenco** heads north. The valley is one of the richest in the world for both the variety and abundance of its mineral crystals, so any walk has the potential of a real find. Within the valley there are several cable ways allowing access to the High Alps and a fine view of the quarries that produce Malenco marble, a green serpentine. At **Chiesa** there is a small museum with exhibits on the history and natural history of the valley. The upper reaches of the valley, which offer excellent winter sport, also offer magnificent   views of the Bernina Alps at all times of the year.

Winter scene, Val Malenco

Beyond Sondrio, back on the Valtellina road, is a succession of very pretty villages, each with magnificent settings. The road to Tirano was called one of the most beautiful in the world by a nine-teenth-century English mountaineer and it is an undeniable claim.

 Ponte in Valtellina is one of the most important artistic sites in the valley. The church of San Maurizio is excellent, with a Romanesque bell tower, a fresco by Luini and a bronze tabernacle. Elsewhere there are other fine buildings, the church of Madonna di Campagna with a fine series of frescoes, and a monument to a local man, Guiseppe Piazzi, who discovered the first asteroid. The town also has two museums, a small diocesan collection beside the church of San Maurizio, and one dedicated to the area, in Via Ginnasio.

At **Chiuro** the minor valley road climbs through vine-covered hills, with excellent views and a succession of small valleys each with a

Family walking at Chiesa, Val-Malenco

stream edged with water polished rocks. **Teglio** is the old capital of the valley, indeed the village gave the valley its name. The Romanesque church of San Pietro has an eleventh-century campanile; Palazzo Besta is the finest sixteenth-century villa in the valley with a wonderful courtyard surrounded by two storeys of arcades and frescoed walls. On the ground floor of the villa is a small museum with a good collection of items from Valtellina's pre-history.

Near Teglio a side valley leads steeply to **Aprica**, Valtellina's major winter sports area and one of Italy's more famous resorts. Cableways give access to high plateaux and fine walking, and the town has a small museum of local artwork and natural history. From Aprica a road leads to Brescia's Val Camonica.

The tour stops at **Tirano**, where the road starts its climb to the Stelvio Pass. Tirano was, historically, an important valley town, and

PLACES OF INTEREST IN VALTELLINA

Natural History Museum
Morbegno
Exhibits on valley bird and plant life, mineralogy and fossils.

Erosion Pillars
Postalesio
Weird conglomerate earth pillars, occasionally supporting large boulders. A freak of nature (see Marone, in Brescia chapter).

Museum
Chiesa, Val Malenco
History and natural history of the valley.

Diocesan Museum
Ponte in Valtellina
Collection of religious items.

Ethnography Museum
Ponte in Valtellina
History and folklore of the area.

Museum
Teglio
Collection on pre-history of Valtellina housed in magnificent sixteenth-century *palazzo* with arcaded courtyard and external frescoes.

Museum
Aprica
Small museum of local art and craft work.

Museum
Tirano
Local history, art and craft work.

has villas built by the Viscontis and Pallavicinis amongst others. From the town a road leads north, passing the church of the Madonna di Tirano, a famous pilgrimage church built in the early sixteenth century to commemorate a miracle of 1504. This has a very fine doorway and a rich interior. The town also has a small ethnographic museum. Just beyond the church is the Swiss-Italian border.

8 AROUND BRESCIA

B rescia, the capital of the province that bears its name, is Lombardy's second city, with around 225,000 inhabitants. It sits at the mouth of the Val Trompia, built at the base of two of the last hills of the pre-Alps (here known as the Brescian Alps) as the mountains make their last sweep down to the Lombardian plain.

What is given here is an itinerary that allows the visitor to see what are, by common consent, the major Brescian buildings and art works, though those who explore the town will find that much of interest has, of necessity, been excluded. Starting at the top (on Colle Cidneo, the oldest part of the town), the **Castle** is the first building to be visited. Although it seems, at first glance, to be a single structure, it is in fact a complex array of buildings dating from the first century. Roman remains of a temple and later fortification works are preserved, as are the remains of a fifth-century church to San Stefano. There is a Byzantine arch from the same period, and the Mirabella Tower is from the thirteenth century — though even this has been constructed on a Roman base. The castle itself was started by the Viscontis in the fourteenth century, with additions and modifications right through to the sixteenth century.

Within the castle buildings are two museums. The one devoted to the Risorgimento is housed in a part of the castle known as the 'Grande Miglio', the Great Mile — now almost the only link with the Mille Miglia, the 'Thousand Miles', a car race around Italy starting from Brescia, which was famous in its day, finally being stopped in 1957 when car speeds had increased to the point where spectator and driver deaths had become alarming. The museum contains items on the city's part in the struggle for Italian independence. Here too is the Luigi Marzoli Museum of Arms, one of the finest collections of its kind in Europe, and a fitting reminder of Brescia's ancient industry, though the arms are not restricted to the medieval period.

The castle stands in a large and very good park, landscaped into a large garden, and this also contains a small zoo. From the grounds go eastward across the hill to the church of **San Pietro in Oliveto** from where the view is excellent. The church is delightfully sited, surrounded by olive trees, and is twelfth century with two very fine sixteenth-century cloisters. From the church go south down Via Piamarta which has the remains of the town's only surviving Roman gate. It is named for San Eusebio, and dates from the first century.

Go left at Via dei Musei, as far as the building complex often called the Monastery of San Salvatore and San Giulia. The complex consists of several linked religious buildings, the whole being of such importance that it is on the UNESCO list as being worthy of special preservation. It is being very carefully restored and will eventually

house the city's main museum. At present the **Christian Museum** is on the site, as is part of the **Modern Art Gallery**, though even that is

not (at the time of writing) in its complete, final form.

There was a Benedictine nunnery on this site from AD753 when Desiderius, Duke or King of the Lombards, or his wife Ansa, founded one dedicated to San Salvatore. The three cloisters which remain are from a later, fifteenth-century building, though some of the materials used — capitals and columns — are from the earliest convent. The

basilica of **San Salvatore** is of the ninth century, though built on the earlier church, and little remains except the dignified crypt. **Santa Maria in Solario** is a twelfth-century Romanesque church, with frescoes from the sixteenth century. The last church is of **San Giulia**, built in the fifteenth and sixteenth centuries, and it too has fine frescoes. The Christian Museum contains many relics from the monastery, all of great historical interest. Several pieces are, however, not only rare and priceless, but of immense beauty. The Lipsanoteca is an ivory reliquary dating from the fourth century and restored to its original form earlier this century. The smooth slabs of ivory are included in place of missing slabs. The reliefs on the box show scenes from the Old and New Testaments. The lid is closed with a medieval lock. The Cross of Desiderius dates from the time of the founder, or a little later, but includes a painted glass cameo from the third or fourth century. The cross is gold, inlaid with semi-precious stones and coloured glass, and is a major work of art. Equally fine is a series of ivory diptychs. Each is two leaves of ivory hinged together: diptychs were given to officials appointed to high public office. One of the museum's examples dates from the fifth century.

West along Via dei Musei from the Christian Museum is one devoted to an earlier age, the **Roman Museum**, standing in the best preserved remains of that age in the city. The first remains seen are those of a theatre of the first century AD standing on what would have

been the edge of the Roman forum. Next is the museum, standing within the remains of the Capitoline Temple built in AD73 by the Emperor Vespasian but lost under a landslide and rediscovered only in 1823. Though heavily restored, what remains of the steps and colonnade is excellent. Beyond, original portals allow access to the museum. The finest of the items here is the *Winged Victory*, a bronze — probably gilded in its original form — of the first century AD. The wings and draped clothing are beautifully worked, and it is intriguing to speculate what was once held in the outstretched hands. There are also six bronze portraits of the emperor from the second and third centuries, as well as stone and mosaic work from the site.

From the Roman Museum, continue westward and then turn left into Via Mazzini to see the **Queriniana Library**, founded by Cardinal Querini in the mid-eighteenth century and containing about a third of a million volumes, some very rare, and housed in an excellent baroque building.

West again is Piazza Duomo in which stand both the old (the Rotonda or Duomo Vecchio) and new (Duomo Nuovo) **Cathedrals**. The older building, the Rotonda, is late eleventh century in Romanesque-Gothic style but with an interesting circular design, austere enough to pass for a fortress rather than a cathedral. It is an interesting building, not obviously beautiful but certainly imposing. Inside there are some interesting works of art, including a reliquary with sections of the True Cross and a Holy Thorn. But everywhere inside, the curved walls allow that imposing exterior to reach the mind.

The New Cathedral is sixteenth century (baroque), constructed of white marble and with a now green lead dome. Though started in the sixteenth century the building was not completed until the dome was finished in 1825, though there is no lack of wholeness. Inside, the cathedral is cold, almost bleak, with few treasures.

North from the cathedrals, and still in the *piazza*, is the **Broletto**, the thirteenth-century Town Hall above which is Brescia's oldest tower, the **Torre del Popolo** — the People's Tower. The Broletto was replaced as Town Hall in the fifteenth century by the **Loggia** that stands in Piazza Loggia, due west from the Broletto. The Loggia is a masterpiece of Renaissance architecture, the contrast of the ground floor arches, first floor windows and the decorated balustrade giving the building a beauty that is enhanced by the use of white marble. The roof is new, built in the mid-eighteenth century to replace the original which was burned down in a fire of 1575.

The Loggia stands on the western corner of Piazza Loggia, the southern side of the square having what looks like an early, smaller version, the Monte di Pietà Vecchio. In the façade of this Renaissance building (of the sixteenth century) is a collection of inscribed Roman stones, so many in fact, that it could be viewed as an outpost of the Roman Museum.

From the Loggia, go northward along Via San Faustino, to reach the church of **San Faustino and San Giovita**, dedicated to the patron saints of the city. Inside there are excellent paintings, but the church is known chiefly for the frescoes of Giandomenico Tiepolo depicting stories from the saints' lives.

Go back along the same street — at the patron saint's feast day it is a thronging mass of people — and enter Contrada del Carmine to see the church of the Madonna del Carmine, considered one of the finest examples of fifteenth-century Lombardian Gothic architecture.

PLACES OF INTEREST IN BRESCIA

Colle Cidneo
Oldest part of the town, dominated by the Visconti castle which houses the Risorgimento and Marzoli Arms Museums. The fine gardens house the city's zoo.

Christian Museum
Via dei Musei
Treasures of early Christian art, some from the monastery of San Salvatore. Items include the magnificent 'Cross of Desiderius'.

Roman Museum
Via dei Musei

Items from Brescia's Roman era including first-century *Winged Victory* in bronze.

City Art Gallery
Palazzo Martinengo da Barco, Via Martinengo
Art collections including many great masters, and masters of the Brescian school.

Natural History Museum
Via Ozanam
Very modern building for collection formerly housed in castle. Exhibits include wildlife of the area.

The church is in brick, a most striking material, studded with coloured ceramic, and this innovative use of materials is carried on inside where there is a piece of monumental sculpture known as a 'Deposition', in multicoloured terracotta, also dating from the fifteenth century.

South from the church, but best reached by returning down the Via San Faustino, is the church of **San Giovanni** in Contrada San Giovanni, a narrow street going south from Via Capriolo. The church contains a series of altarpieces by Moretto and Romanino, sixteenth-century Brescian artists — one of the true treasures of Brescian art.

Nearby, in Via Pace, is the **Torre della Pallata**, the Pallata Tower, which dominates the city at this point. The tower is thirteenth century, buttressed in the fifteenth century. A good fountain at its base takes the edge off its bulk.

Now follow the Via Cairoli, a road with a large number of fine *palazzi*, chiefly of the eighteenth century, interspersed with lighter, arcaded houses from as early as the fifteenth century. Turning left into Corso Giacomo Matteotti, continue to the church of **San Nazzaro and San Celso** a fine eighteenth-century building containing paintings by Moretto, and a polyptych by Titian which is a true masterpiece. Close by, in Corso Martiri della Liberta is the church of **Santa Maria del Miracoli**, a fine Renaissance church in Botticino marble

Lake Iseo

with excellent relief sculptures both inside and outside.

A right turn from Via Percellaga, a continuation of Corso Martiri della Liberta, leads to the Piazza Mercato, flanked by sixteenth-century porticoes, with statues and an array of elegant buildings. Then go eastward to Corso Zanardelli, with the Grand Theatre to the left and the Tourist Office to the right, behind the pavement café. Straight on is Corso Magenta, and turns right and then left lead to Via Martinengo da Barco where the **City Art Gallery** is housed in the Palazzo Martinengo da Barco, a sixteenth-century building, restored a century later, behind the Lebanon cypresses. The art gallery contains work by Raphael and Tintoretto, as well as other great masters, and many masters of the Brescia school. Those not already satiated by museums might also like to visit the city's **Natural History Museum**, a new building in Via Ozanam.

From Brescia three parallel valleys, runing north–south, can be reached, two containing lakes. These are dealt with from west to east.

Val Camonica and Lake Iseo

From Brescia the N 510 main road goes direct to Iseo town and the lake that bears its name. Those preferring the *autostrada*, or arriving on it from farther afield, take the Palazzolo exit, head north and arrive at the lakeside village of Paratico from where a drive around the southern lake shore reaches Iseo.

The road from Brescia passes through **Rodengo-Saiano** where there is an architecturally important fifteenth-century Cluniac abbey with frescoes by Brescian artists and friezes in multi-coloured ceramics. The abbey is currently being restored by the Italian Government, and when complete will be a fine addition to the list of 'places to visit'. Further on, at **Provaglio d'Iseo**, there is a Romanesque church with fifteenth-century frescoes, while above the village to the north is the church of the Madonna del Carno, interesting in its own right, and offering the first and one of the finest views of the lake.

Lake Iseo is the fifth largest of the northern lakes, being 24km (15 miles) long and 5km (3 miles) wide at its widest point. However, at that widest point the lake is almost filled by Monte Isola, the largest island in any of the lakes, or in any lake in Europe, at over 3km (2 miles) long and about 2km ($1^1/_4$ miles) wide. The lake narrows down to only 1km ($^1/_2$ mile) towards the northern end, but those tempted to swim it should bear in mind that it is around 250m (820ft) deep at its deepest.

Although it is possible to drown in only a few metres of water if things go wrong, these depths do seem to have a psychological effect.

At the southern end, as the lake ends onto the plain, there is a large peat bog, the 'Torbiere', famed for its water-lilies and marsh weeds. The marshland is a protected area for wildlife and is also important archaeologically, having yielded evidence of pile-mounted lake dwellings. Elsewhere too, the lake surround is famous for its plant life, its sheltered position between two high mountain ridges helping to provide an ideal climate for plant growth. At the northern end, the high ridges on the edge of the lake actually fall into the water as high cliffs, producing some of the most spectacular scenery on any of the lakes.

The village which shares the lake's name is the outstanding holiday resort on the lake with, at the Sassabonek, a tourist centre which is the most impressive of any of the resorts visited. In addition to the normal rectangular swimming pool, there is a circular one which is irresistible. Elsewhere the village has much of interest, a fine twelfth-century church with a Romanesque campanile, and the remains of the Oldofredi Castle, now incorporated into a village community centre.

From Iseo a winding road climbs up the mountain ridge that borders Lake Iseo's eastern shore, crossing the Passo del Tre Termini and making its way through a series of pretty villages down into the Val Trompia. This route goes instead along the lakeside road to Pilzone.

Pilzone is a small, quiet village, inland from a small headland liberally sprinkled with hotels and camping sites. Beyond the head-land the view northward is dominated by Monte Isola, which can be reached by the lake steamer from **Sulzano**, which is a fine sailing centre. The village has some very good houses, gathered together in delightful streets close to the lake edge, the wooded cliffs of Monte Isola making a compelling background to views of the lake. At the back of the town there is a cobbled street leading off up the mountain, taking the visitor through a series of beautifully set small villages and, finally, at 965m (3,165ft), reaching the fifteenth-century church of **Santa Maria del Giogo**. The view from the top of the ridge, which dips then rises again to Monte Rodondone, is over the top of Monte Isola to the western shore and the northern section of the lake — excellent, and none the less satisfying for having been so easily achieved.

Those who take the short boat trip across the lake to Monte Isola

Oldofredi Castle, Iseo

are immediately surprised by its quietness, the reason for which becomes clear the moment they start along the street of Peschiera Maraglio. There are no cars!

Monte Isola is not an island in the accepted sense, consisting of one giant mountain, pushed 400m (1,310ft) out of the lake — the peak is 600m (1,970ft) above sea level, but the lake surface is itself at about 190m (620ft). In places the peak, which has a plateau summit, drops so steeply that the tree cover cannot always cling to the slope, and white streaks of cliff are exposed. Perched on top of the island peak, half hidden among the chestnut trees, is the church of the Madonna della Ceriola, a place of pilgrimage for centuries.

The view from the peak is, of course, expansive, but those with limited time (and energy) may choose to spend it instead on a walk from Peschiera Maraglio to Sensole, to Siviano or on to Carzano, from each of which boats return around the island to Sulzano. From Carzano boats also cross to Sale Marasino, from where a return boat crosses the channel between island and mainland to reach Peschiera. This trip offers a close-up view of the steepest of the island's cliffs.

Peschiera is a fishing village, indeed Monte Isola is a fishing island, only tourism representing a sizeable alternative industry, and has that timeless air that characterises fishing ports. Elsewhere the villages are similar, little collections of red-tiled houses on each side

Pilzone

of narrow, cobbled streets, the villages linked by lanes that wind through chestnut woods, olive groves and vineyards.

At **Sensole** there are the ruins of a fifteenth-century Oldofredi castle, while **Siviano** has a Martinengo tower from the same period. Flowers have encroached on these places, on virtually every square centimetre of bare soil. In spring the island is yellow with broom, in autumn purple with heather, in between countless colours with countless flowers. Small wonder the island has been so loved by painters.

Back on the mainland the road leads to **Sale Marasino**, a pleasant village dominated by its beautiful eighteenth-century church. The church interior is as fine as its exterior. Near the lakeside there is the Villa Martinengo standing in excellent gardens which contain the remains of a first-century Roman villa. From the village a track leads up through the terraces on the hillside to the top of Punta Almana at 1,391m (4,560ft). Not surprisingly this is a good viewpoint, but the walk, at 8km (5 miles) and around 1,100m (nearby 3,610ft) requires enthusiasm and considerable time.

Beyond Sale Marasino there are excellent beaches and good camping sites up to **Marone**, where there are the ruins of an early Roman villa and, housed in the local library, a fine collection of photographs which are the work of a local photographer, Lorenzo Antonio Predali, taken during the first half of this century. From the

PLACES OF INTEREST AROUND LAKE ISEO AND VAL CAMONICA

Marshland of Torbiere
Near Iseo
Area of outstanding interest for its marsh plants and wildlife.

Photographic Collection
Marone
Collection of the work of Lorenzo Antonio Predali, a local photographer, covering the years 1896-1950. Situated in the town library.

Erosion Pyramids
Above Marone
Weird conglomerate pillars of earth, occasionally supporting large boulders. A freak of erosion (see Postalesio in chapter 7).

Santa Maria della Neve
Pisogne
The poor man's Sistine chapell! A fifteenth-century church with frescoes by Girolama Romanino.

Tadini Gallery
Lovere
Collection of paintings, sculpture, ceramics and arms in nine-teenth-century *palazzo*.

Bögns of Castro and Zorzina
Huge vertical cliffs of rock at the road edge.

Museum
Cividate Camuno
Local items, chiefly of the town's important past, and the history of the valley.

National Park of Rock Engravings
Capo di Ponte
World renowned area for rock carvings dating from Neolithic to Roman times. Guided tours available.

Centre for the Study of the Prehistory of Valcamonica
Capo di Ponte
Collection of the more important finds from the valley.

Viewpoints
Santa Maria del Giogo, above Sulzano
Madonna della Ceriola, Monte Isola
Fraine, above Pisogne
Vigolo, above Tavernola Bergamasca
Punta del Carno, near Tavernola Bergamasca

village a road into the mountains allows access to some excellent walking country, and also to **Zone**, a finely set village in a valley of beech and fir woods. But the best of the sights hereabouts are to be found just below the village of **Cislano**, at an obvious hairpin bend with limited parking to the right. Here are the *piramidi di erosione*, erosion pyramids. Uneven glacial erosion, caused by the layering of the strata, has created eerie pillars of earthy conglomerate some tens

of metres high. They look at first glance like termite nests, but invariably they are topped by a granite boulder, precariously balanced. Though not unique in alpine Europe, this collection of pyramids is reckoned to be the finest and offers one of the most unusual views that will be encountered.

Vello is another pleasant little fishing port beyond which the road excavates a way through the almost sheer cliffs of the Corna Trentapassi, emerging only briefly to offer a tantalising glimpse of the Bögn di Zorzino on the western lake shore. Beyond is **Pisogne**, the gateway to Val Camonica, a fine town dominated by a fourteenth-century tower, the Torre del Vescovo, which is the town's symbol. There is a good square, with porticoed surrounds and the church of Santa Maria della Neve which is famous as the poor man's Sistine Chapel, such are the quality of the frescoes by the artist Romanino.

From the village a road leads to the terrace of Fraine, with fine views of the Val Camonica, and on up the **Valle di Palotto**, in the

Sulzano

upper reaches of which there is a good winter sports area.

From Pisogne the Val Camonica leads off towards the High Alps, to points beyond the scope of this book. This route will follow it only as far as Capo di Ponte and the National Park of Rock Engravings. But first it crosses the valley to go down the west side of Lake Iseo.

On the western shore the first town is **Lovere**, second only to Iseo as a tourist resort on the lake. It is a delightful place, built on terraces so that it seems to tumble down the hill slopes into the lake. It is also very old: on Monte Cala are the remains of a Celtic fort from the fourth or third century BC. Not surprisingly, the rest of the town's buildings are considerably younger, though still old, and very interesting. There are three towers, the Alghisi and the Soca from the thirteenth century and another from the fourteenth century, and a number of very interesting churches. The Palazzo Tadini dates from the nineteenth century, a fine building holding the Galleria dell'Accademia Tadini, a small gallery of paintings, sculpture, ceramics and some arms. The *palazzo* is open to the public, both for the collection and also for a summer season of concerts and, for those with good enough Italian, lectures.

The terraced nature of the town makes it good for walking — odd perspectives and angles are continuously cropping up — and the area around the town is also good for exploring. Most visitors passing through eventually feel the tug of the Bögn, but before giving in to it,

Erosion pyramids, Zone

a short excursion, about 10km (6 miles), can be made to the tiny Lake Endine, tucked away in the Val Cavallina. This is a very secluded lake with a minimum of tourist amenities, but in a superb setting. Just the place for those who really want to be away from the mainstream, to discover Italy quietly and at their own pace.

Alternatively, instead of following the main road to Lake Endine, turn off for **Castro** to find an ancient, once-fortified town sheltering under its long-empty *rocca*. There is a wealth of steep, narrow streets and an old, ruined tower. And beyond is the Bögn of Castro, the first of the two Bögns. The second, the Bögn of Zorzino, creates its own enclosed bay. The Bögns are huge sheets of limestone plunging vertically from the slopes of Monte Clemo into the lake. Some people believe they are best viewed from across the lake, but although such cliffs are foreshortened at close range, and the full form cannot be grasped, their size and power can be better appreciated.

Beyond the second Bögn is **Riva di Solto**, a picturesque fishing village beyond which the road is excellent, with views to Monte Isola and of the slopes of Monte Creo, which advances on the road and eventually smothers it, forcing it to disappear into a tunnel.

Opposite Monte Isola is **Tavernola Bergamasca** with a few forlorn ruins of a fourteenth-century castle tower. From the village a road goes up into the hills, to the villages of **Parzanica**, only comparatively recently reached by road and still unspoilt, and **Vigolo** with good views of the lake. Good views are also available from the Punta del Carno, where the lake has an elbow. Near here is a natural well, known as the 'Giant's Pot'.

Beyond is **Predore**, noted for its vineyards and also for the numerous archaeological finds, chiefly Roman, made in the area. The town also has the ruins of a castle, and a curious tower which was cut in half in the fourteenth century.

Sarnico is a terminus for the lake steamer and will be well known to enthusiasts of motor boat racing. Factories here make good boats, and the lake at this point is used for international competitions and record breaking attempts. The town's architecture is a mixture, with the remains of old fortifications, a centre consisting of old buildings typical of the lake's fishing ports, and some works by Sommarciga, a major Italian art nouveau architect.

Return to Iseo is now made through **Paratico**, where, it is said, Dante once stayed in the now ruined castle, and **Clusane**, a village noted for its roast lake tench — *tinca al farno con polenta* — and with the Castello del Carmagnola, a fifteenth-century castle.

Returning to Pisogne, an exploration of the Val Camonica can begin. In the valley, through which the Oglio river flows, the first place of consequence reached is **Boario Terme**, a town that has built up, like the spas of England, around its thermal springs. Here there are four springs supplying warm, mineralised water to the Thermal Establishment — a fine building set in magnificent, wooded parkland — for use in various ways to treat a variety of ailments. The spa is Italy's third biggest and specialises in liver and intestinal problems.

Also at Boario, or rather near to it, the famous rock engravings begin, the first being visible in Parco di Luine. The valley became famous when the first of the engravings (into the relatively soft Permian sandstone) was discovered, fame that grew rapidly to international status when the extent and age of the works was realised. Today almost 200,000 individual works have been catalogued, the engravings showing a range of subjects, but chiefly hunting scenes,

scenes from ordinary life and religious themes. The Naquane Rock in the Parco della Incisioni Rupestiri — the National Rock Engravings Park — has 900 figures carved on it. In age the carvings cover some 8,000 years from the Neolithic era through to Roman times, a truly amazing depiction of life as civilisation dawned. In 1979 UNESCO gave the site international protection as being of world importance.

The National Park is centred on **Capo di Ponte,** where the study centre for the carvings was set up in the 60s. Between Boario Terme and Capo di Ponte there are several villages of interest. **Cividate Camuno** was the valley's chief town in Roman times and contains excellent remains of that period, some displayed in the town museum. **Breno** is the valley's most important town today, set in the valley below a fourteenth-century castle which still has complete towers and, every schoolchild's dream, real underground dungeons. The key to their door can be borrowed from the Town Hall! In the church of Sant' Antonio and in the *Duomo* there are fine frescoes, while the town museum has much of interest from the local area, including some carvings.

Val Trompia

The Val Trompia is immediately north of Brescia. Indeed, the river Mella which flows through the valley, also flows through the western part of the city, and the ridges which form the valley only fall onto the plain as the outskirts of Brescia are reached. Val Trompia runs parallel to Val Camonica, separated by the ridge of Monte Guglielmo, and crossed only once, to the south, by the road from Iseo which runs over the Tre Termini Pass to Concesio.

The road to Val Trompia passes, at **Mompiano** on the outskirts of Brescia, the Trebbi Botanical Gardens which has a fine collection of plants and can be visited on request. Further on, **Concesio** is the valley's first town, and is famous as the birthplace of Pope Paul VI. Beyond the town the valley is quite industrialised as far as **Sarezzo**, and to **Lumezzane** in a side valley (the Val Gobbia) from Sarezzo. From Lumezzane a road links to the Val Sabbia. The industrial valley here is famous for its metal working, producing high-quality cutlery and kitchenware. This industry is a link with the history of Val Trompia, and specifically the next town, **Gardone Val Trompia**, which was once famous for the making of arms and armour. Today Gardone is world famous for the production of firearms, especially hunting guns. The arms industry here was first started by the

Accademia Tadini, Lovere

 Venetians, and another side to the Republic's influence can be seen in the church of Santa Maria degli Angeli, a fine, cloistered church, which has a number of paintings by artists of the Venetian school. The local Brescian school is also represented, the church's frescoes being by Paolo da Brescia.

Val Trompia proper, from a tourist's point of view, starts at Brozzo. From there the valley (named from the Triumplini, a Celtic tribe that lived among the Ligurian Alps) is a landscape artist's dream: an array of greens, more than can be counted or appreciated, orchards of apples, plums and cherries and a sprinkling of copses and larger woods, chiefly of chestnut trees.

 Tavernole sul Mella is the ancient capital of the valley, and from it **Marmentino** can be reached, a lovely village set in lush meadows with chestnut and beech woods. In winter the skiing is good, though facilities are lacking. The same comment can be made of **Pezzaze** and **Pezzoro** which are reached from the valley village of **Lavane**. In summer they make fine starting points for walking on Monte Guglielmo, 1,950m (6,400ft).

 Beyond Lavone a side valley can be followed to **Irma**, a clean, neat village in a magnificent position with expansive views to blue hills and walks over flower-studded meadows or through pine forests. **Bovegno**, at a height of 750m (2,460ft) as the valley begins to rise steeply, is equally well sited, and here some of the houses have more

Villa Faccononi, Sarnico

than a hint of the Tyrol to add a picturesque touch. Pineta Park has fine pine woods to stroll in, and the church of San Giorgio has some interesting wood carvings.

At **Collio** the river Mella is a fast flowing stream of clear water running over a rock-strewn bed with mossy stones and wooded banks. The village itself is beautiful: white houses and red roofs, geraniums in the niches of old walls, blue pine woods in the background and meadows of startling green, their terraces sharply drawn by shadows. The village is a winter sports centre and has a cable car to a higher plateau, and a ski jump.

Beyond, **San Colombano** is the last valley village, another centre of winter sports. From there, torturous roads lead north to link with Val Camonica at Breno, and south to Val Sabbia at Anfo on Lake Idro.

Val Sabbia and Lake Idro

The Val Sabbia runs from Gavardo (a town on the main road from Bresica) to Salo on Lake Garda, and on to Ponte Caffaro at the northern end of Lake Idro, and in it flows the river Chiese that both feeds and drains that lake. It is a valley of considerable scenic interest, with the added advantage of having a lake. As with Val Trompia, Val Sabbia is a place for the walker and the country

PLACES OF INTEREST IN VAL TROMPIA

Trebbi Botanical Gardens
119 Via Montini, Mompiano
Private gardens on the outskirts
of Brescia, on the road to Val
Trompia. Fine collection of
plants.

**Church of Santa Maria degli
Angeli**
Gardone, Val Trompia

Cloistered church with good
paintings and frescoes.

Pineta Park
Bovegno
Beautiful pine woods in magnifi-
cent surroundings.

enthusiast, although Lake Idro does add an extra dimension to a visit.

 Gavardo, where the valley starts, is a pleasant town, split in half by the Chiese which appears to wash the foundations of the houses on both its banks. The town museum, the Museo del Gruppo Grotte, deals with the history of the Grotte mountains to the north of the town, mountains that form the western side of the valley and which separate Val Sabbia from Val Trompia. It has prehistoric and Roman items, and a fine skeleton of a cave bear.

From the town the main road follows the valley, but a minor road on the opposite side of the river leads to **Vallio Terme**, a spa town whose mineral waters are used chiefly in the treatment of kidney and liver complaints. The spa's Hydropathic centre is open from April to October. The water is also bottled locally and is available for sale.

At **Tormini** the main road divides, the right fork going to Salo and Lake Garda, the left continuing along the eastern bank of the Chiese. The route follows the left road to **Vobarno**, which has the remains of a medieval castle, and a fine bridge dating from the mid-sixteenth century, of Venetian construction. The town is one of the valley's chief industrial centres.

 Sabbio Chiese has a natural fortress, a *rocca*, that was once topped by a medieval castle, but is now transformed (in best swords into ploughshares fashion) into two churches. That might not seem so unusual, but here the churches are one on top of the other! There is a single campanile, still with the fish-tail crenellations so popular on the Lake Garda castles.

Beyond Sabbio Chiese the valley narrows: at **Barghe** the church has been built into the rocks of the mountain ridge, so close does it encroach, and roads from here, on both sides of the valley, lead to beautifully set mountain villages which offer fine views and excellent walking. **Nozza** is the old capital of the valley, while nearby **Vestone** still has the valley's most important market on the first Monday in the month. Also here are the Ruscino Botanical Gardens, which include many plants local to the Val Sabbia. From Vestone, roads again lead off to the mountains on both sides of the valley, the road north going to a series of fine villages. One, **Forno d'Ono**, is probably the most beautiful of all the mountain villages, nestling below a gorge carved by a mountain stream and surrounded by meadows. In the Italian sunlight, which always seems so bright and 'clean', the shadows in the gorge and on the meadow terracing paint the most evocative pictures.

Lavenone has a fine collection of very rich houses and considerable scenic attractiveness. Just beyond the village the jagged peaks of Corna Zeno and Corna Alta dominate the valleys of the Abbioccolo and Canale to the left (north), while soon Idro unfolds ahead. Idro is the highest lake in Lombardy at 368m (1,207ft) above sea level and is 11km (7 miles) long, reaching 2km (1$\frac{1}{4}$ miles) wide, and with a maximum depth of 368m (1,200ft). In places on its shore the surrounding mountains fall so steeply into it that from a distance they seem to rise straight out of the water. Despite that, there is a road, in one place tunnelled, along its western bank, the eastern bank being only sparsely populated.

The village of **Idro** is off the main road at the point where the Chiese river leaves the lake, and further along the western shore are the new villages of **Vantone** and **Vespa**. The first has several good camping sites, and from the second the visitor can walk to Prato della Fame, where the rocky backbone of Monte Calva dips into the lake and from where the lake views are the finest. From Vantone a road leads into the mountains, to several good villages and the mountainenfolded Lake Valvestino — all very fine walking country.

Travelling up the western shore from Idro, **Anfo** is found about half way along, built on a terrace sloping down to the lake. Nearby, the private castle on the Rocca d' Anfo was built by the Venetian Republic and was the headquarters of Garibaldi's forces in 1866. The church of Sant' Antonio has a twelfth-century campanile and contains some good paintings, including a fine set of Renaissance frescoes.

Beyond Anfo a road off left can be taken to **Bagolino**, a beautiful village of narrow streets and piled-up houses, thought by many to be the most picturesque village in the Val Sabbia, though, strictly, lying in a side valley. It also has, in the fifteenth-century church of San Rocco, one of the most important churches in the whole valley, the

Barghe, Val Sabbia

PLACES OF INTEREST IN VAL SABBIA

Museum
Gavardo
Items from area's pre-history
and Roman era. Includes
skeleton of a cave bear.

Sabbio Chiese
Medieval castle converted into
two churches, one on top of the
other.

Ruscino Botanical Gardens
Vestone

Interesting collection of plants,
including many local to the Val
Sabbia

Church of San Rocco
Bagolino
Fifteenth-century church with
excellent series of frescoes by da
Cemmo.

Viewpoints
Proto della Fame to Lake Idro
Bondone to Lake Idro

importance lying in the fine series of frescoes by da Cemmo.

Ponte Caffaro is the last village of Val Sabbia, the last village of Lake Idro and, indeed, the last in Lombardy, for when the Caffaro, one of the lake's inflowing rivers, is crossed, the traveller enters Trentino. Until 1918 the river marked the boundary not between two of Italy's regions, but between Italy and Austria. In the village there are the ruins of the castle of Santa Barbara from which there are fine views of the interesting 'quadri' squares on the Pian d'Oneda. The plain was reclaimed by Benedictine monks in the tenth century and is very fertile. In 1861 it was divided into lots, each separated from its neighbour by an irrigation ditch, which gives it its curious pattern. A better view is obtained by leaving the main road beyond Ponte Caffaro, crossing the Caffaro and Chiese rivers and going to Trentino's first village, Baitoni, and on to **Bondone**. From there both the Pian, the lake and the upper Chiese valley can be seen.

9 LAKE GARDA

At 370sq km (145sq miles), Lake Garda is the largest of the Italian lakes. The shallow shoreline in the south produces excellent beaches which, coupled with the area's very mild climate (in part due to the huge volume of water that acts as a storage radiator), its closeness to large population centres and its distance from the other large lakes means that the entire perimeter of the lake's southern shore seems to have been taken over by holidaymakers. Do not let that observation deter you from visiting however. The near Mediterranean climate is of itself worth a trip, and it also encourages a luxuriant and very varied plant growth. The southern lake has much of interest and, in Sirmione, one of the most extraordinary towns on any of the lakes visited. The northern tip of the lake, cut fjord-like into its enclosing hills, is also worthwhile, the backdrop of hills to the blue lake waters never failing to stir the imagination.

Southern Lake Garda

The lake tour begins at **Desenzano del Garda** on the main railway from Milan to Venice, which has its own exit from the A4 *autostrada*. Desenzano also has a pleasant little harbour, being an important terminus for the lake steamers. The Roman link is strong here in Desenzano, the remains of a third century AD Roman villa having been discovered not far from the harbour. Finest of the remains are the very large multi-coloured mosaics that have been compared favourably to those at Pompeii. Next to the villa a small museum contains some finds from the site, together with other items from a locally excavated prehistoric site. Of particular interest is the collection of very early Christian glassware.

The Roman link is maintained at Capo la Terra, the higher part of the town, where there are remains of a castle, constructed spasmodi- cally from the thirteenth to the fifteenth centuries to guard against attacks by marauders from the north. The castle stands on the

Sunset over Lake Garda

Windsurfing on Lake Garda

remains of a Roman fort, so the strategic merits of this spot must have been obvious 1,000 years ago. The Romans had a market here, chiefly for grain, and Desenzano held its position as an important market town right through to its time under Venetian rule. Even today there is a market every Tuesday — a good day to come to absorb the atmosphere of the lively, small-town Italian market.

A stroll along the tree-lined lake front should take in the old harbour: Desenzano has two harbours, a large modern one that is the terminus for the lake steamers and an older, more picturesque one that nudges its way into the town. If time permits, do also try to visit the local church, Santa Maria Magdalene, dating from the late sixteenth century and including a notable painting of the Last Supper by the eighteenth-century Venetian artist, G.B.Tiepolo.

Away from the lake, some 4km (2¹/₂ miles) further on is **Lonato**, perched on a hill with a fine view of Desenzano. There is much of interest crammed into this typically airy but small town. It has a cathedral with a fine dome beside an excellent central *piazza*. There is a library here with 40,000 books, some of great rarity and, in the Fondazione da Como, a museum, chiefly of statuary but also with paintings and furniture.

On the other side of Desenzano (to the east) and again inland, are two sites, close to each other and historically inseparable, which will be a must for all interested in the Napoleonic campaigns. At **San Martino della Battaglia**, on 24 June (Midsummer's Day) 1859 a Piemontean army under Vittorio Emanuele II defeated the right wing of the Austrian army here, while Napoléon III, a few kilometres to the south at Solferino, crushed the main body of the Austrians, a victory commemorated in name by a bridge over the Seine in Paris. The day had few equals in the Wars of Italian Independence, but it also has a significance that was even more far-reaching. At **Solferino**, a Swiss, J. Henri Dunant, was on holiday, and was so appalled by the sufferings of the wounded of both sides after the battle that he wrote an account, *Souvenir of Solferino*, which was published in 1862. This account was instrumental in the setting up of the International Red Cross, and a memorial was erected at Solferino in 1959, the centenary of the battle. The memorial, of marble sent by nations from all over the world, stands beside the *rocca*, a hugh tower built by the Scaligeri much earlier than the battle, in 1022, though restored in the early seventeenth century. In contrast the round tower of San Martino does commemorate the battle. It is 64m (210ft) high and houses a museum with exhibits on the campaign. From the top, the view over the Lombardian plain is excellent. Each of the sites has an ossuary, a sad reminder of suffering even if one of the world's finest charities was a direct result of it, and a museum.

Returning to the lakeside it seems impossible to escape from images of war, because the castle at **Sirmione** is another. It is difficult however, to be distracted by grim thoughts from the beauties of the Sirmione peninsula. It starts straightforwardly enough, with a drive from the village of Colombare, but travelling about 3km (around 2 miles) to the end, it narrows remarkably down to a mere 120m (400ft) wide in places. Eventually drivers must leave their cars and walk to the town, because although the bridge connecting the 'i' of the peninsula to the 'dot' above it is car width, the town excludes all but essential vehicles.

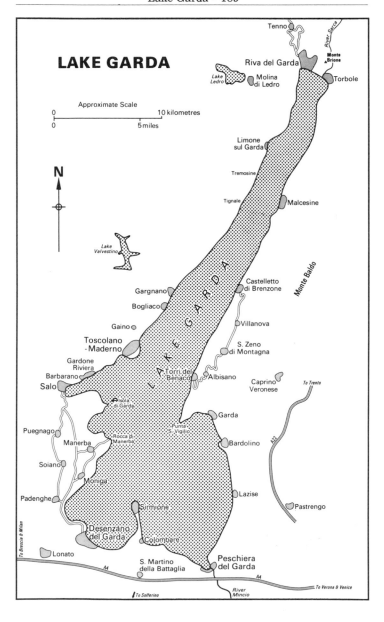

LAKE GARDA

The castle, Sirmione

Peschiera

But though the bridge takes the visitor into the town, it feels as if you are actually entering the Scaligeri castle, which dominates the view rightwards. The Scaligeri built both the castle and the town walls in the fifteenth century when they were lords of Verona, using Roman foundations for their fortress. Inside the castle retains the machinery for a drawbridge, and the near perfect preservation of the upper battlements gives a good idea of the method of protection, by sentinel post and removable foot-bridges.

The castle, which also includes an embattled quay, must by sheer position have defended the entire southern end of the lake. It is an enchanting building, the fish-tail shaped battlements giving it a fairy tale quality, the archetypal child's castle.

Beside the castle is the town, which occupies about half of the 70 or so hectares (180 acres) that the peninsula's head comprises. Into that small area are packed an astonishing variety of things. For the

PLACES OF INTEREST ON THE SOUTHERN SHORE OF LAKE GARDA

Museum
Lonato
Fine collection of statuary, together with paintings and furniture.

Roman Villa
Desenzano del Garda
Fine multi-coloured mosaics.

Museum
Desenzano del Garda
Includes items from Lavagnone, a local Bronze Age site, and collection of early Christian glass.

Tower and Museum
San Martino
Church/Ossuary, Museum and Rocca
Solferino
All commemorating the battles of 24 June 1859. The *rocca* at Solferino is an eleventh-century castle.

Memorial
Solferino
Red Cross memorial. Built in marble sent by nations of the world.

Castle
Sirmione
Enchanting thirteenth-century castle including a fortified harbour.
Not to be missed.

Grotte di Catullo
Sirmione
Romantic remains of a Roman villa, set in olive groves. Site museum has best of excavated finds, including fine mosaics and frescoes.

Viewpoints
Tip of Sirmione peninsula

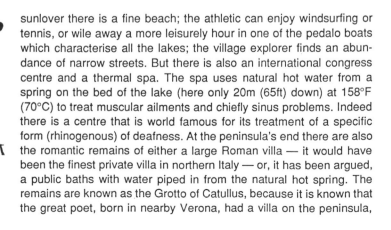

sunlover there is a fine beach; the athletic can enjoy windsurfing or tennis, or wile away a more leisurely hour in one of the pedalo boats which characterise all the lakes; the village explorer finds an abundance of narrow streets. But there is also an international congress centre and a thermal spa. The spa uses natural hot water from a spring on the bed of the lake (here only 20m (65ft) down) at 158°F (70°C) to treat muscular ailments and chiefly sinus problems. Indeed there is a centre that is world famous for its treatment of a specific form (rhinogenous) of deafness. At the peninsula's end there are also the romantic remains of either a large Roman villa — it would have been the finest private villa in northern Italy — or, it has been argued, a public baths with water piped in from the natural hot spring. The remains are known as the Grotto of Catullus, because it is known that the great poet, born in nearby Verona, had a villa on the peninsula, and wrote glowingly of it several times, but there is no hard evidence to link him with this specific site. A small museum holds the best of the excavated finds.

Also worthy of note is the church of San Pietro in Mavino, built in the eighth century on the site of a pagan temple. It is beautifully positioned among trees and has some fine thirteenth- and fourteenth-century frescoes. Outside is a bell monument to the dead and wounded of all wars.

Continuing eastward along the lake from Sirmione, the visitor soon crosses the border from Lombardy to Veneto reaching, at **Peschiera del Garda**, the start of the 'Olive Tree Riviera', the name given to that part of the shoreline of Lake Garda which lies within Veneto. Peschiera has been fortified since earliest times. The Romans had a presence here, and in medieval times there was a castle and a walled harbour, proof of the importance of the site where the Mincio river leaves the lake. The castle was demolished and the wall made extra strong during the time of the Austrian occupation when the town formed part of the occupying army's primary defence, a quadrilateral with, at its corners, Peschiera, Verona, Legnago and Mantua. It is the ruins of those defences that now encompass the town. In 1917, King Vittorio Emanuele III came here with allied commanders and decided to hold the Piave line, pivoted around Peschiera, to the last man.

Peschiera today is a pretty town with pleasant gardens to relax in, a fine multi-arched bridge across the Mincio and several good Renaissance buildings. The Austrian defences are interesting, and be sure to watch the hour chimed on the Town Hall clock in the main square, by the beaks of two bronze eagles. It is also a good place to explore the wine growing area of Lugana which lies to the south.

Also south, about 8km (5 miles), is the Villa Sigurta with a large, superbly laid out park that can be toured either by car along specially prepared roads or on foot. There are fine lawns, ponds and grottoes, the whole having been conceived by Count Sigurta over the last half century, as an example of peace and brotherhood through nature.

After crossing the river, turn northward to follow the eastern shore of Lake Garda, driving along the Gardesana Orientale.

The Eastern Shore

The first spots visited on the eastern side of the lake are not actually on the lakeside. Just outside Peschiera, on the road to Lazise, is

Gardaland, with numerous rides which are free after paying the entrance fee. Further on towards Lazise is the Caneva Aquatic Sports Park with a large variety of water chutes and pools and inland, at **Pastrengo**, is the Garda Safari Park, with a conventional, drivable safari park area, a zoo and a model dinosaur park.

On the shore line **Lazise** is the first town reached after going past several pleasant villages and a fine line of camp sites — the whole eastern shoreline is, virtually, a beach to one side, a camp site to the other — each with good beaches, and sunsets, behind the hills that hem in Val Trompia, which are themselves worth a trip to Italy. Especially good is Pacengo which also has a church with some fine paintings.

Lazise is both impressive and charming, with parts of the old arched and embattled town wall on three sides, the lake on the fourth and the still strong remains of a castle of the Scaligeri. The castle is private and cannot be visited. One interesting point here is the use of fish-tail battlements, and the delightful continuation of their use in one of the lakeside buildings. From this castle a chain could be drawn across the harbour mouth, the town being known as 'The Key to the Lake' by the Venetian Republic who maintained warships here. The harbour itself is delightful, an array of small boats with a backdrop, from the church side, of fine three-storeyed buildings, each, in typical fashion, with a balcony.

Above Lazise, on the road through Vallesana, is **Calmasine**, a pretty village worth the detour for its view out over Lazise to the lake, with the peninsula of Sirmione in sharp relief and the hills north of Brescia on the skyline.

Alternatively, continue along the Gardesana Orientale to reach **Bardolino**, which also had a castle, the tower of which now forms part of a hotel. Bardolino is famous for its wine, and the vineyards from which it is produced spread up the hillside (too far south to be Monte Baldo as yet) that rises not too steeply here. The whole of the town and its surrounding area lives up to the name of Olive Riviera: not only are there olives and vines, but also avenues of cypresses and other trees which crowd in on roads and houses alike.

The village contains five churches, each of considerable interest, but if time is limited then be sure to visit San Zeno, a tiny building dating from the eighth century, and San Severo, a magnificent eleventh-century building.

As would be expected on this holiday riviera, the holidaymaker is well catered for. The harbour area provides good sport and there is

Bardolino

a good beach for swimming. In the town centre, the main street has a row of shops specialising in the necessities of beach life along one side, while the opposite side of the street is equipped with a line of typically Italian cafés and restaurants, some with road (rather than pavement) seating, to the confusion of the motorist.

Villa Abertini, Garda

North again are two huge lumps of rock, like the humps on a camel though flatter on the top, the larger of which has given its name to both

Garda

the town and the lake at its foot, for this is the *rocca* of **Garda**. Not surprisingly the rock was used as a fortress from earliest times. Today the visitor who walks up (allow about 45 minutes) is treated to a fine view, can wander through a luxuriant natural garden, and gaze at all that remains of the final castle.

In the town at the base of the *rocca* there is a hotel named after Queen Adelheid, and the Palazzo del Capitani which was once occupied by the Captains of the Lake — an imposing building, arched at ground level. Also look for Villa Albertini, a romantic, castle-like villa where the treaty for the annexation of Lombardy to Piemonte was received by King Carlos Alberto in 1848, a prelude to the Risorgimento. Look too for the town museum, which includes items on its important history and some of the better rock engravings discovered near Punta San Vigilio. Those tempted to look for the real thing at the Point should note that they are now very, very difficult to find.

Outside **Costermano**, a village on the hill above Garda, is a German war cemetery, holding 22,000 German soldiers of World War II. It is a most moving place where lie, not enemies, but fellow human beings.

The lake at Garda is a bay formed by the hooked nose of land poking out into the water to the north of the town. This is **Punta San Vigilio**, one of the highlights of any tour of Lake Garda. At the tip of the nose of land are a little church, to San Vigilio of course — a simple, dignified building, a statue in a niche in the wall which is only visible from across the water, and the private sixteenth-century Villa Guarienti. The buildings stand among tall, dark cypresses, the whole vision mirrored in the calm lake waters. But equally fine is the view from the tip, either south across the bay to Garda, or westward, across the lake to Manerba and Gardone. Alternatively, on the northern side of the tip, the secluded Serene Bay offers marvellous views, with a beautiful mixture of greens and blues.

At **Torri del Benaco** there is yet another Scaligeri castle and, again in keeping with its southern neighbours, the site has been fortified virtually continuously since Roman times. The castle still has attached to it part of the old town walls, which give a delightful period quality to the town and its picturesque harbour. But like the other towns on the eastern shore, this one has made significant concessions to tourism. The lake's only car-ferry links Torri to Maderno, and there is a good panoramic view of the town as you approach — the castle, the red-tiled houses, the backdrop of trees and the ridges of Monte Baldo. Equally good is the view from **Albisano**, a village set on the hill above Torri, and reached by a winding road from the lakeside. An even better view, taking in almost the entire lake, though not directly of Torri del Benaco, can be seen from **San Zeno di Montagna** about 6km (4 miles) further on along another winding road. Continuing along the road from San Zeno, through a collection

PLACES OF INTEREST ON THE EASTERN SHORE OF LAKE GARDA

Villa Sigurta
Near Peschiera
Superb landscaped parkland of large seventeenth-century villa, conceived as a monument to the brotherhood of man.

Gardaland
Near Peschiera
Garda's 'Disneyland', with numerous rides and attractions. Includes water rides and cork-screw roller coaster.

Caneva Aquatic Sports Park
Near Peschiera
Large collection of water chutes and pools.

Garda Safari Park
Pastrengo
Safari park, zoo and dinosaur park.

Rocca di Garda
Excellent views and plant-life. Remains of old castle.

Museum
Garda
Items on the town's history and rock engravings from Punta San Vigilio.

Punta San Vigilio
Delightful little church and fine mid-sixteenth-century villa set in cypress groves. Beautiful views across lake and Serene Bay.

Castle
Torri del Benaco
Remains of Scaligeri castle and part of old town wall, ancient harbour site. Holds museum with exhibits on lake fishing, olive growing, marble working and the local rock engravings.

Orrido del Sandolino
Villanova
Fine gorge that is very difficult and arduous to reach.

Church of San Zeno
Castelletto di Brenzone
Romantically sited twelfth-century church.

Funivia
Malcesine to Monte Baldo
Expansive views from the summit.

Castle/Museum
Malcesine
Wonderfully sited early four-teenth-century Scaligeri castle. Magnificent views from castle towers. Holds Museum of the Lake dealing chiefly with fishing, and the Pariani Museum dealing with J.W. Goethe's visit to the town. Not to be missed.

Palazzo dei Capitani
Malcesine
Excellent fifteenth-century building, formerly home to the Venetian Captains of the Lake. Occasional exhibitions.

The Giant's Pots
Nago
Smooth hollows scooped out of the rock by glacial meltwater.

Viewpoints
Calmasino
Albisano
San Zeno di Montagna
Monte Brione, above Torbole

An aerial view of Malcesine

  of little hamlets (from **Villanova** the energetic enthusiast can walk/ scramble to the *orrido* (gorge) of Sandolino) the visitor can reach Castelletto di Brenzone direct. The coast road is pleasant, but the views from the higher road make the detour worthwhile, though some will want to backtrack a few hundred metres to visit the twelfth-century church of San Zeno (not be be confused with the hill village of that name) — a romantically sited building.

Malcesine castle

Castelletto is the first of a collection of villages which are known collectively as Brenzone, though that name — said to derive from Bruncione, one of Charlemagne's paladins — is usually applied to Porta, the largest of the collection, about 4km (2¹/₂ miles) north of Castelletto. But Castelletto is probably the nicest, an ancient village retaining its character. The Piazza dell 'Olivio is almost too good to be true: tall trees, balconies covered in flowers and creepers, arched entrances, external staircases, shuttered windows — all the elements of the essential lake village.

Malcesine is the last of the towns of the eastern shore that lie in Veneto, is among the most famous, and offers the most interesting itinerary of any on the Riviera of Olives. It also offers the most spectacular view, with its impressive Scaligeri castle, a huge, almost complete building perched right at the lake edge with a tall square central tower that dominates the town from any direction. The approach to the town gives a very good view of the castle, and also of the Val di Sogno, a peaceful valley with flowers and fine villas. Offshore is Isola Val di Sogno, the Island of the Valley of Dreams.

Malcesine is a wonderful place, beloved over centuries by writers and artists. It is an apparently haphazard array of excellent buildings; unexpected eruptions of tall shady trees; a picturesque harbour almost totally enclosed and lined on two sides by arcaded, balconied buildings; and over everything the castle, tier upon tier of white stone, embattled walls and towers, competing for height with dark green cypresses and winning, finally, with the tower. From the tower the view to the town is worth every step of the climb. The castle, built in the early fourteenth century, houses the Museum of the Lake, and among its exhibits are models and drawings of the transportation of Venetian war galleys across land for launching at Torbole.

Within the town any walk will pay dividends, but be sure to see the fifteenth-century Palazzo dei Capitani, the palace of the Venetian Captains of the Lake near the harbour, which is now the Town Hall, a most impressive building with its pillars and arcaded windows. Do not miss the view across to the tiny Island of Olives and be sure also to find the inscribed stone headed:

HINC
J. W. GOETHE
ARCEM DELINEAVAT

because there can be few towns anywhere which have raised a memorial to an arrest. The arrest occurred on 13 September 1786 when Johann Wolfgang Goethe visited Italy for the first time. At that time the border between Austria and Italy lay between Torbole and Malcesine, so on present day terms Goethe was already in Italy as he made his way from one town to the other. In Malcesine he was impressed by the castle and paused to sketch it. He was seen, and promptly arrested as an Austrian spy, having no small difficulty in proving his innocence as a citizen of the Republic of Frankfurt. When he was released the great man saw the funny side of it all, writing a humorous account in his *Italian Tour.* The castle's Pariani Museum deals with Goethe's visit.

In Via Novene Vecchia, which lies almost directly inland from the castle, the visitor can take a 15-minute ride in a *funivia* that rises 1,650m (5,410ft, over a mile) to the flank of Monte Baldo. At the top of the *funivia*, where in summer time the pylons of the winter sports chair lifts stand like forlorn skeletons, the visitor is only 450m (1,475ft) and 6km (about 4 miles) from the actual high point of the long ridge along a well used path. The last part of the ridge is rocky, and the ridge is steeply sided, so great caution should be exercised, but the views are spectacular. Many however, settle for the more immediate

Riva del Garda

panorama from the cable car terminus. Monte Baldo has been called the 'Botanical Garden of Italy' for the profusion of both species and growth, and the rarity of some species on its flanks, and two nature parks have been set up on the mountain to preserve the flora and the insect, bird and animal life that lives on, and in, it. The Selva Pezzi Park is high on the peak, one boundary running along the ridge through the highest tops, the other lying on the flank above Malcesine. The Gardesana Orientale Park lies above the lakeside road from Malcesine to Torbole, starting about 4km (2¹/₂ miles) outside of Malcesine, and continuing for about 5km. Each park is crossed by waymarked paths — a map of these is available at the Information Centre — though the paths through the higher park do necessitate taking the cable car and some high-level walking.

Beyond Malcesine the Gardesana Orientale follows the lake edge, hugged on its eastern side by the steep wooded flank of Monte Baldo, so tightly in places that the road engineers had to resort to tunnelling. There are villages though, and a row of very fine camping sites each with its own beach. Between Casello and Piano di Tempesta (where, until 1918 when some of the Tyrol was transferred to Italy, the route would have crossed into Austria) the visitor now crosses into Trentino, leaving Veneto and its Riviera of Olives.

The first town in Trentino is **Torbole**, on the eastern bank of the Sarca river which is Garda's main feeder. The approach is a great sight: the Gardesana Orientale has reached its northern limit, and the road turns westward towards the town, which lies on flat land broken by wedges of white rock as the pre-Alps to the north descend into the lake. The lake here is very deep, the enclosing ridges giving it a fjord-like appearance, and is, at this northern extremity, excellent for sailing and windsurfing. The sailors take advantage of the consistent winds — blowing from the north in the morning, from the south in the afternoon. The town is grouped around its main harbour (there are several other harbours and landing stages) and in its older parts is very picturesque.

It was from Torbole that Goethe sailed to Malcesine and arrest. A plaque below a medallion image of the writer notes the visit, a memorial to the fact that is was here, Goethe maintained, that he began to write *Iphigenia*. Be sure also to visit the public gardens, for a peaceful stroll in the shade of olive trees beside a quiet stream.

Equally peaceful is a walk in **Nago**, a quiet village behind Torbole in which to escape the bustle of the larger town. There you can visit the Marmitte dei Giganti, the Giant's Pots, a dozen smooth hollows scoured out by the action of whirling glacial meltwater. Also, stroll among the ruins of Penede castle, almost returned now to nature, but offering good viewpoints for Torbole and the lake. It is one of the viewpoints recommended in a series of walks and rides mapped out in a small booklet available at the Azienda Autonoma di Soggiorno (19 Via Lungolago Verona, on the lakeside). Another of the recommended viewpoints should not be missed: the one reached by taking the short but winding road to the top of Monte Brione, the wedge-shaped ridge on the opposite side of the Sarca. The panorama from there is very interesting as well as being expansive — the Sarca valley can be seen, as can the valley of Lake Loppio giving access to the *autostrada* for the Brenner Pass — and is the best of any on the northern end of the lake.

The Western Shore

Only 4km (2¹/₂ miles) and the river Sarca separate Torbole from **Riva del Garda**, though Riva is not visible until the wedge of Monte Brione has been passed, the road rounding and finally breaking through the rock mass. Riva is the largest town at the northern end of the lake, though not as big as Desenzano where the tour started.

Not only is it large — especially in comparison with the smaller, more manageable, villages of the Riviera of Olives — it is also very prosperous, a prosperity which it carries in sophisticated rather than gaudy style. For while Riva is the most popular holiday centre with the largest number of tourists (the lake is sometimes an astonishing sight, such is the profusion and colourfulness of the windsurfers) and as a result, the largest number of hotels, cafés etc, it also retains much of its fishing/trading port atmosphere. Nowhere is this better seen than in the main square that fronts onto the lakeside — the water laps at your feet as you contemplate the harbour, its quays angled to provide a safe haven. The square is the Piazza Tre Novembre and is dominated by the huge but simple Torre Apponale, a clock tower from the thirteenth century. The Palazzo Pretorio is a century newer, the Palazzo Communale, a century later again. Between them are medieval arches and porticos. Elsewhere parts of the old town wall, as well as three wall towers, have been incorporated into newer buildings.

Only a step away from the main square is the moated castle, the *rocca*, built by the Scaligeri in the twelfth century, though altered on several occasions, to defend the town against lake-borne pirates rather than land-borne adventurers. The castle is open to visitors, and offers, in addition to the building itself, a museum in which are many of the artefacts from the Lake Ledro lake dwellings as well as interesting exhibits on the history of the town. The *rocca*'s approach, over a double-arched bridge and old drawbridge, is utterly irresistible.

Also in connection with Lake Ledro, it is worth noticing the Ponale Hydroelectric Power Station in Riva, powered by water from that lake, which is brought along a pipe 6km (4 miles) long. A more exciting fall of water is to be seen about 4km ($2^1/_2$ miles) north of Riva beside the road to Tenno. Here the Cascata del Varonne falls nearly 90m (almost 300ft) in two leaps, each in a tightly enclosed, dark gorge that amplifies the noise and concentrates the spray.

Also northwards but still within the town, on Via Roma, the road to Arco, is the church of the Inviolate with an octagonal interior in baroque style and containing stucco and gilded work of considerable interest. The ceiling of the octagonal cupola is especially good.

A little way south of the town, on the road along the lake's western shore, there is a *funivia* offering a 5-minute ride to the top of the Bastione on which there is an early sixteenth-century round tower built by the Venetians, and from which there are excellent panoramic views. This outcrop, and others around Riva, were fortified by the

Austrians during World War I, and though the artillery was ordered not to shell the town when the Italian army advanced in 1915, it was badly damaged by the fighting. Fortunately, much that is interesting has survived.

The road south from Riva is the Gardesana Occidentale, a fine road that bores its way innumerable times through the steep cliffs that fall into the lake and delivers the traveller speedily to his chosen spot on the lakeside. The first chosen spot on this route is soon after the *funivia*, where an older road that also tunnels its way southwards is followed. After the second tunnel the road heads up the valley of the Ponale river passing, almost immediately, the noted, but frankly disappointing Cascata del Ponale. The gorge of the river itself is much less disappointing, the road being on a shelf cut out from the rock. At the pleasant village of **Molina di Ledro**, there is, near the lake shore, a small museum that deals with the lake dwellings found near the village during construction work, in 1929, for the pipeline to the hydroelectric station at Riva. If the power station has demanded more water than the lake inflow is supplying, the fall in the lake level reveals some of the nearly 15,000 wooden stakes that the lake dwellings comprised. The site, and another found more recently, are now confidently ascribed to the Bronze Age. Altogether this is a most interesting site.

Lake Ledro itself, though small — it is about 3km long and, on average, 1km wide (2 miles by $^1/_2$ mile) — is a beautiful lake, well sited among high hills, but with a wide enough valley to give flat land at the shoreline, so there is ample space for several good camping sites and beaches. **Pieve de Ledro**, at the opposite end of the lake from Molina, is the valley's holiday resort, a pleasant village with good sports facilities.

Back on the Gardesana Occidentale (which can only be regained by returning along the same road, though it is, of course, straightforward to continue from Lake Ledro into the upper Val Sabbia and down to Lake Idro) the drive south is through a succession of tunnels. The entrance to one marks the boundary between Trentino and the Brescian province of Lombardy, and is where the route crosses into the Riviera del Garda. The first town reached in Lombardy is **Limone sul Garda**, named after the lemon trees which, it is believed, were grown here for the first time in Europe. They still grow here, in terraces overlooking the lake and in numerous greenhouses which they share with oranges and mandarins. Elsewhere there are olive groves and other trees typical of Mediterranean areas, indicative of a very good

Limone sul Garda

climate. Limone has a beautiful old quarter associated with the old fishing port, with picturesque houses, arches, window boxes, balconies and shutters all piled on top of each other. And above it all are the white cliffs of Cima di Mughera, speckled with plant life in many shades of green.

Today Limone has expanded outwards from the old fishing port, reaching across two rivers, the Pura and San Giovanni torrents, between which, up on the hill, is the church of San Pietro. This formerly stood in a village, where now there is only an olive grove. It is an ancient church and on one outside wall notable events in the history of the village are inscribed, remembering the pestilence of 1630, the poor olive harvest of 1822, the cold winter of 1857, but not the death of the community it served.

From Limone a road above the Gardesana Occidentale leads to **Tremosine** and **Tignale**, collections of small villages on plateaux apparently hewn out of the high rocks of the pre-Alps. The church of Madonna di Montecastello in Tignale, built in the ruins of a Scaligeri castle, typifies the area. It is magnificently sited, with panoramic lake views, and is itself very beautiful with good frescoes and paintings, four on copper being attributed to Palma the Younger. This is one of the most beautiful areas anywhere on Garda. There are meadows full of flowers, with dairy farms, some making and selling butter and cheese, gentle wooded slopes, huge rock faces — the village of

Pieve is perched right on the edge of a precipice and from the lake it seems to hang in space — and waterfalls. It is an ancient landscape — evidence of Etruscans and Gauls have been discovered — and full advantage of its timeless qualities can be taken by following any of a series of waymarked trails that criss-cross the ridges and valleys. Details of these are on a pamphlet issued by the Tourist Offices at Gargnano and Limone, as well as in Tignale and Tremosine themselves. It is advisable to obtain the leaflet because some of the routes, though well marked, are for experienced walkers only, and also because it has a good panoramic map of the area. Since the plateaux also have good restaurants and excellent sports facilities, they can be thoroughly recommended as excellent holiday centres.

From either the high plateaux or the Gardesana Occidentale, the visitor will arrive at **Gargnano**, a well known, and well loved sailing town — the Centomiglia sailing competition brings boats from all over Europe to the lake here in September. The winds on Lake Garda are dependable, but the lake does also suffer from spasmodic winds that bring cool air down from the pre-Alps and Dolomites. These winds, and the more continuous morning and afternoon winds, seem more persistent than on the other lakes and Garda appears more rarely to be flat calm. For the sailors this is a bonus, though not for some residents. One patch of green, set among high cliffs and, before the road, provisioned by boat alone, was known as 'Hungry Meadow' because the lake's fierce winter winds prevented boats from landing.

One of most interesting aspects of Gargnano is the array of terraced citrus orchards beside the town, eager farmers having pressed every last square centimetre of soil into service. Equally good is the Franciscan monastery, dating from the thirteenth and fourteenth centuries, with a fine cloister.

From the village a road leads to Val Toscolano and Lake Valvestino, named after the valley beyond it; from the lake's northern end a road winds down to Lake Idro; another, which winds even more, can be used to explore the lonely, isolated villages of Valvestino itself. The valleys are excellent and the lake (dammed and used as a source of hydro-electric power) well set, but the area does not have the beauty of the high plateaux that have already been visited.

Back in Gargnano, walk along the lake shore, admiring the lines of the Villa Feltrinelli, home to the Italian government during the time of the Salo Republic, though Mussolini himself stayed in another villa of the Feltrinelli family also in the town, which is now home to foreign students from the University of Milan when they attend summer

Vineyards above Bogliaco

courses in the Italian language.

The sixteenth-century town hall still bears the marks of an
Austrian bombardment of 1886. Cannon balls and a stone memorial
bear witness to this event. On the lakeside are locals who grow fruit
on the hillside terraces and bring it here to sell. No fruit tastes better
than the sun-warmed, fresh and ripe fruit from these stalls.

Away from the lakeside the town has older, picturesque areas: in
one alley the houses are bridged at first floor level, the visitor walking
under a succession of stone arches, each with its own light. And
everywhere the window boxes are alive with colour.

Within the commune of Gargnano are several outlying villages. In
one of these, **Bogliaco**, is the Villa Bettoni, an eighteenth-century
building of immense size and majestic lines that contains an art
gallery with a fine collection of art from the same period. The villa is
open to visitors on request. Another lakeside village, **Villa**, was
visited by D.H. Lawrence who, it is claimed, was inspired by his stay
to write *Lady Chatterley's Lover*.

The next town is, in fact, two — **Toscolano**, of Etruscan origin,
now linked to **Maderno**, of Roman origin, across the diameter of a
circular blob of land thrust into the lake about 5km (3 miles) south of
Bogliaco's Villa Bettoni. From Toscolano, which is reached first (a
village famous for its paper mills), a road leading up the valley of the
Toscolano river reaches Gaino, an excellent viewpoint. The river has

PLACES OF INTEREST ON THE WESTERN SHORE OF LAKE GARDA

Castle
Riva del Garda
Twelfth-century castle surrounded by moat. Fine courtyard. Castle has museum with items from Ledro lake dwellings, and on history of the town.

Church of the Inviolate
Riva del Garda
Interior in baroque style, with good stucco and gilded work.

Cascata del Varonne
Near Riva del Garda
Waterfall in enclosed gorge. Water drops 90m (300ft) in two leaps.

Funivia
Riva to Bastione
Short cable car to plateau with sixteenth-century Venetian round tower and fine views.

Museum
Molina di Ledro
Museum devoted to finds from two sets of lake dwellings found locally. Exhibits include a reconstructed hut at the lakeside.

Tignale/Tremosine
High plateaux above the lake between Gargnano and Limone sul Garda. Breathtaking views of mountains and lakes with a fine series of walks to explore the best of the scenery. The church of Madonna di Montecastello in Tignale is outstandingly positioned. Not to be missed.

Villa Feltrinelli
Near Gargnano
Elegant villa, now part of Milan University.

partly helped create the button of land that supports the two villages, but its aid has created fertile, rather than picturesque land. The villages have turned this to advantage, every spare piece of soil having been utilised in the growing of trees or shrubs, adding a real garden feel to any walk.

Maderno is the terminal port for the lake's car ferry (from Torri Benaco), but has much more than that to offer any visitor. The basilica of Sant' Andrea is a fine twelfth-century Romanesque building, with some Byzantine additions, and contains the painting, *The Virgin and the Angel*, by Paolo Veneziano. Across from the church is an Ionic column topped by the winged lion of St Mark, Maderno being the only village of Lake Garda that retains such a memory of the rule of the Venetians. Also nearby is a statue of Sant' Ercolano, on an extremely tall pedestal, now only the local patron

PLACES OF INTEREST ON THE WESTERN SHORE OF LAKE GARDA -continued

Villa Bettoni
Bogliaco
Fine eighteenth-century villa with good gallery.

Venetian Column
Maderno
Ionic column topped by the Winged Lion of St Mark, symbol of the Venetian Republic.

Hruska Botanical Gardens
Gardone Riviera
Magnificent gardens in superb setting. Not to be missed.

Vittoriale degli Italiani
Gardone Riviera
Quite remarkable montage of buildings, curios and parkland. Home of Gabrieli d'Annunzio. Also museum of memorabilia of d'Annunzio, including plane from 1918, and car from 1919.

Museum
Salo

Civic museum, with exhibits from history of town and area.

Church of Madonna di Carmine
San Felice
Fourteenth-century church with beautifully restored fifteenth- and sixteenth-century frescoes.

Museum
Manerba del Garda
Museum of life and folklore of the Valtensi.

Castle
Padenghe
Medieval castle with houses built within the walls.

Viewpoints
Madonna di Montecastello, Tignale
Gaino, above Toscolano-Maderno
Rocca di Manerba

saint, but once the protector of the lake and its voyagers.

Beyond Maderno is a small bay created by the Toscolano-Maderno semi-circle, and a similar but smaller combination of towns which is **Fasano-Bornico**. This is a pleasant town and the only one that historians agree definitely existed as such in Roman times. Next comes **Gardone Riviera** marking one end of a much more defined bay, the Gulf of Salo. It must have become apparent that the Riviera del Garda on the western shore is more sheltered and hence has a better climate for plant life than Veneto's Riviera of Olives. The climate was noted in the late nineteenth century by Dr Ludovic Rohden, a German expert in climate, who did much to popularise the area. So famous did it become that the Austrian Emperor had the Villa Alba built here in 1904, though he never actually stayed in, or visited, it.

Any lingering doubts on the climate will be cast aside with a walk through the parks of Gardone or, indeed, on any walk at all through the town. But most of all it is obvious at the Hruska Botanical Gardens, named after Professor Arthur Hruska who lived here until his death in 1971, where 2,000 varieties of plants and flowers thrive, and where there are the finest rock-gardens in Italy, if not in Europe. No visit to Gardone, or for that matter to Lake Garda itself, should fail to include a visit to the gardens, which are in Via Roma that leads off northwards from Corso Zanardelli near Piazza Marconi, close to the steamer landing stage.

Those who follow Via Roma will eventually reach the Vittoriale degli Italiani, though it is easier to go directly along Via Panoramica which leaves the lake road just north of the Torre San Marco — a fine tower. Il Vittoriale was built for Gabriele d'Annunzio, one of Italy's larger-than-life historical figures. He was a poet, with a verse style that has been described by most words from sensuous to decadent, and in later life he was a military leader whose style in that field was equally flamboyant. The Vittoriale complex is open to the public, and contains many mild surprises, together with the odd major one. At one point, between the cypresses, there is a ship, the *Puglia* — no ordinary ship, being in part original and in part stone; at another there is a magnificent open-air theatre. This, together with the concert hall, is administered by the Fondazione del Vittoriale, and regular festivals are held in the summer months. Throughout the grounds there are memorials to d'Annunzio, including his tomb at the top of a hugely elaborate, three concentric-ringed mausoleum that also holds the tombs of several of his war comrades. In addition, the villa is a museum to the man, poet and soldier.

A walk along the Gardone lakeside is one of the great pleasures of a trip to Lake Garda, but the town has much more than such good, but conventional, pleasures. The Barbarano stream which runs into the western edge of the town can be followed back to the hills, through little gorges and over little falls, past old iron forges and the occasional water-wheel. At San Michele a detour can be made to the tiny church, set among hills crowned with chestnut trees. And even when the Barbarano is finally crossed, the town of Salo, lying at the back edge of the square lake gulf that bears its name, is equally elegant.

But first, between the two, is the Palazzo Martinengo, a sixteenth-century villa that played a part, in the latter part of that century, in the tale of murder and intrigue that is recalled in John Webster's play *The*

Salo

White Devil. The *palazzo*, named after a Brescian family whose name is synonymous with the history of that city, is open to visitors who request permission in writing.

Salo, beyond the *palazzo*, has a fine cathedral, built in Gothic style in the fifteenth century, with a now familiar dome. Inside it is a towering combination of dark stone and colourful paintings, with a floor of an unusual, but very effective, geometric design. Some of the artwork is both excellent and of historical interest.

In complete contrast, the Whiskythek in Lungolago — on from the cathedral, but still on the lakeside — reputedly has every brand of whisky in the world on its shelves.

As if to maintain its reputation for diversity, Salo has two other claims to fame. The brothers Bertolotti lived here, both musicians, and one of whose sons was Gasparo da Salo who is credited with having invented the violin. An excellent statue of the great man at work on a violin can be seen on the first floor of the sixteenth-century Palazzo Municipale, the Town Hall. Centuries later Salo was created capital of its own republic (the Republic of Salo) which was formed by Mussolini towards the end of World War II when the Italian Fascist state had collapsed and Il Duce's world was crumbling.

But aside from these tales, Salo is an excellent place to wander around, another town which makes the most of its considerable assets of climate and position. The Palazzo Fantoni, near the

Manerba del Garda

cathedral, houses the Biblioteca Atenco, a library with a great number of rare books. Closer to the lake, in the fourteenth-century Palazzo del Capitano Rettore attached to the Town Hall, the Town Museum houses exhibits of Salo's history.

From Salo the main road leaves the lake, making directly for Desenzano, but there is merit in taking the minor road that stays close to the shore. Between Porto Portese and San Felice del Benaco the view is dominated by Isola di Garda, the lake's largest island, on which is a magnificent villa set in equally good gardens — shades of Isola Bella — but private property which can only be viewed from afar, either from the lakeside or from a round-the-island boat trip.

In **San Felice**, at the head of the Valtensi, a valley running parallel to the lake shore, the sanctuary of Madonna di Carmine has fine fifteenth- and sixteenth-century frescoes, recently and lovingly restored. At **Manerba del Garda** there is a rocky headland offering fine views over the lake, the *rocca* being known (not a compliment) as Dante's profile! Manerba also holds the Museum of Valtensi.

Moniga del Garda has a wonderful little port — take advantage, it is the last — and a medieval castle, while at nearby **Padenghe** there is a castle within the walls of which houses have been built, so that it now appears as a hill-top walled hamlet.

10 VERONA

V erona is a very old city, so old that its true origins are unknown, though it is known that by the first century BC it was already an important Roman city, built on an S-bend of the river Adige, and on important roads going north through the Alps and east to west across the Lombardy plain. In terms of its Roman past, Verona is second only to Rome itself in the quality of its surviving structures, and its amphitheatre, smaller only than Rome's Colosseum and the one at Capua, is arguably the most magnificent of all such structures.

Verona maintained its importance into the Middle Ages. Berengar died here in 924, and Otto I stayed during his mission to free Adelheid on nearby Lake Garda. As a free state the city was ahead of its time, forming the Veronese League before the formation of the Lombard League, and defeating Barbarossa in 1164 before joining with Milan to defeat him decisively in 1176 at Legnano. Following this there were severe feuds between rival rich families within the city, one of which formed the basis for a story by the sixteenth-century writer Luigi da Porto. His story involved the Cappelletti and Montechi families whose names, anglicised to Capulet and Montague, were taken by Shakespeare when he adopted the story for *Romeo and Juliet*, still perhaps the most famous association that the city offers tourists.

The feuding stopped when the city was taken by Ezzelino da Romano, a savage tyrant who ruled, or dictated, until his death around 1260. Next came Mastino della Scala, first of a family which was to give Milan's opera house its name, and whose name, Scaligeri, is associated with so many of the fish-tail embattled castles seen on Garda's shore. Mastino in Italian means mastiff, and many subsequent members of the Scaligeri had their names prefixed by *can* (dog), as a mark of respect. The most famous ruler was Francesco della Scala, who was known as 'Cangrande', Great Dog, under whose rule Verona had its greatest sphere of influence, and reached great artistic heights. Dante, the greatest early European writer who was banished from Florence, came here and received Cangrande's protection, dedicating the third section (*Paradise*) of the

An aerial view of Piazza dell' Erbe

Divine Comedy to him. In keeping with the dog allusions, one later member of the family, not noted for his thoughtful dignity, was Canrabbiaso, Mad Dog.

A later Scaligeri, the second Great Dog, Cangrande II, built the city's castle, but by the end of the fourteenth century the family's rule was at an end, Verona falling firstly to the Viscontis and then becoming part of the Venetian Empire. During the four centuries of Venetian rule the city grew in stature, its artistic development being greatly assisted by the presence of the brilliant Renaissance architect Michele Sanmicheli and the artist Andrea Mantegna.

Ultimately the Venetian Empire collapsed, and the city was occupied in 1796 by the French. The following year saw the 'Pasque Veronesi', the Veronese Easter, when the city rose and killed the new ruler's men who were quartered there, an uprising that was swiftly avenged with considerable damage to the city's fabric. Thereafter the city was held by French or Austrians until the Risorgimento when it became part of the unified Italy.

The swift tour of the city will start in Piazza Bra — the name deriving from the Latin *pratum*, a meadow. Here the **Arena**, the Roman amphitheatre, immediately takes the eye. The Arena is elliptical, the structure originally covering a site measuring 152m by

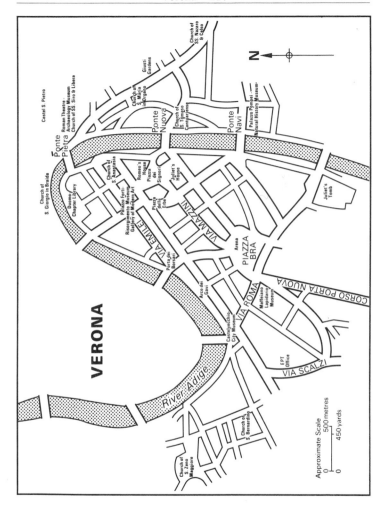

VERONA

Castel S. Pietro

Church of S. Giorgio in Braida

Ponte Pietra

Roman Theatre
Archaeology Museum
Church of SS. Siro & Libera

Church of S. Maria in Organo

Giusti Gardens

Church of SS. Nazaro & Celso

Ponte Nuovo

Church of S. Tsimaso Cancujarense

Ponte Navi

Palazzo Pompei
Natural History Museum

Duomo
Chapter Library

Church of S. Anastasia

Romeo's House

Piazza dei Signori

Juliet's House

Palazzo Forti–
Risorgimento Museum
Gallery of Modern Art

Piazza delle Erbe

VIA MAZZINI

Juliet's Tomb

VIA EMILEE

Porta dei Borsari

Arco dei Gavi

Arena

PIAZZA BRA

CORSO PORTA NUOVA

VIA ROMA

Maffeiano Lapidary Museum

Castelvecchio
City Museum

EPT Office

VIA SCALZI

River Adige

Church of S. Bernardino

Church of S. Zeno Maggiore

Approximate Scale
0   500 metres
0   450 yards

123m (499ft by 403ft). The arena floor measures 74m by 44m (243ft by 144ft). The whole was built of local stone in the last years of the first century AD. When first built the structure had a three-tier perimeter wall, only a small section of which, known locally as the *ala* (the wing), remains, following a destructive earthquake in 1183.

Inside, the amphitheatre is wonderfully imposing, and it takes a moment to remember that amid this splendour gladiators died on the sandstrewn floor. Thankfully, the only spectacles to be seen here today are operas performed duing a season that runs from mid-July to the end of August.

Piazza Bra is a spacious square, one of the largest in Italy, with elegant buildings on all sides and a formal fountain garden at its centre. The wide pavements, the *Listone*, of the north-west side are ideal for stolling, and while doing so, be sure to notice Sanmicheli's **Palazzo Guastavera**. On the corner of Via Roma is the **Museo Lapidario Maffeiano** with the oldest collection of ancient inscriptions in Europe.

North-east from Piazza Bra is Piazza dell' Erbe occupying, almost exactly, the position of the Roman forum. It is a delightful place, one of the most picturesque spots in the whole of Italy with its array of umbrellas protecting its fruit and vegetable market, stallholders and shoppers. In the square there is much of interest: just relax and stroll, but do not fail to see the **Palazzo della Ragione**, founded in the twelfth century, but much altered except for the tower, the Torre delle Carceri; or the **Arco della Costa** beside it, the Arch of the Rib, so called because of the whale's rib that hangs by it. On the north-western side is the baroque **Palazzo Maffei** from the seventeenth century with, beside it, the **Torre del Gardello** from the fourteenth century. In front of the *palazzo* is the **Colonna di San Marco**, the lion symbol of the Venetian empire, destroyed after the Pasque Veronesi, but now restored. Note too, the fourteenth-century fountain with a statue. The statue is Roman, but the bizarre head is not original, making the whole thing a bit odd, but it is revered as the Madonna Verona. The 84m (276ft) **Torre dei Lamberti** beside the Palazzo della Ragione can be climbed to improve the view.

A little way from the *piazza* is Via Cappello, and the **Casa di Giulietta**, Juliet's House. It is an exquisite house, thirteenth century with a façade of golden brown brick and a balcony of cream marble. The house is probably too old for the legend, the climb to it too difficult, and the legend may have no basis in truth. The name of the street is, apparently, from a dubious inn sign that once hung at the house — 'Il Cappello'. But if this was not Juliet's house, it should have been.

For lovers of the story there is also **Romeo's House**, on the corner of Via delle Arche Scaligeri, near Piazza dei Signori, whose history is even more dubious and which does not have anything like the romantic appeal of Casa di Giulietta.

Piazza dei Signori is reached through the Rib Arch. By contrast to Erbe it is small, quiet and dignified. To the right on entering, another

The Roman Arena at Verona

Piazza dei Signori

archway leads to the Old Market, a beautiful courtyard formed within the Palazzo della Ragione. Here is a first glimpse of the red and white horizontal zebra stripes that will become so familiar on the tour of the city. In the old courtyard they act as a perfect backdrop to an elegant stairway.

In the centre of Piazza dei Signori is a statue of Dante, his back to the **Loggia del Consiglio**, an elegantly arcaded and painted fifteenth-century Renaissance building, crowned by statues of famous men of Verona, including Catullus and Pliny the Elder. To Dante's left is the **Palace of the Scaligeri**, a much altered twelfth-century building with the familiar fish-tail battlements. Beside the palace an archway leads to the small Romanesque church of **Santa Maria Antica** beside which are the **Tombs of the Scaligeri**, an extraordinary assembly of monuments damaged by an earthquake in 1976, but now almost restored.

The tombs can be seen as marvels of Veronese art of the thirteenth and fourteenth centuries, or an over-elaborate self-indulgence. Their nicest part is the exquisite wrought iron grille surrounding them, which incorporates the five-ringed ladder used by the family as a symbol. The equestrian statue of Cangrande that surmounts the topmost pyramid of his tomb is a masterpiece by an unknown artist, and is a copy, the original being in the city's Castle Museum.

Going north from the tombs, the visitor passes, in Via Emilei, the

The Roman Ponte Pietra at Verona

Palazzo Forti where Napoléon stayed, and which now houses the city's **Risorgimento Museum**, covering the period from the Pasque Veronesi to final unification, and the **Modern Art Gallery**. Nearby is the church of **Sant' Anastasia**, the largest in the city, and in a beautiful position beside the river. The main doorway is superb, though the façade in which it is set is unfinished, 700 years after work began. Inside, do not miss the *gobbi* (hunchbacks), who support the Holy Water stoups at the first column bases, the terracotta scenes from the life of Christ, and some good frescoes.

In contrast to the church, the city **Cathedral** (*Duomo*), further north, seems disproportionate — too many changes of idea, too much over-emphasis. It was once described as 'architecture in colour' which seems a back-handed compliment. Inside however, it is light and spacious and has a superb Titian altarpiece — *The Assumption* — his only work in the town and worth the journey to see. Near the *Duomo*, the **Chapter Library** can be visited. Founded in the eighth century, it contains many interesting and valuable texts.

From the *Duomo* cross Ponte Pietra, one of the two original Roman bridges though little is of that age now. The bridge was almost completely destroyed in 1945, but the stones were dredged from the river and faithfully restored to position. Ahead now is the **Castel San Pietro**, an Austrian fortress which dominates the **Roman Theatre**. The theatre, which was not re-discovered until the early nineteenth

PLACES OF INTEREST IN VERONA

Arena
Piazza Bra
Magnificent Roman amphithe-
atre, perhaps the finest in
existence. Operas are performed
during a season mid-July to
August.
Not to be missed.

Museo Lapidario Maffeiano
Via Roma
Europe's oldest collection of
inscribed stones. Includes
Greek, Roman and Etruscan
work.

Torre dei Lamberti
Piazza dell' Erbe
84m (276ft) tower started in the
twelfth century but not completed until the fifteenth. Lift or
stairs take visitors to an expansive city view.

Juliet's House
Via Cappello
Fine thirteenth-century house
with balcony. House is romantically correct, if historically
dubious, as the Capulet family
house.

Tombs of the Scaligeri
Piazza dei Signori
Elaborate, cathedral-like tombs
to members of the Scaligeri
family, including Cangrande.

**Risorgimento Museum and
Gallery of Modern Art**
Via Emilei
Housed in Palazzo Forti, an
eighteenth-century building,
once the home of Napoléon.

Church of Sant' Anastasia
Corso Sant' Anastasia
Large thirteenth-century church

with fine doorway and interesting
art work.

Chapter Library
21 Piazza del Duomo
Contains many early and
valuable texts.

**Archaeological Museum and
Roman Theatre**
Via Santa Chiara
Roman Theatre, items from
which are housed in old convent
building.

Giusti Gardens
2 Via Giardino Giusti
Italian-style gardens of sixteenth-
century *palazzo*.

Natural History Museum
Palazzo Pompei
Famous museum in fine
sixteenth-century *palazzo* by
Sanmicheli.

Juliet's Tomb
Via del Pontiere
Remains of Capucin convent with
stone sarcophagus said to be
that of Juliet. Also small museums of detached frescoes.

City Museum
Castelvecchio
Fine collection of art and craft
work in magnificent Scaligeri
castle. Not to be missed.

Basilica of San Zeno Maggiore
Piazza San Zeno
Magnificent Romanesque church
with excellent cloisters. Artwork
includes triptych by Mantegna.
Not to be missed.

City Zoo
Via Citta di Nimes

century is thought to be older than the Arena. The view from the top of the seating tiers, both of the theatre and the city, is excellent. Also on the site are small fourteenth-century churches to **San Siro** and **San Libera**, and an **Archaeological Museum** — reached by lift from the back of the theatre — with items from both the theatre and Verona's Roman past.

If, after crossing Ponte Pietra, a left turn instead of a right is taken, the church of **San Giorgio in Braida**, will be reached. This contains many fine paintings, and the cupola is by Sanmicheli.

Going east from the Scaligeri tombs, the river is crossed by way of Ponte Nuovo, and, in Piazza San Tomaso is a church dedicated to **San Tomaso Cantuariense** — Thomas of Canterbury — in which the architect Sanmicheli is buried. A little north is the church of **Santa Maria in Organo**, the interior of which is covered in frescoes and has some exceptionally fine woodcarving. Note especially the Palm Sunday carving of Christ on a donkey.

Eastward are the Giusti Gardens, the Italian-style gardens of the sixteenth-century Palazzo Guisti. Here, as one would expect with the formal Italian style, are statues, fountains and well defined flower beds. But there is also a maze and some beautiful, very old, cypresses. South-east from the gardens, the church of **San Nazaro** **e San Celso** has some fine paintings.

South from the Scaligeri tombs, at the western end of the Ponte Navi, is the basilica of **San Fermo Maggiore**, colourful in stripes of red brick and yellow stone. The basilica is actually two churches, a lower, Romanesque one from the twelfth century and an upper, Gothic one from the fourteenth century. Beside the basilica is a fine campanile, most unusually topped by a stub spire. The campanile is also in marble and brick, but here the builder was not successful in his layering! Inside, the basilica has a magnificent wooden ceiling, superb frescoes and some fine monuments.

On the other side of the Ponte Navi is the city's **Natural History Museum**, housed in Sanmicheli's Palazzo Pompei. The museum is considered to be one of the finest of its type in Italy and has an especially good collection of local fossils.

Continue to the south instead of crossing Ponte Navi, to reach the grounds of a former Capuchin convent, of which only the cloisters and a small chapel remain. Here is a fourteenth-century stone sarcophagus that tradition ascribes to Juliet. There is also a modern bust of Shakespeare, and a small museum of detached frescoes.

West from the Scaligeri tombs is the **Porta dei Borsari**, a Roman

Castelvecchio

gateway derived from the word *bursarii*, Latin for tax collectors, this being a tollgate into the old city. The gateway is an imposing double archway of marble, and is inscribed '*Colonia Verona Augusta*'. Further along the riverside road is another Roman archway, the **Arco dei Gavi**. This formerly stood elsewhere in the city and was demolished by the French being rebuilt here from its original fragments supplemented with new material, in 1932. The arch is older, more delicate, and more beautiful then the Borsari Gate.

Next comes the Scaligeri castle, the **Castelvecchio**, one of the undoubted highlights of a tour of Verona. The castle was built by Cangrande II in the years around 1350 and was subsequently used by the Venetians as a college, by the French, and Austrians as a barracks and it was here that Count Ciano, Mussolini's son-in-law, was tried in 1944. The castle is quite magnificent, embodying all of the features seen in the Garda castles and setting them in a superb riverside position. The river itself is crossed by the Ponte Scaligero, a bridge incorporated into the original design as part of the defences. During World War II the bridge was almost totally destroyed, but has been lovingly restored to its former massive glory.

Today the castle holds the **City Museum**, which houses some very fine items including the original equestrian statue from the tomb of Cangrande I, works by Mantegna and Paolo Veronese, some fine early and Renaissance sculpture, jewellery and gold, medieval

Ponte Scaligero, Castelvecchio

glass, a collection of ancient firearms, detached early frescoes and many works from the Veronese and Venetian schools.

West from the castle the church of **San Bernardino** has some good frescoes and a fine chapel — Cappella Pellegrini — by Sanmicheli. North from here is **San Zeno Maggiore** thought by many to be the most beautiful Romanesque church in northern Italy. The basilica, dating from the early twelfth century, dominates a large, paved square, its own façade being dominated equally by a huge rose window. To one side of the church is an elegantly slender twelfth-century campanile in similar golden stone, while on the other side stands the embattled tower of a former monastery, looking out of character in its red brick and heavy design. Behind the church, its cloisters are breathtakingly beautiful, arcaded with a tiled roof, above which are two tiers of red and yellow striped walls each with its own tiled roof.

The basilica doors consist of forty-eight panels of bronze depicting biblical scenes, dating chiefly from the twelfth century with a few added in the thirteenth century when the doors were enlarged. The bronze reliefs are in one sense very primitive in layout and characterisation, but are very dynamic, foreshadowing the change to come in the nature of art.

The basilica of San Zeno Maggiore ✗

Inside, the basilica is very simple, elegantly so, with a minimum of artwork. There is a porphyry bowl in the north-west corner that some say was given by San Zeno, an African, to the Roman Emperor Gallienus in the fourth century, but that legend says was placed here by the devil, though quite why he should want to is not clear. There is also a triptych by Andrea Mantegna — partly a copy, as some of the original is in the Louvre having been removed by Napoléon. The church's crypt holds an urn containing the remains of San Zeno.

FURTHER INFORMATION

ACCOMMODATION

Hotel reservations cannot be made through ENIT offices. They do, however, hold lists of organisations who can book hotels, (normally 4 or 5-star), in all major tourist areas. The tourist (APT) offices in the regional centres, the local tourist offices (Aziende Autonome di Cura e Soggiorno — AACST) in larger towns/villages, and the Pro Loco offices in small villages also hold lists of hotels.

Camping is popular all over Italy. The tourist offices will provide details of sites and their standard. Alternatively, two lists can be obtained. The first contains details of all of Italy's sites, some 1,600, and must be purchased (19,000 lire in 1987). The second is an abbreviated list and is free. Each can be obtained from:

Centro Internazionale Prenotazioni
Federcampeggio
Casella Postale 23
50041 Calenzano
Firenze
☎ 055 882391

The Italian Alpine Club owns most of the **Mountain Huts** in upland Italy. The huts offer cheap overnight accommodation with basic facilities. Details from:

Club Alpino Italiano
Via Foscolo 3
Milano
☎ 02 802554 or 8057519

The Italian Youth Hostel Association has over fifty **Youth Hostels** in Italy, including Bergamo, Como, Domaso, Milan, Riva del Garda and Verona. Information can be obtained from:

Associazione Italiana Alberghi per la Gioventu
Palazzo della Civiltà del Lavoro
Quadrato della Concordia
00144 EUR Roma
☎ 06 5913702

In addition several of the larger towns have **Student Hostels** available to visiting students. Ask about *Casa della Studente* at the Milan Tourist Office. Milan is the only town in the area with such a hostel.

MISCELLANEOUS INFORMATION

Credit Cards
All major credit cards (Access, Visa, American Express etc) are taken at most large restaurants, hotels and shops. Eurocheques and traveller's cheques are also

accepted. The notable exceptions are filling stations which, as a rule, do not accept anything but money or fuel coupons.

Banks are normally open 8.30am-12.30pm, 3-4pm, Monday-Friday only.

Currency Regulations

The Italian monetary unit is the Lira (plural = Lire). No traveller may import or export more than 400,000 lire (1986 regulation — please check to ensure this amount remains valid), or may re-export traveller's cheques valued at more than 1,000,000 lire unless they have completed customs form V2 on entry.

Customs Regulations

Normal EEC customs regulations apply. The Italian age limit for the import of duty-free alcohol and tobacco is 17. Normal personal equipment — cameras, jewellery etc — can be taken into the country, but professional photographers need an AFA Carnet for the importation of their equipment.

Entry into Italy

No visa is required for stays of less than 3 months for holders of passports from Britain, Canada or the United States. A valid passport is required.

Health Care

British travellers have a right to claim health services in Italy by virtue of EEC regulations. Form E111 — available from the Department of Health and Social Security — should be obtained to avoid complications.

Canadian and American tourists will need to check the validity of their personal health insurance to ensure they are adequately covered.

If drugs are prescribed by a doctor and these are dispensed at a pharmacy (*farmacia*), a minimal local tax is payable which will not be re-imbursed.

For Emergency Service (Fire and Police as well as Ambulance) ring 113

For immediate attention at airports, railway stations or hospitals look for the sign PRONTO SOCCORSO

Holidays, Festivals

Italy has the following national holidays:

New Year's Day
Epiphany
Easter Monday
Liberation Day (25 April)
Labour Day (1 May)
Assumption Day (15 August)
All Saint's Day (1 November)
Christmas (25 and 26 December)

In addition, some towns celebrate the patron saint's day with a holiday. Museums etc also occasionally close on other saint's days.

Most of the major festivals in the area are mentioned in the text, but are gathered here for completeness:

Bergamo, Donizetti Theatre opera season, variable dates — ask at tourist office
Milan, La Scale opera season, December-June
Stresa, Musical Weeks in August and September

Verona, Arena opera season, July-August
Verona, Film Festival, June
In addition courses for visitors are run at:
Arcumeggia — on the History and Techniques of Frescoes, July
Gargnano — on Italian language and culture, summer (information from Universita degli Studi, 7 Via del Perdono, Milano)

Police Registration
All tourists must register with the police within 3 days of entering the country. If you stay at a hotel, campsite etc this registration will be carried out for you.

Post and Telphone Services
Stamps (*francoboli)* are sold at both Post Offices and tobacconists. Post Offices are normally open from 8.30am-2pm, some in large towns remain open until 7 or 8pm. Tobacconists are normally open from 8.30 or 9am-1pm and from 3.30 or 4-7.30 or 8pm.

Phones in phone-booths occasionally take coins — usually 200 lire coins — but these, and all older phones, take *gettone*, a 200 lire token available at post offices, tobacconists, bars and some news stands.

Some bars will allow you to phone, taking a note of the time of the call and charging you when you have finished. This is more convenient, but there may be a bar 'surcharge' and the phone will not have a meter advising you of time or cost.

In larger towns look for the SIP 'shop' where you can phone from a sound-proof booth and a meter will advise you of cost. Again you pay after your call.

The dial codes from Italy are:
Great Britain   00 44
Canada   00 1
USA   00 1

And remember to leave out the first zero of your home country number — eg to dial the Italian Tourist Office in London (01 408 1254) from Italy, dial 00 44 1 408 1254.

Tipping
Tipping rules are similar to those that apply at home.

Voltage
220v ac, 50 Hertz (cycles/sec)

MUSEUMS AND PLACES OF INTEREST

Please note: most museums charge for admission; opening times are subject to slight alteration from year to year.

Around Brescia

Brescia City

Arms Museum
Colle Cidneo
Open: 10am-12noon, 3-7pm Tuesday, Wednesday and Friday; 3-7pm Saturday; 10am-12noon Sunday.
☎ 030 44176

Christian Museum
Via dei Musei
Open: 9am-12noon, 2-5pm daily except Monday.
For information ☎ 030 45052

City Art Gallery
Palazzo Martinengo da Barco
Open: 9am-12noon, 2-5pm Tuesday-Thursday; 9am-12noon Saturday; 2-5pm Sunday.

Natural History Museum
Via Ozanam
Open: 8.30am-12noon, 2-5pm
daily except Monday.
☎ 030 397693

Risorgimento Museum
Colle Cidneo
Open: 9am-12noon, 2-5pm
Wednesday, Thursday and Friday;
2-5pm Saturday; 9am-12noon
Sunday.

Roman Museum
Via dei Musei
Open: 9am-12noon, 2-5pm
Tuesday, Thursday and Friday;
9am-12noon Saturday; 2-5pm
Sunday.
☎ 030 46031

Zoo
Open: 9am-12noon, 2.30-6.30pm
daily except holidays.

Lake Iseo and Val Camonica

Centre for the Study of the Prehistory of Valcamonica
Capo di Ponte
Open: 8am-12.30pm, 2-5pm daily
except Sunday.
☎ 0364 42091

Museum
Cividate Camuno
Open: 9am-2pm weekdays except
Mondays; 9am-1pm Saturdays and
Sundays.
☎ 0364 44301

National Park of Rock Engravings
Capo di Ponte
Open: 9am-1 hour before sunset,

daily except Monday.
☎ 0364 42140

Photographic Collection
Marone
Open: 7-9pm Monday and
Thursday; 3-6pm Wednesday;
5-7pm Saturday.
For information ☎ 030 980209
or 981361

Santa Maria della Neve
Pisogne
Open: 9am-6pm daily.

Tadini Gallery
Lovere
Open: May-August, 3-6pm
Monday-Saturday; 10pm-12noon,
3-6pm Sundays and Holidays;
September-mid-October 2-5pm
Monday-Saturday; 10am-12noon,
2-5pm Sundays and holidays.
☎ 035 960132

Val Trompia

Trebbi Botanical Gardens
119 Via Montini, Mompiano
Open: By request.
☎ 030 395762

Val Sabbia

Museum
Gavardo
Open: March-October, 10am-
12noon, 3-5pm Thursday, Sunday
and holidays only.
☎ 0365 31410

Ruscino Botanical Gardens
Vestone
Open: By request.
☎ 0365 81138 or 0365 81714

Around Varese

Varese City

Baroffio Museum
Sacre Monte
Open: May-September, 10am-12noon, 2.30-5.30pm daily except Monday.
For information ☎ 0332 226040

Observatory
Monte Campo dei Fiori
Guided tours (individuals or parties) must be booked in advance.
☎ 0332 235491 or contact Tourist Information Office, Varese.

Pogliaghi Museum
Sacre Monte
Open: April-September 10am-12noon, 2.30-5.30pm daily except Monday.
For information ☎ 0332 226040

Sacre Monte
For information ☎ 0332 226040

Town Museum
Villa Mirabello
Open: 9.30am-12.30pm, 2-5.30pm, Tuesday-Saturday, 9.30am-12.30pm Sundays. Closed Monday and Holidays.
☎ 0332 281590

Tre Croci
Monte Campo dei Fiori
For information ☎ 0332 284624

Villa Ponti
Biumo
Gardens only 10am-sunset.
For information ☎ 0332 284624

The Varese Lakes

Gliding Club
Calcinate del Pasce
Weather dependent!
For information ☎ 0332 284624.

Museum
Golasecca
Open: 9am-12.30pm, 3-6.30pm daily. ☎ 0332 964032

Pipe Museum
Gavirate
Open: By request at building.
☎ 0332 743334

Solvini Gallery
Cocquio-Trevisago
Open: 4-7pm Wednesday, Saturday and Sunday only.
☎ 0332 602161 or 602152

Villa Ponti
Isolino Virginia
Open: June-September 2.30-6pm Friday, Saturday and Sunday only. Tours available Saturday and Sunday only. Contact Varese Museum or Tourist Office for details.
☎ 0332 284624 or 281590

Valcuvia

Arcummegia
Avoid times when village is crowded (fêtes etc) as parking will be impossible.
For information ☎ 0332 283604 or 650110

Villa Bozzolo
Casalzuigno
Open: June-September 3-7pm, Saturday and Sunday only.
For information ☎ 0332 650110

Valganna

Museum
Ganna
Open: By request at the building.
☎ 0332 719795

Valceresio

Butti Gallery
Viggiu
Open: 9am-12noon, 3-6pm daily
except Monday.
☎ 0332 486106

Museum
Besano
Open: 10am-12noon, 4-6pm daily.
☎ 0332 910268

Museum
Induno Olona
Open: 3-5pm Friday, 10am-
12noon Sunday.
☎ 0332 200000

Villa Cicogna Mozzoni
Bisuschio
Open: April, May and October
9am-12noon, 2-6pm daily; June-
September 9am-12noon, 3-7pm
daily.
☎ 0332 471134

South of Varese

Archaeological Zone
Castelseprio
Open: At any reasonable time.
☎ 0332 825386

Museum/Church Complex
Castiglione Olona
Open: Winter 2.30-5pm Tuesday-
Friday, 10am-12noon, 2.30-
5.30pm Saturday and Sunday.
Closed Monday. Summer 10am-
12.30pm, 3-6pm Tuesday-Sunday.
Closed Monday.

Transport Museum
Malnate
Open: By request at the building.
☎ 0332 425390

Bergamo and the Surrounding Valleys

Bergamo City

Accademia Carrera
Piazza dell' Accademia
Open: 9.30am-12.30pm, 2.30-
5.30pm daily except Tuesdays and
Holidays.
☎ 035 399426

Archaeology Museum
Piazza Cittadella
Open: 9am-12noon, 3-5.30pm
Wednesday, Thursday and Friday;
3-6pm Saturday and Sunday.
Closed Mondays and holidays.
☎ 035 242839

Botanical Gardens
Porta San Alessandro
Open: April 2-5.30pm Saturday,
Sunday and Monday only; May-
June 3-7pm Saturday, Sunday and
Monday; 9.30am-12noon Wednes-
day, Thursday and Friday.
For information ☎ 035 242226 or
232730

Campanile
Piazza Vecchia
Open: 10am-12.30pm, 3-6.30pm
daily except Monday.
For information ☎ 035 242226 or
232730

Church of Santa Maria Maggiore
Piazza Duomo
Open: 7.30am-12.30pm,
3-6.30pm daily (7pm April-
October). ☎ 035 219955

Colleoni Chapel
Piazza Duomo
Open: 9am-12noon, 3-6pm daily
☎ 035 219955

Diocesan Museum
3 Via Donizetti
Open: By request.
☎ 035 211001

Donizetti Museum
9 Via Are
Open: 8.30am-12noon, 2-5pm
weekdays only. Closed on
holidays.
☎ 035 237374

Donizetti's Birthplace
14 Via Borgo Canale
Open: June-September 10am-
12noon, 3-6pm Saturday and
Sunday only. At other times by
request.
☎ 035 247116

Natural History Museum
Piazza Cittadella
Open: 9am-12noon, 2-5pm daily
except Mondays and holidays.
☎ 035 233513

Risorgimento Museum
Rocca
Open: May-September 9am-
12noon, 3-6pm Sunday, Monday,
Wednesday and Thursday; 9am-
12noon Saturday.
October-March 10am-12noon,
3-5pm Sunday, Monday and
Wednesday; 10am-12noon
Saturday. Closed on holidays
For information ☎ 035 242226 or
232730

Sotto il Monte
Near Bergamo
Open: 8am-12noon, 2-7pm daily.
For information ☎ 035 791195 or
791277

Val Seriana

Astronomical Clock
Clusone
Open: By request at the Tourist
Office.
☎ 0346 21113

Cascata del Serio
One of Europe's highest waterfalls,
hydro-electric station permitting.
Ask at Tourist Office for times
☎ 035 242226 or 232730

Fantoni Foundation
Rovetta
Open: Mid-May-mid-October
3-5pm daily.
☎ 0346 72944

Funivia
Albino to Selvino
For information ☎ 035 222107

Museums
Gandino
Open: By request
☎ 035 745425

Oratorio dei Disciplini
Clusone
Open: By request at the Tourist
Office.
☎ 0346 21113

Val Brembana

Church of San Tome
Almenno San Bartolomeo
Open: 10am-12noon, 3-5pm daily
except Friday.
☎ 035 640241

Funivia
San Pellegrino Terme
For information
☎ 0345 21020

Grotte delle Meraviglie
Sedrina
Open: Certain Sundays from June
to September 2.30-6.30pm.
☎ 035 235114 or 246069

Grotte del Sogne
San Pellegrino Terme
Open: June-September 8am-
12noon, 2-6pm daily.
For information ☎ 0345 21020

Museum
Zogna
Open: 9am-12noon, 2-5pm daily
except Monday.
☎ 0345 91473

Sondrio Town

Valley Museum
Villa Quadrio
Via 4 Novembre
Open: 9am-12noon, 2.30-5pm
Monday to Friday. Closed at
weekends.
☎ 0342 213305

Valtellina

Diocesan Museum
Ponte in Valtellina
Attached to parish church of San
Maurizio. Entry by request.
☎ 0342 482158

Ethnography Museum
Ponte in Valtellina
Attached to school in Via Ginnasio.
Entry by request.
☎ 0342 482222

Museum
Aprica
Open: By request. ☎ 0342 746112

Museum
Chiesa Valmalenco
Open: July and August 5pm-7pm

daily; all other months 4.30-
6.30pm Saturday only.
☎ 0342 451150

Museum
Teglio
Open: May-September 9am-1pm,
2.30-5.30pm daily; October-April
9am-2pm daily.
☎ 0342 780268

Museum
Tirano
Open: June-September 10am-
12noon, 3-7pm daily; October-May
3-5pm Saturday; 10am-12noon
Sunday.
☎ 0342 701181
or 701349

Natural History Museum
Morbegno
Open: May-October 3.30-5.30pm
Tuesday, Thursday, Saturday and
Sunday only; November-April
3-6pm Tuesday, Thursday,
Saturday and Sunday only.
☎ 0342 602451

Lake Como

Como City

Baradello Castle
9am-12noon, 2-6pm Monday,
Thursday and holidays.
☎ 031 592805
or 557849

Civic Museum
Palazzo Giovio and Palazzo
Oliginati
Via Vittorio Emanuele II
Open: 9.30am-12noon, 2-5pm
Tuesday-Saturday; 9.15am-
12.15pm Sunday.
Closed Monday and holidays.
☎ 031 271343

Funivia to Brunate
For information ☎ 031 265592

Temple Sacrarium
Via per Brunate
Open: 2-6pm Sunday only.
☎ 031 277407

Temple Voltiano
Open: April-September 10am-
12noon, 3-6pm daily except
Monday; October-March 10am-
12noon, 2-4pm daily except
Monday.
☎ 031 559976

Villa Olmo
Park and Gardens open: 8am-6pm
daily except holidays. Villa:
sometimes closed for conferences.
☎ 031 557404

The Western Shore

Boat Museum
Pianello Lario
Open: 2.30-6.30pm Saturday;
10.30am-12.30pm, 2.30-6.30pm
Sunday.
☎ 0344 87235 or 87267

Funivia
Argegno to Pigra
For information ☎ 031 265592

Isola Comacina
For information ☎ 031 265592

Palazzo Gallio
Gravedona
Open: 9.30am-12.30pm, 3-5.30pm
weekdays only.
For information ☎ 031 265592

Villa Carlotta
Tremezzo
Open: March-October 9-11.30am,
2-4.30pm daily, April-September
9am-6pm daily.
☎ 0344 40405

**Villa del Balbianello
(Il Balbianello)**
Lenno
Open: Easter-mid-October 10am-
12noon, 4-6pm Tuesday only.
Can only be reached by boat from
Lenno or Campo.
☎ 0344 55120

Villa Passalacqua
Moltrasio
Open: 9am-12noon, 3-6pm
Thursday only.
☎ 031 290541 or 290373

The Eastern Shore

Abbey of Piona
For information ☎ 031 265592

Funivia
Versasio, near Lecco, to Piani d'
Erna
For information ☎ 031 265592

Museum
Esino Lario
Open: May-September 9am-
12noon, 3-7pm Saturday and
Sunday.
For information ☎ 0341 860111

Museum (Palazzo Belgioiaso)
Lecco
Open: 10am-12.30pm, 2.30-
5.30pm daily except Monday.
☎ 0341 481249 or 481247

Museum
Primaluna
Open: July and August only 4.30-
6.30pm Saturday and Sunday
only.
☎ 0341 980253

Ornithological Museum
Varenna
Open: June-mid-September 10am-
12noon, 3.30-6pm weekdays;
10am-12noon Saturday and

Sunday, mid-September-May
3-5pm Thursday and Saturday
only.
For information ☎ 031 265592

Orrido
Bellano
Open: Easter-September 9.30am-
12.30pm, 1.30-6pm daily except
Wednesday.
NB: If there has been torrential rain
the gorge may be closed as the
water rises above the ropeways.
For information ☎ 031 265592

Villa Cipressi
Varenna
Open: June-September 4-7pm
weekdays only (10am-12noon,
4-7pm Saturday and Sunday as
well in July and August).
☎ 0341 830113

Villa Manzoni
Lecco
Open: 10am-12.30pm, 2.30-
5.30pm daily except Monday
(10am-1pm holidays).
☎ 0341 481249 or 481247

Villa Monastero
Varenna
Open: June, July, August 9am-
12noon, 2-7pm daily, April,
September, October 9am-12noon,
2-5pm daily.
☎ 0341 830139 or 830179

The Southern Shore

Buco dei Carpi (Carp Hole)
Lezzeno
For information ☎ 031 265592

Museum of Silk
Garlate
Open: By appointment.
☎ 0341 681306

Orrido
Nesso
For information ☎ 031 265592

Town Museum
Erba
Open: 9.30am-12noon daily;
closed Sunday and Monday.
☎ 031 643133 or 642092

Villa Melzi d'Eryl
Bellagio
Open: Gardens and villa chapel
only 9am-6.30pm daily.
☎ 031 950318

Villa Serbelloni
Bellagio
Open: 10am-4pm daily except
Monday. ☎ 031 950204

Lake Garda

Southern Shore

Castle
Sirmione
Open: April-September 9am-6pm
daily (9am-1pm holidays);
October-March 9am-1pm daily.
☎ 030 916468

Grotte di Catullo
Sirmione
Open: 9am-dusk daily except
Mondays and holidays.
☎ 030 916157

Museum
Desenzano del Garda
Open: 10am-5pm daily except
Monday.
For information ☎ 030 9144209 or
9141510

Museum
Lonato
Open: June-September 10-
11.30am, 3-5pm daily. At other
times by request.
☎ 030 9130060

Ossuary Chapel
Solferino
Open: June-August 8.30am-1pm,
2-7pm.
For information ☎ 030 45052

Roman Villa
Desenzano del Garda
Open: March-October 9am-5pm
daily except Monday; November-
February 9am-4pm daily except
Monday.
For information ☎ 030 9144209 or
9141510

San Martino della Battaglia
and Solferino
Tower, San Martino
Museum, San Martino
Museum, Solferino
Rocca, Solferino
Open: June-August, October-
December 9.30am-12.30pm, 1.30-
7pm daily except Tuesday; March,
April 9am-1pm, 2-5pm daily,
except Tuesday; May, September
8.30am-1pm, 2-7pm daily except
Tuesday.
For information ☎ 030 45052

Eastern Shore

Caneva Aquatic Sports Park
Near Peschiera
Open: Times vary annually, but are
roughly mid-May-end of June, and
September 10am-8pm daily; July,
August 10am-11pm daily.
☎ 045 7590633

Castle
Torri del Benaco
Open: May-September 9am-
12.30pm, 4.30-8pm daily;
October-March 9am-12.30pm,
3-5pm daily.
For information
☎ 045 626120

Castle/Museum
Malcesine
Open: May-September 9am-8pm
daily; October-March 9am-1pm,
3-6pm Saturday and Sunday only.
☎ 045 7400837

Funivia
Malcesine to Monte Baldo
For information ☎ 045 7400024

Gardaland
Near Peschiera
Open: April-September 9.30am-
sunset daily; *but* mid-July-end of
August 9.30am-midnight; March,
October 9.30am-sunset Saturday
and Sunday only.
☎ 045 7551397 or 7551764

Garda Safari Park
Pastrengo
Open: March-October 9am-6pm
daily; November-February 10am-
4pm.
☎ 045 26675

Museum
Garda
Opening times under review.
For information ☎ 045 7255194

Palazzo dei Capitani
Malcesine
Open: 8am-8pm daily.
☎ 045 7400024 or 7400346

Villa Sigurta
Near Peschiera
Open: March-November 9am-
sunset Thursday, Saturday,
Sunday and holidays.
☎ 045 7950203

Northern and Western Shore

Castle
Riva del Garda
Open: 8.30am-12noon, 2.30-
6.30pm daily except Monday.
For information ☎ 0464 514444

Funivia
Riva to Bastione
For information ☎ 0464 514444

Hruska Botanical Gardens
Gardone Riviera
Open: March-October 8.30am-
dusk daily.
For information ☎ 0365 20347

Museum
Manerba del Garda
Open: May-September 10am-
12noon, 4-6pm daily; October-April
3-5pm Saturday; 10am-12noon,
3-5pm Sunday.
☎ 0365 53007

Museum
Molina di Ledro
Open: 9am-12noon, 1-6pm daily
except Monday.
For information ☎ 0464 514444

Museum
Salo
Open: June-September 10am-
12noon, 5-7pm daily except
Monday; October-May 10am-
12noon, 4-6pm Saturday and
Sunday only.
☎ 0365 21423

Villa Bettoni
Bogliaco
Open: By request during the
working day.
For information ☎ 0365 71222

Villa Feltrinelli
Near Gargnano
Permission to view may be
granted. Ask at Tourist Office
(☎ 0365 71222)

Vittoriale degli Italiani
Gardone Riviera
Open: 9am-12.30pm, 2-5.30pm

(later in summer) daily. On
Mondays the d'Annunzio Museum
is closed.
☎ 0365 20130

Lake Lugano

Swiss Lugano

Note: not all of the following places
are mentioned in the text, but they
are included here for
completeness.

Archives Museum
Strada di Gondria, Lugano City
Open: 10am-12noon, 2.30-5.30pm
weekdays only.
☎ 091 510271

Botanical Park
Carona
Open all year at any reasonable
time.

Casa Tencalla
Bissone
Open: Easter-October 10.30am-
12noon, 2-5pm daily except
Saturday.
☎ 091 687342

**Cog Railway to Monte
Generoso**
For information ☎ 091 214664

Customs Museum
Gandria
Open: Easter-October
2.30-5.30pm daily. ☎ 091 239843

Funivia
Lugano to Monte San Salvatore
For information ☎ 091 214664

Funivia
Melide to Carona
For information ☎ 091 214664

Funivia to Monte Bre
For information
☎ 091 214664

Gallery
Mendrisio
Open: 2-6pm Wednesday,
Saturday and Sunday.
☎ 091 463655

Gallery Ziist
Rancate
Open: March-November 9.30am-
12noon, 2-5pm daily, except
Monday.
☎ 091 464565

Museum
Meride
Open: 8am-6pm daily.
☎ 091 463780

Museum
Stabio
Open: 2-5pm Tuesday, Thursday,
Saturday and Sunday.
☎ 091 471418

Natural History Museum
Via Cattaneo, Lugano City
Open: 9am-12noon, 2-5pm daily
except Sunday and Monday.
☎ 091 237827

Scherrer Park
Morcote
Open: March-October 9am-5pm
daily (guided tours on Tuesday
and Thursday).
☎ 091 692125

Swissminiatur
Melide
Open: March-October 8am-6pm
daily (8am-10pm in July and
August).
☎ 091 687951

Vela Museum
Ligornetto
Open: March-November 9am-
12noon, 2-5pm daily except
Monday. ☎ 091 472850

Villa Ciani
City Park, Lugano City
Open: 10am-12noon, 2-5pm daily
except Monday. ☎ 091 236162

Villa Favorita
Castagnola, Lugano City
Open: Good Friday-2nd Sunday in
October 10am-12noon, 2-5pm
Friday and Saturday, 2-5pm,
Sunday. ☎ 091 521741

Wilhelm Schmid Museum
Bre
Open: Easter-mid-October 10am-
12noon, 3-5pm daily except
Monday.
For information ☎ 091 214664

Italian Lugano

Casino
Campione d'Italia
Restaurant opens from 12noon,
gaming rooms open from 3pm.
☎ 091 687926

Grotte di Rescia
Claino-Osteno
Open: 2-6pm Saturday and
Sunday only.
Those camping at 'Campeggia
Rescia' may ask for permission to
enter at any time. Others may
☎ 0344 65240

Museum
Cavargna
Open: 2-5pm Sunday. At other
times by request.
☎ 0344 63162

Museum
Ponna d'Intelvi Superiore
Open: By request.
☎ 031 269317

Museum
Scaria
Open: July-mid-September 3-5pm
daily.
☎ 031 840400

Museum
Valsolda
In preparation
For information
☎ 031 265592

Orrido
Claino-Osteno
For information ☎ 031 840143

Lake Maggiore

The Piemonte Shore

Alpine Garden
Alpino
Open: July-September 9am-
12.30pm, 2-6pm daily except
Monday.
For information ☎ 0323 30150

Chimney Sweep's Museum
Santa Maria Maggiore
In course of re-construction.
For information ☎ 0321 27238

Funivia
Stresa to Il Mottarone
☎ 0323 30295

Isola Bella
Stresa
Open: March-October 9am-
12noon, 1.30-5.30pm daily.
☎ 0323 30557
5-minute boat trip from Stresa
commencing 6.35am, April-
September. Last boat leaves Bella
7pm, but 7.35pm from 1 June
onwards.

Isola Madre
Stresa/Verbania
Open: March-October 9am-
12noon, 1.30-5.30pm daily.
☎ 0323 31261
Half-hour boat trip from Stresa
commencing 7.20am, April-
September. Last boat leaves
Madre at 6.40pm.

Isola Pescatori
Stresa
10-minute boat trip from Stresa
commencing 6.35am, April-
September. Last boat leaves
Pescatori 6.55pm, but 7.30pm
from 1 June onwards.

La Torbiera Safari Park
Agrate Conturbia
Open: Spring/summer 10am-7pm
daily; Autumn 10am-5pm daily;
Winter closed.
☎ 0322 802136

Malpaga Castle
Cannero Riviera
Not open to the public, but boat
trips to view can be made from
Cannero.

Museum
Arona
Open: By request.
Ask at Palazzo de Filippi or
☎ 0322 2577

Museum
Cannobio
Open: By request.
☎ 0323 7232

Museum
Craveggia
Open: By request.
☎ 0324 94521

Museum
Gurro
Open: By request.
☎ 0323 76100

Museum
Lesa
Open: July and August only. Hours to be announced. Ask at local Tourist Office, or ☎ 0323 30150 for information.

Museum
Mergozzo
Open: By request.
☎ 0323 80247
or 0323 80291

Museum
Sanctuario, Re
Open: By request at the church or ☎ 0324 97046

Paesaggio (Landscape) Museum
Pallanza-Verbania
Open: 9am-12noon, 3-5pm daily except Monday.
☎ 0323 502418

Statue of San Carlo Borromeo
Arona
Open: April-October 8.30am-12.30pm, 2-7pm daily; November-March 8.30am-12.30pm, 2-6pm daily.
☎ 0322 3601 for information.

Umbrella Museum
Gignese
Open: April-September 10am-12noon, 3-5pm daily.
☎ 0323 20444 or 20067

Villa Pallavicino
Stresa
Open: March-October 9am-6pm daily.
☎ 0323 32407

Villa Taranto
Pallanza-Verbania
Open: April-October 8.30am-sunset daily.
Gardens only open to public.
☎ 0323 506667

Zoo Safari del Lago Maggiore
Pombia
Open: April-September 10am-7pm daily; October-March 10am-dusk daily except Tuesday and Friday.
☎ 0321 95126 or 956431

The Lombardian Shore

Borromeo Castle
Angera
Open: 9.30am-12.30pm, 2-6pm daily (3-7pm in July/August).
☎ 0332 931300

Ceramics Museum
Cerro del Lago Maggiore
Open: 2.30-6pm Tuesday, Wednesday, Thursday (3.30-7pm July/August). Closed Monday.
☎ 0332 666530

Funivia
Laveno to Sasso del Ferro
☎ 0332 668012

Museum
Angera
Open: 3-5pm Monday, Thursday and Saturday.
At other times by request.
☎ 0332 931133

Museum
Luino
Open: 2.30-6pm Wednesday, 2-6pm Saturday. ☎ 0332 532057

Museum
Sesto Calende
Open: 8.30am-12.30pm, 2.30-6.30pm daily except Monday (10am-12noon, 3-6pm on holidays)
☎ 0332 922489

Sanctuary of Santa Caterina del Sasso
Near Reno
Open: 8.30am-12noon, 3-6pm daily.
☎ 0332 647172

Studio of Sergio Tapia Radic
177 Via Labiena, Laveno
Open: Shop hours.
☎ 0332 666377

Lake Orta

Calderara Collection
Vicciago (near Ameno)
Open: May-mid-October 10am-12noon, 3-6pm daily except Monday.
☎ 0322 99192

Isola San Giulio
Boat trips available during daylight hours.
For information
☎ 0322 905501

Museum of Musical Instruments
Quarna Sotto
Open: August only daily 4-7pm. At other times by request.
☎ 0323 826141
or 0323 826264

Sacre Monte di Orta
Orta San Giulio
For information   ☎ 0322 905501

Milan

Ambrosiana Art Gallery
Piazza Pio XI
Open: 9.30am-5pm daily except Saturday. Closed on certain days in August. ☎ 02 800146

Aquarium
2 Viale Gadio
Open: 9am-12noon, 2-5pm daily except Monday.
☎ 02 872847

Archaeological Museum
15 Corso Magenta
Open: 9.30am-12.15pm, 2.30-5.30pm daily except Tuesday.
☎ 02 806598

Basilica of San Ambrogio
Piazza San Ambrogio
Open: 10am-12noon, 3-5pm Monday and Wednesday-Saturday, 3-5pm Sunday and holidays. Closed Tuesdays and all of August.
☎ 02 872059

Basilica of San Eustorgio
Piazza San Eustorgio
Open: 9am-12noon, 3.30-6.30pm daily except Wednesday.

Brera Gallery
28 Via Brera
Open: 9am-2pm Tuesday-Saturday, closed Monday, 9am-1pm Sunday (open holiday Mondays, but then closed on the Tuesday).
☎ 02 808387

Church of San Marco
Piazza San Marco
Hours to be announced. (See Tourist Office).
☎ 02 809662

Church of San Maurizio
15 Corso Magenta
Open: 9.30am-12noon, 3-6pm Wednesday only.

Church of Santa Maria della Passione
2 Via Vincenzo Bellini
Open: 10am-12noon, 3-5.30pm daily; (Sunday: afternoon only)

Cinema Museum
Palazzo Dugnani
(2 Via Manin)
Open: 9.30am-12.15pm, 2.30-
5.30pm daily except Monday (open
holiday Mondays).
☎ 02 6554977

Duomo Museum
Palazzo Reale
Open: 9.30am-12.30pm , 3-6pm
daily except Monday (open holiday
Mondays). ☎ 02 860358

Francesco Messina Museum
10 Via San Sisto
Open: 9.30am-12.15pm, 2.30-
5.30pm, Tuesday, Thursday,
Saturday and Sunday only.
☎ 02 871036

Leonardo's *Last Supper*
Piazza delle Grazie
Leonardo da Vinci's famous
fresco.
Open: 9.30am-1.30pm, 2-6.30pm
Tuesday-Friday; 9.30am-1.30pm
Saturday, Sunday, Monday.
☎ 02 4987588

Manzoni Museum
1 Via Morone
Open: 9am-12noon, 2-4pm
Tuesday-Friday and holidays.
☎ 02 871019

Museum of Contemporary Art
Palazzo Reale
Open: 9.30am-12.30pm, 2.30-
5.20pm daily except Monday (open
holiday Mondays).
☎ 02 6208 ext 3943

Museum of Contemporary History
6 Via San Andrea
Open: 9.30am-12.15pm, 2.30-
5.30pm daily except Monday
(open holiday Mondays).
☎ 02 706245

Museum of Modern Art
16 Via Palestro
Open: 9.30am-12noon, 2.30-
5.30pm daily except Tuesday.
☎ 02 6236, ext 3943

Museum of Naval Education
21 Via San Vittore
Open: 9.30am-12.15pm, 2.30-
5.30pm daily except Monday (open
holiday Mondays).
☎ 02 487270

Museum of Science and Technology
21 Via San Vittore
Open: 9am-5pm daily except
Monday (open holiday Mondays).
☎ 02 462709

Natural History Museum
55 Corso Venezia
Open: 9.30am-12.30pm, 2.30-
5.30pm daily except Monday.
☎ 02 6208, ext 5405

Planetarium
57 Corso Venezia
Lectures (in Italian) at 9am on
Tuesdays and Thursdays, 3pm
and 4.30pm on Saturdays and
Sundays.
Schools by appointment.
☎ 02 225181

Poldi Pezzoli Gallery
12 Via Manzoni
Open: 9.30am-12.30pm, 2.30-
5.30pm daily except Monday.
(Sunday: afternoon only, Tuesday
and Wednesday: evening closing
at 6pm)
☎ 02 794889

Risorgimento Museum
23 Via Borgonuovo
Open: 9.30am-12.15pm, 2.30-
5.30pm daily except Monday.
(open holiday Mondays).
☎ 02 803549

Scala Museum
Piazza della Scala
Open: 9am-12noon, 2-6pm daily;
9.30am-12noon, 2.30-6pm
holidays.
☎ 02 807041

Sforzesco Castle
Open: 9.30am-12.15pm, 2.30-
5.30pm daily except Monday (open
holiday Mondays).
☎ 02 6236, ext 3963 or 3940

Siloteca Cormio
21 Via San Vittore
Open: 9am-5pm daily except
Monday (open holiday Mondays).
☎ 02 434154

Zoo, Public Gardens
Open: November-February
8.30am-4.30pm Monday-Saturday,
8.30am-5.30pm Sundays and
holidays.
March-October 8.30am-7pm
Monday-Saturday, 8.30am-7.30pm
Sundays and holidays.
☎ 02 6554365

Verona

Archaeological Museum and Roman Theatre
Via San Chiara
Open: May-September 8.30am-
7pm daily except Monday;
October-March 8.30am-1.30pm
daily except Monday.
☎ 045 8000360
or 33974

Arena
Piazza Bra
Open: May-September 8.30-
6.30pm daily except Monday;
October-April 8.30am-5.30pm daily
except Monday.
☎ 045 23204

Basilica of San Zeno Maggiore
Piazza San Zeno
Open: 7am-12.30pm, 3.30-6.30pm
daily.

Chapter Library
21 Piazza del Duomo
9.30am-12noon Monday, Tuesday,
Wednesday and Friday only.
Closed August and September.
☎ 045 596516

Church of Santa Anastasia
Corso Santa Anastasia
Open: 7am-12noon, 3-5pm daily .

City Museum
Castelvecchio
Open: 8.30am-7pm daily except
Monday.
☎ 045 28812 or 594734

City Zoo
Via Citta di Nimes
Open: 8.30am-sunset.
☎ 045 28656 or 38590

Guisti Gardens
2 Via Giardino Giusti
Open: May-September 9am-8pm
daily; October-April 9am-6pm.
☎ 045 38029

Juliet's House
Via Cappello
Open: 8.30am-7pm daily except
Monday.
☎ 045 38303

Juliet's Tomb
Via del Pontiere
Open: 8.30am-7pm daily except
Monday.
☎ 045 25361

Museo Lapidario Maffeiano
Via Roma
Open: 8.30am-7pm daily except
Monday.
☎ 045 590087

Natural History Museum
Palazzo Pompei
Open: 9am-7pm daily except
Friday.
☎ 045 21987

Risorgimento Museum and Gallery of Modern Art
Via Emilei
Open: 8.30am-7pm daily except
Monday.
☎ 045 21903

Tombs of the Scaligeri
Piazza dei Signori
Closed for restoration, though
visible from the street. Ask at
Tourist Office for details.
☎ 045 8000065

Torre dei Lamberti
Piazza delle Erbe
Open: May-September 8.30am-
1.30pm daily except Monday.
☎ 045 32726

PHONE NUMBERS FOR LAKE STEAMERS

Como 031 273324 or 260234
Garda 030 9141321
Iseo 035 971483
Lugano 091 515223
Maggiore 0322 46651 or 2352
(Arona)
0323 30393 (Stresa)
0323 42321 or 503220 (Verbania)
Orta 0322 844862

SPORTS

Water Sports
Apart from Lakes Varese and
Comabbio which are closed to
swimmers because of pollution,
swimming is allowed in all the
lakes and each town (indeed
virtually all camp or holiday sites)
is provided with its own beach.
Swimming is, in general, very safe,
with gently sloping — though
frequently stony — lake bottoms.
There are places where the lake's
are shelved, but these are easy to
spot, the general lie of the fore-
shore land giving the clue. If there
are steep cliffs, take care. The lack
of tides and currents adds to the
safety, the chief hazard the
swimmer faces is the wash from a
ferry or the occasional trainee
windsurfer.

The lakes are *the* place to
learn or practice board sailing. The
dependable winds, normally
blowing from the north in the
mornings, and from the south in
the afternoons and evenings, and
the combination of warm sun and
warm water, do much to encour-
age the beginner, and to give the
expert the opportunity to display
his skills. On all the lakes the
winds are stronger and more
dependable the further north the
sailor travels.

All the above comments on
windsurfing apply equally well to
dinghy or yacht sailors. All major
villages and many hotel and camp
sites have public launch points and
berthing arrangements. If in doubt,
contact the local Tourist Office.

Walking
The lake foreshores are more for
strolling than walking, but the
ridges that confine the lakes and
the high valleys that link them,
offer enormous potential for the
more committed walker. Though
some of the peaks rise to 8,000ft
or more (above about 2,500m)
there are many cableways offering

easy access to high ridges, and the mountains themselves are, in the main, pre-Alpine, that is, rounded and grassed, rather than rocky and angular.

The Lombardy Tourist Authority produce an excellent leaflet 'Trekking in Lombardy' giving details of superb 7-day treks in the region's uplands. In the area covered by this book they include Valsassina to the east of Lake Como; Valmasino and Valmalenco, near Sondrio; the upper reaches of Val Seriana, north of Bergamo; and the upper part of Val Camonica, north of Brescia and Lake Iseo. Each of the itineraries uses mountain huts or small hotels for sleeping, and offers a daily walk of around 5 hours. Even those who feel that to devote a full week to such a tour is to give too much time, should consider including a one day walk in their holiday; some of the upland scenery is magnificent, the views to the lakes quite superb and there is always the chance of seeing some of the unusual alpine animals.

As walking increases in popularity more towns are recognising the enormous potential that the ridges which form their back gardens offer to complement the lakeside front gardens. Many places now have waymarked paths — the Tremosine/Tignale area above the western shore of Lake Garda being the finest example — that offer short, half-day, walks. Those wanting a greater freedom, but not wanting to take to the mountains, should consider the longer trail which is waymarked from Cernobbio to Sorico, staying above Lake Como's western shore

at all times and visiting Val d'Intelvi. The walk is usually accomplished in 4 days, but any section, Cernobbio to San Fedele, San Fedele to Grandola ed Uniti, Grandola to Garzeno, and Garzeno to Sorico, is worthwhile.

As a complete change, there is a waymarked geological trail that traverses the interesting section of the High Brianza near Canzo, to the south of Lake Como.

Winter Sports

Obviously these are limited to the upland area, and in the main have limited facilities when compared to the internationally famous resorts such as Bormio. They do offer a very different holiday however, quieter, less bustling, and many summer tourists book hotels for a winter return. The major resort within the area covered by the book is Aprica, near Sondrio, which has excellent facilities and snow, and is developing into a major resort.

Hunting Fishing

Italy is one of the few European countries which still has a strong hunting tradition, a tradition frequently at odds with Europe's new ecological movement. Details on seasons, licences etc can be obtained at the local tourist offices.

Both the lakes and the rivers that feed them offer considerable scope for the fishermen. Again details on times, licences etc are obtainable at the tourist offices.

Golf

There are golf courses at Gignese, Premeno, Ascona (Switzerland), Luvinate, in the vicinity of Lakes Orta and Maggiore, and near the city of Varese.

Pellio d'Intelvi, Menaggio, Annone di Brianza and Cassina Rizzardi serve Lake Como. Grumello di Monte is near Lake Iseo, and Semmacampagna lies to the east of the southern tip of Lake Garda.

Horse Riding

Horses are available for hire or trek at: Oleggio, Castello, Lossone (Switzerland), Mesenzana, Marchirolo, Ghirla, Caravate, Brenno Useria, Cantello, Varese, Bodio. Cargenno and Angera near Lakes Orta, Maggiore and Lugano.

At Grandate ed Uniti, Magriglio, Canzo, Poncia and Alzate, Brianze, near Lake Como.

At Boario Terme, near Lake Iseo, and at Lonato, Desenzano, Manerba and Padenghe near Lake Garda.

Swimming Pools

Public pools are available at: Meina, Lesa, Baveno, Verbania Pallanza, Luino, Marchirolo, Besozzo, Comerio, Induno Olona, Castiglione Olona, Varese, Azzate, and Ispra near Lakes Orta, Maggiore and Lugano.

At Como, Cernobbio and Lecco near Lake Como, at Iseo, Crone (near Idro) and Collio near Brescia and at Cisano, Salo, Manerba and Padenghe near Lake Garda.

THE ITALIAN LANGUAGE

Italian is a straightforward language, with each letter being pronounced, and always being pronounced in the same way.

There are differences in pronunication from English however:

c before *e* and *i* is pronounced *ch*, eg *dolce* - dole chay, *cinque* - chin kway
elsewhere *c* is pronounced *k*
ch is pronounced *k*
g before *e* and *i* is pronounced *j*
elsewhere *g* is hard
gh is pronounced as a hard *g*
gl is pronounced *ly*
gn is pronounced *ne*
h is silent
sc before *e* and *i* is pronounced *sh*
elsewhere *sc* is pronounced *sk*
z and *zz* are pronounced *ts*, though occasionally as *ds*

Si — Yes
No — No
Per piacere or per favore — Please
Grazie — Thank you
Prego — You're welcome, OK
Va bene — That's alright
Buongiorno — Good morning/ afternoon
Buona Sera — Good evening
Buona Notte — Good night
Dov'e. . .? — Where is. . .?
Quando? — When?
Che cosa? — What?
Quanta costa? — How much?
Parla inglese? — Do you speak English?
Non capisco — I do not understand
Possa avere? — Can I have?
Puo dirmi? — Can you tell me?
Vorrei — I would like

aperto — open
chiuso — closed
caldo — hot
freddo — cold
grande — big
piccolo — small

buono — good
cattivo — bad
cambio — currency exchange

zero — 0
uno — 1
due — 2
tre — 3
quattro — 4
cinque — 5
sei — 6
sette — 7
otto — 8
nove — 9
dieci — 10

cento — 100
mille — 1,000
   but
duemila — 2,000
cinquemila — 5,000
   etc
primo — 1st
secondo — 2nd
terzo — 3rd

Domenica — Sunday
Lunedi — Monday
Martedi — Tuesday
Mercoledi — Wednesday
Giovedi — Thursday
Venerdi — Friday
Sabato — Saturday

Gran Bretagna — Great Britain
Canada — Canada
Stati Unita — United States
inglese — British
canadese — Canadian
americano — American

In the Hotel
una camera — a room
due, tre camera — two, three
   rooms
con bagno — with bathroom
con doccia — with shower
con gabinetto — with toilet

giorni — days
una settimana — one week
la colazione — breakfast

Motoring
Accendere i fari in Galleria — Use
   headlights in tunnel
Accostore a destra (sinistra) —
Keep right (left)
Avanti — Walk (seen at pedestrian
   lights)
Divieto di Sosta or Sosta Vietata
   — No parking
Entrata — Entrance
Lavori in Corso — Road works
   ahead (literally workmen in the
   road)
Pericolo — Danger
Polizia Stradale — Highway police
Rallentare — Reduce speed
Senso Unico — One way
Senso Vietato — No entry
Sosta Autorizzata — Parking
   allowed (followed by times)
Uscita — Exit
Vicolo Cicco — No through road
Zona Pedonale — Pedestrian zone

USEFUL ADDRESSES

Consulates

Great Britain
7 Via San Paolo
Milan
Open: 9am-12noon, 2.30-4.30pm
daily except Saturday.
☎ 02 803442 (02 862490 at nights
and during holidays)

United States of America
32 Piazza Repubblica
Milan
Open: 9am-12noon, 2-4pm daily
except Saturday.
☎ 02 652841/5

Canada
19 Via V Pisani
Milan
Open: 8.45am-12.30pm, 1.30-
5.15pm daily except Saturday.
☎ 02 657045 (02 654600 at night
and during holidays)

ENIT (Italian Tourist) Offices

Great Britain
1 Princes Street
London W1R 8AY
☎ 01 408 1254

USA
500 North Michigan Avenue
Chicago 1
Illinois
☎ 0312 6440990

Suite 1565
630 Fifth Avenue
New York
NY
☎ 0212 245 4961/4

Suite 801
360 Post Street
San Francisco
☎ 0415 392 6206/7

also, c/o Alitalia at:

Suite 530
223 Permieter Center-Parkway
Atlanta
Georgia
☎ 0404 2239770

8350 Central Expressway
Dallas
Texas
☎ 0214 6928761

Canada
Store 56
Plaza 3, Place Ville Marie
Montreal
Quebec
☎ 0514 8667667/9

also, c/o Alitalia at:

120 Adelaide Street West
Toronto
☎ 0416 3631348

Tourist Offices in Italy

Most of the lakeside towns and the
majority of the larger mountain
villages have tourist/accommoda-
tion offices.
  The main provincial (APT)
offices are always found in the
provincial capitals, and these are
listed below.

PIEMONTE
The main provincial office close to
Lakes Orta and Maggiore is at:

Novara
2 Corso Cavour
☎ 0321 27238

though for information on the
sections of Lakes Orta and
Maggiore that lie in Piemonte it is
better to contact offices at:

Orta San Guilio
26 Piazza Motta
☎ 0322 90355

Stresa
3 Piazzale Europa
☎ 0323 30150

LOMBARDY
The regional office for Lombardian
tourism is at:

Milan
Via Marconi
Beside the cathedral (the Duomo)
☎ 02 809662

The Lombardian provincial offices
are at:

Bergamo
4 Via Vittorio Emanuele
☎ 035 242226

Brescia
36 Corso Zanardelli
☎ 030 45052

Como
17 Piazza Cavour
☎ 031 269491/262091

Sondrio
28 Piazza Garibaldi
☎ 0342 214461

Varese
5 Piazza Monte Grappa
☎ 0332 283604/284454

VENETO
The main provincial Veneto office
close to Lake Garda is at:

Verona
20 Via Carmelitani Scalzi
☎ 045 8000065

though for Lake Garda itself it is
advisable to contact the local
village offices, chief of which is at

Malcesine
Palazzo dei Capitanai
☎ 0451 600044

TRENTINO/ALTO ADIGE
The main provincial Trentino office
close to Lake Garda is at:

Trento
132 Corso 3 Novembre
☎ 0461 980000/895111

though for Lake Garda itself it is
advisable to contact the local
village offices, chief of which is at:

Riva del Garda
Palazzo dei Congressi
☎ 0464 54444

The Tourist Offices can assist with
all queries regarding accommodation, local festivals etc as well as
some more interesting items. For
example, Varese has a list of
farms where the visitor can live
and work for a few days, a
fascinating chance to see Italian
life at first hand.

Italian Automobile Club (ACI)

Head Office
8 Via Marsala
00185 Rome
☎ 06 4998

Regional Offices
16 Via A Maj
Bergamo
☎ 035 247621

16 Via 25 Aprile
Brescia
☎ 030 40561

79 Via le M Masia
Como
☎ 031 556755

12 Via A De Gasperi
Domodossola
☎ 0324 2008

43 Corso Venezia
Milan
☎ 02 7745

36 Via Rosmini
Novara
☎ 0321 30321

12 Via Milano
Sondrio
☎ 0342 212213

6 Via Pozzo
Trento
☎ 0461 25072

25 Via le Milano
Varese
☎ 0332 265150

INDEX